THE MASS

an historical, theological, and pastoral survey

THE MASS

an historical, theological, and pastoral
survey

by

Josef A. Jungmann, S.J.

translated by
Julian Fernandes, S.J.

edited by
Mary Ellen Evans

THE LITURGICAL PRESS

Collegeville   Minnesota

Nihil obstat: William G. Heidt, O.S.B., S.T.D., *Censor deputatus. Imprimatur*: ✝ George H. Speltz, D.D., Bishop of Saint Cloud. July 31, 1975.

Printed by The North Central Publishing Company, St. Paul, Minnesota, U.S.A.
ISBN 0-8146-0887-6.

"It is through the liturgy, especially the divine Eucharistic Sacrifice, that the work of our redemption is exercised. The liturgy is thus the outstanding means by which the faithful can express in their lives, and manifest to others, the mystery of Christ and the real nature of the true Church."

—*Constitution on the Sacred Liturgy*

Editor's Foreword

This magisterial distillation of liturgical history and commentary on the postconciliar reform became a posthumous work on January 26, 1975, when Father Josef Jungmann died at Innsbruck as a very "young man" of some eighty-seven years.

It was not given to Father Jungmann to see the publication of this his final book; and that is a pity, for, as he had confided to us earlier, since in his "life's work" he had had to limit himself most often to the "liturgical forms" of the Mass, he had accepted gladly an American publisher's invitation to present also the "theological and pastoral implications of the holy Mystery." This, as he continued, "I could do both historically and systematically; and in this way I could hope to present a well-rounded picture." Even so, he did have the satisfaction of following the work of translation as done by Reverend Julian Fernandes (at the time the author's student at the Canisianum, now a priest of the Jesuit province of India).

At each step in the process of translation and publication the objective has been that of making the text as intelligible as possible to the English-speaking lay person, without reducing the work's value as a resource-book for theologians, the parish clergy, and students for the priesthood. To the end of serving this two-way goal, we have converted into the vernacular practically all technical terms and quotations from other languages (using authorized translations if such exist), and prepared an analytical Table of Contents to provide "a path through Jungmann," so to speak. On the other hand, we have preserved all but the most esoteric of the author's academic references, and for maximum retrievability have indexed both the text and any notes that introduce new material.

As a concession to both the professionals and the general readers, bibliographical citations have been incorporated in the text when this could be done without causing too much clutter, and it has been done consistently in citations of Sacred Scripture, patristic writings, and the key resources of medieval theology. Moreover, the Greek is transliterated, and those cabalistic-looking patristic short-forms have been spelled out.

Among the many Cyrenian interventions in the production of this work (which has had quite a history), I should mention, first of all, William Eckenrode, who found me for the "Americanizing" operation when initial efforts failed to materialize; Dr. Niels Sonne (then director, now retired) and Lydia Lo (then assistant, now acting, librarian) of St. Mark's Library, General Theological Seminary in New York, and Henry J. Bertels, S.J., librarian, and Edward B. Dunn, S.J., assistant librarian, of Woodstock College Library during its stay in New York — for no end of helpfulness and the freedom of these two almost inexhaustible collections; the ever-gracious staff of New York Public Library and of Union Theological Seminary library; Lysabeth Flynn, who fulfilled heroically the task of transcribing the original revision — which meant decoding my penmanship and pursuing my insert-arrows all over the page — and library scientist Warren Willis, who verified the documentation for her in the Catholic University of America libraries; and Dr. Matthew J. O'Connell, who contributed very significantly to the final, streamlined version. It has been a joy to work with people like these, and a privilege to have had a hand (however "trembling") in introducing a new generation of readers to the author of the classic *The Mass of the Roman Rite*.

M.E.E.

Feast of the Epiphany, 1976

CONTENTS

Contents

Part Two

THE THEOLOGY OF THE EUCHARISTIC SACRIFICE

Part Three

THE LITURGICAL FORM

Part Four

THE SPIRITUAL AND PASTORAL ASPECTS OF THE MASS

THE MASS

an historical, theological, and pastoral survey

PART ONE

Historical Survey

I. THE INSTITUTION OF THE EUCHARIST

A theological study of the Mass must begin with a look at the history of its institution. The New Testament contains two accounts of the events at the Last Supper: that of St. Paul in 1 Corinthians 11:23-25, which recurs in Luke 22:19f. with slight variations, and that of Mark 14:22-24, which corresponds in essentials to the account of Matthew 26:26-28.

1. THE HISTORICAL SOURCES

The two narratives have this in common: their style is set off from the familiar language of the Gospels by a certain dignity of tone and especially by its exotic Semitic coloring. In his work *The Eucharistic Words of Jesus*, Joachim Jeremias has identified sixteen Semitisms in the three Greek verses of Mark. Although Jeremias considers Mark to be the oldest account, most other scholars believe that of Paul to be even earlier. Paul's version is not only the first to have been set down in writing (in the year 54 or thereabouts) but also — since Paul relayed it as something handed down by tradition — it must be traced to its Greek origin in the Christian community of Antioch, where Paul moved in and out about the year 44 (Acts 11:26).

Yet even in the Greek text the Semitic ring of the language points farther back to the first Christian community of Jerusalem. Even the separation of the two Eucharistic actions by means of the full meal in the Paul/Luke account — the presentation of the consecrated bread at the beginning, and the chalice after the meal — is a mark of the oldest tradition. This is all the more true in view of the indications that already among Paul's Corinthians, the two actions were actually continuous and took place only after the meal.

This faithful handing on of the irreducible essentials of the account and, importantly, the reverential preservation of the somewhat foreign idiom, assert that this event is a matter of firmly es-

5

tablished tradition, carefully cultivated in the early Christian communities. For these two accounts are *cult* accounts, and they have their origin in the liturgical life of the communities. There have, of course, been attempts to reconstruct one original account from them, but the resulting forms differ far too widely, one from another. For our review, then, it is better to compare the two accounts side by side, ignoring the purely grammatical differences since they are not to our purpose.

Matthew 26:26-28	*Mark 14:22-24*	*Luke 22:19-20*	*1 Cor. 11:23-25*
During the meal blessed it, broke it, and gave it to his disciples. "Take this and eat it,"	Jesus took bread, blessed and broke it, and gave it to them. "Take this,"	Then, taking bread and giving thanks, he broke it and gave it to them,	. . . The Lord Jesus, on the night in which he was betrayed took bread, and after he had given thanks, broke it and said,
he said,		saying:	
"this is my body."		"this is my body,	which is
		to be given	
		for you.	
		Do this as a remembrance of me."	Do this in remembrance of me."
Then he took the cup, gave thanks, and gave it to them. "All of you must drink from it," he said, "for	He likewise took a cup, gave thanks and passed it to them, and and they all drank from it. He said to them,	He did the same with the cup after eating, saying as he did so:	In the same way, after the supper, he took the cup, saying:
this is my blood, the blood of the covenant, to be poured out in behalf of many		"This cup is the new covenant in my blood,	
for the forgiveness of sins."		which will be shed for you."	Do this, whenever you drink it, in remembrance of me."

2. THE LAST SUPPER A PASCHAL MEAL?

The three Synoptic Gospels, in their account of the Last Supper, supply also some of the circumstances in which the Eucharist was instituted. Thus, it was a feast-day meal on the occasion of the Passover, and the disciples had to find a room where the Master could eat the Pasch with them. From the Synoptics we would conclude that this was in fact the paschal meal itself (see Mark 14:12-17; Luke 22:15); and yet we are faced with the fact that, according to John 18:28, the law-abiding Jews who accused Jesus before Pilate intended to eat the paschal meal only on the following day, which was Friday.

Still, there are many indications that the Last Supper was a paschal meal too, if, as is probable, an anticipated one. Thus, a number of rituals prescribed for the paschal meal were faithfully observed: the meal was taken *in Jerusalem*, even though the city was choked with Passover pilgrims (perhaps as many as 125,000) with no place to stay; and *in the evening*, not at midday as otherwise would have been the case. Jesus and his disciples *reclined* to take the meal, though ordinary meals were taken sitting. The breaking of bread, with which a meal normally began, in this case took place only *during the course* of the meal. Moreover, the guests drank *wine*; they *left something for the poor*; they concluded the meal with a *song of thanksgiving* — all notes of a paschal meal. (Jeremias cites a total of fourteen arguments for the Passover character of the meal.)

Thus, even if the meal itself was not the paschal meal proper, it was partaken in a paschal atmosphere and spirit and had a paschal character. Curiously enough, the New Testament accounts say nothing about the paschal meal itself. They speak instead of Jesus' new Institution, implying that this new Institution was to be the fulfillment of what the paschal lamb symbolized.

That Jesus was the true paschal lamb was a belief current in the first Christian community. Thus St. Paul could say without further elaboration: "Christ our Passover has been sacrificed" (1 Cor. 5:7). In 19:36 John sees in the crucified Jesus the fulfillment of the prophecy concerning the paschal lamb: "You shall not break any of its bones" (Exod. 12:46). Hence the death of Christ on the Cross was regarded as the fulfillment of what was signified by the paschal lamb. The lamb of the Apocalypse as well as the designation of Jesus as "the Lamb of God" develop this figure further.

The same identification underlies also the expression current at the time, that we are redeemed "by his blood." It is the blood of a "spotless, unblemished lamb" (1 Peter 1:19). In the short account of the Last Supper extrapolated from Luke 22:15-18 (evidently a subsequent insertion by Luke), the new food and drink are explicitly distinguished from the paschal lamb, and the new ritual is depicted as replacing the old. Specifically, as Schürmann holds, these verses contain "the account of the paschal meal [as] fulfilled in the new covenant." [1]

The position that this was actually a paschal meal is confirmed by the words and actions reported of the Last Supper. The Jewish paschal meal had a very specific ceremonial, consisting of the following actions:

> 1. The blessing of the day (*kiddush*), and the blessing of the first cup by the father of the house; then the preliminary course of bitter herbs and unleavened bread;
> 2. The paschal ritual itself: the child's question as to the special significance of the day's feast; the first part of the *Hallel* (Psalms 112; 113:1-8 in the Vulgate); the second cup;
> 3. The meal proper, beginning with the blessing pronounced over the bread, which was then broken and passed around the table; the eating of the paschal lamb; the third cup—"the cup of blessing"; the real table prayer, by the father of the house;
> 4. The second part of the *Hallel* (Psalms 113:9–117:29; 135) and the thanksgiving prayer over the fourth cup. (*Adapted from* Strack-Billerbeck 4:41-76).

Now, in all probability Jesus made use of the preliminary act of the paschal meal proper, i.e., the blessing over the bread, to bring home to his disciples the mystery of the new bread; and in the same way, "after supper" he pronounced the words of Consecration over the third cup of wine.

3. THE WORDS OF CONSECRATION AND THE NEW COVENANT

These words of Consecration call for more thorough inspection, for we do not exhaust their significance when we merely establish that they express the Real Presence of the Lord's body and blood in the form of bread and wine. The deeper meaning becomes especially clear in the words over the chalice. For here blood is more than a mere symbol of human life. It is blood *poured out*; and, moreover, the blood of the covenant. In fact, covenant is so

strongly emphasized in Paul/Luke that the chalice itself is referred
to simply as *the covenant,* i.e., the basis of the covenant that is to
exist between God and his new people. In this way the relation is
established with the covenant of Sinai (Exod. 24:5-8), in which,
after the proclamation of the divine law, Moses appeared as the
mediator of the old covenant, offering and sprinkling on the altar
one-half the blood of the bullocks sacrificed, and the other half on
the people, with the words, "This is the blood of the covenant
which the LORD has made with you in accordance with all these
words of his."

Here the Greek word *diatheke* must be (and now generally is)
understood not to mean *testamentary decree,* as Luther wrongly
supposed even in the words of the institution of the Eucharist.
Hebrews 9:16f. is already a new interpretation of *testament,* and
covenant is the correct rendering of *berith.* As noted by J. Behm,
however, the idea does not necessarily presuppose two contracting
parties of equal standing but implies, rather, in the context of salvation history, a plan designed by God for his people.[2]

This covenant, referred to as the *new covenant* in Luke/Paul,
is the covenant that the prophet Jeremias had heralded in 31:31-34;
the covenant that is more than a renewal of the old covenant broken
by the fathers. It also has a new dimension: it "places God's law
within them and writes it upon their hearts" (31:33). Jesus' emphasis on this aspect of the covenant is the more weighty as the
remembrance of the covenant of Sinai already appears so rarely in
the prophets and moreover was pushed into the background of the
people's consciousness by the memory of the departure from Egypt.
But at the paschal meal, so richly reminiscent of Moses, the reference to *covenant* would be immediately intelligible without need
for further explanation.

The blood spoken of here is the blood that is to be shed to
seal the covenant. Hence it is sacrificial blood. Here a cultic notion
is employed as a description, a notion that was particularly vivid
on the day when the paschal lamb was "sacrificed" (Mark 14:12)
and when people everywhere gathered together to share the meal
of the paschal sacrifice.

The present tense of the Greek form — really a survival from
the Aramaic, without a proper future grammatical form — has here
a future meaning. It points to the death on the Cross, for it is by
the death on the Cross and not at the Last Supper that this covenant

is made and sealed (to take the view of J. Lecuyer in *Le sacrifice de la Nouvelle Alliance*, p. 179, as against that of H. Kruse[3]). By his words, then, Jesus announced his sacrificial death at which his blood was to be shed. He himself disposed of his blood. According to the biblical conception, blood is God's rightful share, and man cannot dispose of it "for blood is life" (Deut. 12:23). Hence with this word Jesus laid down his life, as he had already foretold.

The words over the chalice, however, explain also the significance of the surrender of life. The blood will be shed "for you," "for many," and "for the forgiveness of sins."[4] Incidentally, these are expressions used about Ebed-Yahweh, the servant of God in Deutero-Isaias (53:5, 11-12); the word *covenant* is taken from the same context (42:6; 49:8; 53). The parallel between the mysterious "servant of God" and Jesus is drawn in several places in the Gospels: Matthew 8:17; 12:18-22; John 12:38. Jesus himself makes pointed reference to it in Luke 22:37 and certainly alludes to it in the words over the chalice. In Deutero-Isaias the Ebed-Yahweh's self-surrender is characterized as expiatory suffering; this, however, is not conceived as a sacrifice in the traditional cultic sense, for Deutero-Isaias does not place the Ebed-Yahweh's death on a level with the sacrifice of the paschal lamb.

At the Last Supper the Master gives his blood to his disciples to drink so that they may have a share in his life, and in this manner be party to the new covenant he is about to seal with his blood. The sacrifice and the sacrificial meal are there right before them even now (see Exod. 24:11; 1 Cor. 10:16). Mark's explicit statement that "all drank from it" could not have been a merely casual remark, for as J. Betz indicates, among the Jewish Christians there seems to have been a certain amount of opposition — which died out only gradually — to the Eucharistic chalice.[5]

The Paul/Luke account attests to the word on self-surrender in the manner of the servant of God even in connection with the bread: "for you," "given for you" (see Is. 53:12). The form *given* (*didomenon*) need not yet be understood as a term for sacrifice. It may also be understood in the more general sense of a gift, a present. Part of the ritual of concluding a treaty or a covenant was to exchange gifts. But a gift given to God is indeed a sacrifice, as scholars have brought out in their studies on the Eucharist as covenant. Besides, even if this *didomenon* is to be taken in the sense of something presented to the disciples (corresponding to *dedoke*), this giving was the beginning, the anticipation, of the final surrender on the Cross, which will continue in the giving to believers of all times. It is identical with the pronouncement in John 6:51c, "The bread I will give is my flesh, for the life of the world."

4. The Body-Blood Symbolism

Since, according to Paul/Luke, the words over the bread were spoken before the meal and were therefore separated in time from the words over the chalice, one might rightly ask whether in the words over the bread the separation of body and blood could be already understood. First of all, *body* (Greek: *soma*; Aramaic: *gufi*, my body) implied no opposition to *blood* (*haima*); it could as well signify the complete person. Hence no opposition to *blood* could have been read into the words by the disciples.

In liturgical tradition however, which brought the two actions together very soon as already in Mark/Matthew their separation by means of the meal is no longer mentioned, *soma* and *haima* stand side by side as sacrificial terms. Flesh (*sarx* rather than *soma*) and blood comprise one single pair of concepts in the language of sacrifice (Lev. 17:11-14; Exod. 39:17-20; see Heb. 13:11). In one part of the tradition at an early time a symbolism of the sacrificial death was read into the words over the bread, i.e., whenever the word "broken" (*klomenon or thryptomenon*) was added to the original text "my body for you."

5. A Rite of Thanksgiving

In the New Testament tradition the sacramental words do not stand isolated; they are part of the action. According to Jewish custom, at the beginning of a meal (on the day of Pasch, after the meal had already begun: "as they were eating") the father of the house took bread, blessed it with a thanksgiving prayer, broke it, and passed it around to those sharing the meal. At the paschal meal as well as at every feast-day dinner, the real grace at table was said at the end, "over the third cup." Then everyone drank from his cup. At this point in the course of the Last Supper we are told of a striking deviation from custom, parallel to the presentation of bread: the Master gives to his disciples his own chalice — this was normally done only as a special mark of honor to a guest — and invites them to drink from it. "And all drank from it." In this way the significance of this chalice from his own hand is emphasized. The words accompanying the action furnish the explanation.

The thanksgiving prayer over the bread at the beginning of the meal was a short ejaculation: "Praised be Yahweh, our God, the king of the world, who makes bread come forth from the earth" (Mishnah, Berakoth 6:1). It is characteristic that Mark/Matthew describe it with the word *eulogia*, which corresponds more to a short thanksgiving prayer; and that in the second instance, over the chalice, they use the word *eucharistia*. At the breaking of bread, as on other occasions, Jesus must have formulated his words in his characteristic, personal way. For the disciples of Emmaus recognize him by the breaking of bread (Luke 24:30-35). The grace after meals lends itself to even further expansion.

In Jesus' time the grace after meals (*birkatha-mazon*) consisted of three parts preceded by the invitatory, "Let us say the prayer of benediction." In the first sentence God was thanked for sustaining the universe through his goodness and mercy. The second sentence was a thanksgiving for the land that God had given his people for inheritance. This was followed by the thanksgiving, or rather the intercession, for Jerusalem.[6]

The chief emphasis lay on the middle sentence, with its thanksgiving character and its improvisatory capacity to make room for thanking God for his particular works. Such expansion was customary (at least in later times), especially at the paschal meal (Hänggi-Pahl 27). It was on this basis that the prayer became, on the Lord's lips, the vehicle of thanksgiving for all that had come about for the salvation of the world according to God's decree, and all that was now to be accomplished. If in this prayer the Lord had already declared the meaning and purpose of his action and of his coming suffering, then it became all the more reasonable that the words traditionally handed down should have stated the essentials with the greatest conciseness.

For this grace after meals at the Last Supper, Mark/Matthew use *eucharistesas*, a word that stresses its greater weightiness and its thanksgiving aspect as against the less definitive *eulogesas*, used to describe the words over the bread. Paul/Luke employ the same *eulogesas* in the first place and only once — probably after the usage already familiar to them. The basic Semitic text admitted of no distinction between *eulogein* and *eucharistein*. The word for this type of prayer was *barak*, and to this form the Greek *eulogein* corresponds. Hence such a prayer was called in later times *berakah*, and rigid rules drawn up by the Rabbis restricted its use. Of course, no definitive form of *berakah* can be shown to have existed yet in Jesus' time.[7]

An external ritual, too, was prescribed for this thanksgiving after meals. The father of the house had to hold the cup filled with wine, and raise it a hand's breadth above the table. This gesture was a kind of offertory ritual — the same one the psalmist speaks of in Psalm 115:13, "The cup of salvation I will take up" (*calicem salutaris accipiam*), where *accipiam* corresponds to a Hebrew word meaning *to raise up*. That is simply a concrete expression of the mode of thought pervading the entire Old Testament and even the New Testament. Food and drink are gifts which we receive from the hand of God and with which he sustains our life. Hence, before we enjoy them we must raise them up to God and "make them free" by blessing him; we must tender him thanks for them.

The sacrificial rituals developed for this thanksgiving stem from the same root as those acknowledging God's sovereignty, and are based on the same fundamental idea, as is clearly brought out in the Old Testament conception of slaughtering. Right up to the period of the New Testament, the idea persisted that blood shed at slaughter had to be offered to God. Blood as the basis of life belonged to God and had to be poured out before the tabernacle of the covenant or spilled on the ground.

In Peter's vision the command given him to *slaughter* and eat the unclean animals comes in the form *thyson kai phage* (Acts 10:13). As Joseph Sint observes, this *thyson* "is resonant with sacrificial overtones."[8] Thus, at the Last Supper Jesus not only rehearsed the sacrifice of the following day; he also related his action to certain rituals of an offering, and these rituals form a significant starting point for the Church's sacrifice in the subsequent evolution of the Eucharistic celebration.

6. The Last Supper as Sacrificial Meal

The raising of the cup at the Last Supper is not the only ritual that suggested a movement toward God, while anticipating the sacrifice of Golgotha and making it present. There is probably a similar ritual over the bread — as might be implied in the strikingly emphasized word "taking" (*labon, elaben*). While written evidence for such action over bread as a Jewish custom at table is to be found only much later (see Hänggi-Pahl 5-7), still, the liturigcal tradition of the fourth and fifth centuries in the Liturgy of Basil, as well as in that of James, interprets the "taking" (*labon*) of the biblical narrative to mean such a "raising up" (*labon arton epi ton . . . cheiron kai anadeixas soi*).[9] Importantly, however, even the thanksgiving introducing each of the actions points unmistakably toward God. Originally both verbs *eulogein* and *eucharistein* were *intransitive*: to give praise and thanks. But since they were spoken over an object they implied at the same time a sanctification and consecration of that object. Hence already in Justin Martyr, *eucharistein* is used as a transitive verb.

In these two expressions we need not look for sacrificial terms in the strict sense, as some scholars have attempted to do; for here it is enough to understand *giving* in the sense of a movement toward God. The theory of K. G. Goetz (d. 1944) explaining the institution of the Last Supper exclusively in terms of the Old Testament food- and drink-sacrifices has rightly been rejected. This thesis was revived in 1952 to a quite different effect by A. Rehbach, according to whom the food-sacrifice in the Eucharist is closely identified with the sacrifice of the Cross that it re-presents.[10] It must not be overlooked, however, that the Eucharist of the Last Supper was already surrounded by certain rituals in which the sacrifice of the Church could later find expression.

It is not only the Eucharist of which it has been asked, in the name of biblical exegesis, whether it was understood from the beginning as a sacrifice; the same question has been asked also of Jesus' death on the Cross, which is re-presented in the Eucharist. Such a question would be warranted if the word *sacrifice* is understood here simply in the sense of the Old Testament ritual laws. The old concept is applicable to the new event only in an analogical sense. Just as in the New Testament the levitical priesthood and the Temple no longer exist, so too there is no sacrifice in the old sense. But the fact of the sacrifice does exist now in a new form, and along with it a reassessed and purified concept of sacrifice.

We have heard Jesus himself employ some elements of the Old Testament language of sacrifice for a paraphrase of his own action. Indeed, as Sabourin points out in *Rédemption sacrificielle,* lamb, blood, and blood of the covenant are central ideas in the language of sacrifice.[11] Hence it could only be that from the very beginning the idea of sacrifice was applied even to the action of the God-Man. The fact is directly referred to in Ephesians 5:2, "Christ loved you; he gave himself for us as an offering to God, a gift of pleasing fragrance." Finally, in chapter 10 of the Letter to the Hebrews, under the metaphor of the old Temple cult, the new concept has become a dominant theme.

When Jesus explains the meaning of the bread and of the chalice in his hands with the words "This is my body to be given for you . . . my blood which will be shed for you," and thus introduces and anticipates the sacrifice of the Cross, he characterizes even this present action of his as sacrifice, or at least as the prelude to the one sacrifice. And consequently the food and drink to which he invites the Apostles is a sacrificial meal.

A sacrificial meal completed the rite of sacrifice with which the old covenant was sealed (Exod. 24:11). The paschal meal for which people came together was likewise a sacrificial meal, but at the Last Supper the reality takes the place of the shadows. It is this sacrificial meal that is alluded to by Paul in 1 Corinthians when he contrasts the Lord's table with the demon's table and its flesh sacrificed to the gods (10:21). And even in the Eucharistic discourse reported by John, clear reference is made to sacrificial flesh: "The bread I will give is my flesh, for the life of the world" (6:51).

7. THE EUCHARIST AS MEMORIAL

The Gospel account containing the mandate, "Do this in remembrance of me," is cited by Paul in both parts of the double action but is wanting in Mark/Matthew. Strictly speaking, these words did not have to be written down if the mandate was being observed in the actual liturgical practice of the communities. As a rubric that somehow became attached to the text proper, it reveals all the more clearly that Jesus' action at the farewell meal was not merely a symbolic action to point to his coming death and prepare his disciples for it, but that it was an *institution* — the foundation of a custom — that was to remain.

Hence, too, the Last Supper was not a public meal, with guests from outside, but was restricted to the Twelve, the representatives of the new people of God. The mandate was meant only for them. Nor is the New Testament account simply a report, but rather a *cultic* text that reduced the double action to its essentials and had to be repeated in the gathering of the community in order to keep alive the memory of Jesus Christ.

That the account was repeated from the time of the early Church is granted by everyone; now it was necessary to look for an explanation of the fact or, at least, of the words with which it was commissioned. The explanation was believed to be found in Hellenistic sources, where there are institution inscriptions requiring a commemoration (*anamnesis*) on a fixed recurring day; but such an explanation was unnecessary in Judaism because, since the beginning (Exod. 12:14), the paschal celebration had to be performed every year "as a memorial."

The meaning of the memorial can hardly be doubted. True, the theologian Jeremias has proposed the following variation on the mandate to repeat: 'Do this in order that God may remember me — that is, that he may bring about the messianic kingdom.' But his proposal has found little favor and much opposition, as is noted especially in Betz, *Die Eucharistie* 2.1:213f. There is no reason to depart from the obvious and literal meaning of the words as they stand, namely, that his own disciples wish to keep him in remembrance and to remain united with him through this remembrance. The burden thus falls on what Jesus does and on the later consummation of this double action, which *made present* his self-surrender on the Cross.

Farther along in his account St. Paul puts the same thing explicitly: "Until the Lord comes, therefore, every time you eat this bread and drink this cup, you are proclaiming (*katangellete*) his death." To announce in words the Lord's death "until he comes" is not a new mandate that is issued here; it is the same mandate mentioned earlier, but now it is specifically grounded on a reason: "therefore." And it is expressly stated that the new Institution will hold good for the whole interval till the Lord's glorious Second Coming. It is self-evident that the external action is to be accompanied by the proclaiming word, which will then constitute one component of the action. That is to say, the *eulogein-eucharistein* unquestionably participates in the object of the mandate; and that is not the case with the meal proper. In fact the meal is no longer involved. As Neuenzeit observes,[12] Paul argues from an understanding of the Eucharist that prescinds from the meal aspect.

II. FROM THE FIRST COMMUNITY TO HIPPOLYTUS OF ROME

When, after the events of Easter and Pentecost, the Apostles came to a full realization of what had happened, and when, too, the meaning of Jesus' institution of the Eucharist at the Last Supper became clearer to them, they were face to face with a changed situation. What had been at the Last Supper a proclamation and anticipation of Jesus' sacrificial death was now to be memorialized; what Jesus himself had done at the Last Supper, they must now do in his name and according to his instructions.

That they did so, and moreover that they were eager to fulfill the Lord's mandate with the greatest possible fidelity, is evident from the very fact — as well as from the singular nature — of the New Testament accounts of the Institution of the Eucharist. These accounts, with their peculiar form of language, date from the first Christian community of Jerusalem. We find only a few scattered clues as to how the apostles actually fulfilled their mandate, how they integrated the Institution of the Eucharist into the life of the infant Church, how they interpreted their action. Serious decisions had to be taken. In what framework and setting should the memorial be celebrated? on what occasions? in what group of participants? Should it be presided over by an official with a special mandate, or celebrated simply at a round table of equals?

In the New Testament accounts we find only incomplete answers. One thing alone is clear: the infant Church was conducting the celebration right from the beginning, and that with surprising sureness, with uniformity of rubrics and with the same literal, realistic interpretation. The origin of this self-assurance is not in doubt. If the Lord's appearances after his resurrection had any meaning, and if during his appearances he spoke to the apostles about "the things that concern the reign of God" (*ta peri tes*

17

basileias tou theou, Acts 1:3), then confirmation and clearer explanation of what had been instituted at the Last Supper must inevitably have come up.

1. THE EUCHARIST OF THE FIRST CHRISTIANS

a) The "breaking of bread"

The Acts bears witness to the breaking of bread in the first Christian community. In the Didache (14:1) as well as in St. Ignatius' Letter to the Ephesians (20:2), the breaking of bread already stands for the Eucharist. But even earlier, in 1 Corinthians 10:16, "the bread we break" is without doubt the Eucharist. So, too, nothing but the Eucharist could have been meant when the community at Troas "on the first day of the week . . . gathered for the breaking of bread" (Acts 20:7) — all the more so since this is noted incidentally as a self-evident custom, in which it is Paul especially who "breaks bread" (20:11). Thus there is solid ground for the assumption that Luke's use of this expression has a similar sense in Acts 2:42 and 46, even though a full meal besides might well be understood (2:46).

Breaking of bread was an expression current in Judaism as a technical term for the preliminary act of a meal (the father of the house broke the bread), but embracing at the same time the accompanying prayer of thanksgiving and the sharing of the bread with everyone at table. Since this very act was incorporated and elevated in the Eucharist, the breaking of bread must soon have come to prevail as an appropriate frame for the Eucharist. The faithful of the young Church must have come together in little groups for a common evening meal in houses where there was a room suitable for it — as was in fact already the custom among Jews by way of a community meal within the circle of friends (*ḥaburah*). Along with this evening meal the Christians probably celebrated the Eucharist on certain days not recorded for us: "They devoted themselves to the apostles' instruction and the communal life, to the breaking of bread and the prayers" (Acts 2:42).

This passage suggests also a certain priority or order of events. The teaching of the Apostles — the witnesses of the Resurrection — comes first, and then the brotherhood, which implies here a readiness to share, a sentiment of brotherly love that keeps back nothing as one's own (Acts 4:32). Just as Baptism presupposes faith, so the Eucharist presupposes love.[18] "With exultant and sincere hearts they took their meals in common," we read in Acts 2:46.

The knowledge of the victoriously risen Lord and the consciousness of a fellowship with him must have been the reason for this exultation. They knew that at their gatherings, and in particular when they celebrated the Eucharist, it was the Lord who was there "in their midst" as he himself had said (Matthew 18:20). They knew that in the Eucharist was continued the fellowship of the Lord's table enjoyed by his disciples during his earthly life as well as after his resurrection (Luke 24:41-43; John 21:12-13; Acts 10:41). In their sacred meal they saw the beginning and the mystical anticipation of the messianic banquet of which the Lord had spoken in his parables.

Hence, too, the invocation "*Marana tha*, come, Lord!" in the gatherings of the first Christian community. This is one of the few words preserved for us in the original language of their liturgy (1 Cor. 16:22; Didache 10:6; see Apoc. 22:20). In Jesus Christ they recognized their "Lord," their *Kyrios*, who was their host in his invisible presence, and from whose hands they received his flesh and his blood.

b) The Eucharist with an evening meal

It is clear beyond question that in early times the Eucharist was coupled with a meal. In 1 Corinthians 11:17-34 Paul calls the attention of the community of Corinth in the fifties to this fact. It is the "Lord's table," an expression that already implies a combination of the two components. Even in the Didache — hence, toward the end of the first Christian century — the Eucharist was still conjoined to a meal, for the celebration is preceded by a dinner surrounded by the prayers given in our chapters 9 and 10.

This relation is sufficiently suggested already in the invocations joined to the prayers (ch. 10.6): "May grace come down, and may this world pass away, Amen! Hosanna to the house of David! Whoever is holy, let him approach. Whoever is not holy, let him do penance. Marana tha, Amen." (From J. P. Audet, *La Didachè*, p. 423f.). So, too, Jeremias, in *The Eucharistic Words of Jesus* (see pp. 108–25), considers the question settled once and for all. Moreover, the second-century Letter of the Apostles (Epistola Apostolorum, ch. 15; pp. 13f. in the Duensing edition), ascribed to the Lord words invoking the "Agape and my remembrance" (or "my remembrance and the Agape," in the Coptic tradition), though here the reference is to the special case of Easter night.

With the exception of this (far from clearcut) case, the meal associated with the Eucharist is nowhere called *agape*, a term that has since the third century been reserved for a different observance firmly established in the Church, i.e., a meal as a feeding of the poor.[14] A remnant of the old custom of taking the meal during at least the Easter night may well have persisted for a long time. According to the Apostolic Tradition (Traditio Apostolica), of Hippolytus, the newly baptized, after they had received the Lord's body and before receiving the chalice, were to be given a cup of milk and honey (food for children) and another cup containing water (Botte 56–59).

Although this meal came to be thought of as associated with the Eucharist by reason of a certain ritualized order, it could not conceivably have been the paschal meal. The paschal meal, with its characteristic ritual, could be celebrated only once a year; and that is why liturgical accounts of the institution of the Eucharist say nothing about the details of that Last Supper. But this non-paschal meal could have been a feast-day meal, of a kind with which the Sabbath began within the family circle or which might be organized also on other occasions within circles of friends. For at such meals, too, the breaking of bread at the beginning and the chalice of benediction at the end were not unknown.

At all events what had to be repeated as the Lord's Institution was not the meal but what in its original form has been called by Dom Gregory Dix (in *The Shape of the Liturgy*) a "seven-action" *schema*: (1) the Lord took bread; (2) gave thanks; (3) broke it; (4) distributed it with the corresponding words; (5) took the chalice; (6) gave thanks; (7) handed it to his disciples. A first step toward the adaptation to circumstances was to merge the two parts of the double action. The account of the Institution in Mark/Matthew seems to have had this liturgical practice in view.

The effect was a four-action shape: (1) preparing bread and wine; (2) the thanksgiving prayer; (3) the breaking of bread; (4) the communion (pp. 48–50; 78–82). In this formula one may recognize already the "shape" of the structure of the Mass that has since come into common use. Once the two parts were thus conjoined, the meal began to be dissociated from the Eucharistic action, and the Eucharistic ritual could be performed before or after the meal. The next logical step was that this action could also take place by itself, independent of the meal. The exact date of this second step was probably contingent upon local conditions in different places. By the second century, at any rate, it is a fait accompli.

With this development came a significant decision with regard to the external form as well as to the general conception of what the Lord had instituted. All the tables disappeared from the hall except the one on which bread and wine were kept. The dining hall was changed into a place of religious assembly. The expressions *breaking bread* and even *the Lord's table*, which had been associated with the idea of an actual meal, were discontinued. It is only the Protestant Reformers of the sixteenth century who employ the term *supper* for the sacramental ritual dissociated from the meal.

c) A new time and a new name for the celebration

Once the meal was dispensed with, the hour for celebrating the Lord's memorial had to be readjusted also. In Jewish as well as Hellenistic tradition the important meal of the day was the *deipnon*, the evening supper. Now that the Eucharist was no longer to be joined to a meal, it could be shifted to some other time of day outside working hours; for among early Christians Sunday was officially as much a working day as any other. The obvious choice was an early morning hour. This hour had a further recommendation on the same ground that had evidently been decisive in the choice of Sunday: the remembrance that the Lord's resurrection had taken place during the *early hours* of the first day of the week. Express mention of this point is made a little later in St. Cyprian's Letter to Caecilius (Ep. ad Caecilium 63:16).

To this a further justification was added when the practice of initiating the Eucharistic celebration with Scripture readings was introduced, after the example of the Synagogue, since this Jewish service was conducted on the *morning* of the Sabbath. It is probable that the gathering of Christians about which Governor Pliny reports to Emperor Trajan c. 111–13, "on the appointed day . . . before daybreak" (*stato die ante lucem*), was in fact the Eucharistic celebration (Ep. ad Traianum 10:96).

The expression that now emerges is *eucharistia* (St. Ignatius, Letters to the Smyrnians 7:1; 8:1; Ephesians 13:1; Philadelphians

4:1). In the Eucharistic ritual, dissociated from the nonessentials, the thanksgiving prayer is the most impressive element. It is no longer the meal but this thanksgiving prayer recited over bread and wine that now fundamentally determines the character of the service; for while elements of a meal remain with the sacrament and its reception under the species of bread and wine, the celebration as a whole can no longer be called a meal. As Schürmann notes, "The procedure has become completely stylized, relieved of its ordinary meaning, and completely transformed into a symbol." [15] From the very beginning the Communion was not the whole Institution of Jesus, but only an essential component.

The content of the thanksgiving prayer was determined by the very nature of the Institution itself, by the Lord's mandate to recall his memory and by his example at the Last Supper. Such prayer of thanksgiving for the work of redemption and for salvation granted to us in Christ is outlined in several passages in the Epistles, such as Colossians 1:12-22; Philippians 2:5-11; 1 Timothy 3:16; 1 Peter 3:18-21. Almost all the letters of Paul begin with a thanksgiving prayer. The hymns of praise in the Apocalypse (4:11; 5:9-14; 11:17-8; 15:3-4) and the Lord's farewell discourse (John 14–17) have with good reason been cited as well. Some authors still believe that in the prayers in chapter 9 and 10 of the Didache may be traced not only the table grace for the feast-day meal of the Jewish Christians but Eucharistic prayers as well. [16]

d) The Eucharist understood as a sacrifice

The sacrificial aspect of the Eucharistic celebration is brought out also in the Didache (ch. 14:1), "Gather together on the day of the Lord, break bread, and give thanks, but first confess your sins, so that your sacrifice may be pure." Malachi's prophecy about the pure offering is then cited (1:11, 14). Besides proving incidentally that the Eucharist was celebrated on Sundays, this text still more significantly establishes the association of the Eucharist with the concept of sacrifice, providing at the same time safeguards against misunderstanding. Thus it is not just a matter of a ritual to be performed outwardly; the sacrifice must be pure, that is, performed interiorly at the same time. Hence, too, a purifying act of confession at the beginning is demanded.

The text with relevance here is obviously 1 Peter 2:5. Christians, says St. Peter, must be "living stones built as an edifice of spirit into a holy priesthood," to offer up through Jesus Christ spiritual sacrifices acceptable to God. A mere liturgical ritual is hardly what he is describing here. Rather, the focus is on Christian living that is continually integrated with the sacrifice of Christ. It may be that even in the Letter to the Hebrews the reference is to more than mere community assemblies (3:12); the caution against falling away, and especially the *thysiasterion* (13:10) indicate that Paul has the Eucharist in mind. This, however, is still a matter of controversy, and we can draw no absolute conclusions.[17]

e) Ancient elements in the ritual

On the contrary, several details of the form of Eucharistic celebration that have since come down to us make it clear that we here have elements of a tradition dating from the very first Jewish-Christian community. Certain stylistic peculiarities of the prayer to be found in the later liturgies must be traced to this point. The prayer begins with the greeting *The Lord be with you* or *Peace be with you*. Both are biblical, Hebraic forms of greeting used already in the first Christian community (Ruth 2:4; Matthew 10:12-13; Luke 1:28; 10:5; John 20:19, 21 and 26); so, too, the traditional answer *And with your spirit* (Gal. 6:18; Phil. 4:23; Philemon 25).

Then follows the invitation to prayer: *Let us pray, Let us give thanks*; and these formulas, too, have their parallels in the customary prayers of the Jews. The ratifying *Amen* of the people has to this day retained its Hebraic form; in this form it appears, along with *Hosanna* and *Alleluia*, in the Mass of every rite. Even the practice of concluding the prayer with a doxology or doxological term, the last phrase echoing God's eternity, originates in the Synagogue.

These and other traditions borrowed by the Christian liturgies from the liturgical practice of Jerusalem become immediately intelligible if the faithful of the first community (such as the Apostles) frequented the Temple and the Synagogue. They not only took over the Old Testament writings, not only continued to sing the psalms; they drew the very inspiration for their liturgy from the living practice of the Old Testament people of God. Of course, the life of the Church developed not only in a Jewish-Christian climate but after some time in a Hellenistic climate as well. And so in the following pages we shall survey the more important documents that can tell us something about the celebration of the Eucharist within different circles during the subsequent centuries.

2. First and Second Century Testimonies

a) St. Clement of Rome

Eucharist is mentioned only in passing in the Letter of Pope St. Clement I to the community of Corinth A.D. 93–97). Concerning some disrupters of the community he writes emphatically that in the Church there are office-bearers who have received their office from Christ through the Apostles and cannot be arbitrarily deposed (ch. 42:1f.). Their most important service is "to offer up the gifts" in a holy manner (44:4). On the Eucharistic implications of these "gifts" light is thrown from another side when Christ is referred to as "the High Priest of our gift offerings" (36:1); they are our gift offerings, i.e., it is the sacrifice of the Church. Offering them up is the special task of those who have received their mandate from Christ. But ultimately Christ himself is the Priest in the full and proper sense.

b) St. Ignatius of Antioch

The Letters of St. Ignatius of Antioch to the Seven Churches were farewell messages dispatched (c. 110) during his journey to Rome soon after he had been condemned to death — death by beasts. If the Eucharist is mentioned several times in these letters, this fact alone indicates how important a place it occupied in the life of the Church and in the consciousness of the faithful. Thus, the faithful often came together for its celebration; Sunday was chosen to take the place of the Sabbath (To the Magnesians 9:1); at these meetings the Eucharist was celebrated, but only the Eucharist presided over by a bishop or authorized by him could be counted as legitimate (Smyrn. 8:1). Ignatius speaks with great emphasis of the solidarity of the community around the bishop and his presbyterium. Effective prayer was that offered by the bishop together with his entire community. "But whoever keeps away from the altar (or: from the place around the altar, *thysiasterion*) deprives himself of the divine bread" (Eph. 5:2).

There were Christians who kept away from the Eucharist and from the common prayer because they did not believe that the Eucharist was Christ's flesh in which he had suffered and risen

(Smyrn. 7:1); here Ignatius refers to the Docetists, who denied love. Hence Ignatius himself calls the Eucharist *agape* (8:2). At this love feast the one bread is broken, the bread that is the elixir of immortality (Eph. 20:2). Side by side with the divine bread, which is the body of Christ, he mentions also the drink, which is his blood (To the Romans 7:3).

That the Eucharist is a sacrifice is not expressly stated, but neither is it by any means denied. Even if *thysiasterion* need not be taken to mean *altar* (Eph. 5:2; see Magn. 7:2; Philad. 4), the term still implies that the bishop with his community was considered to constitute a locus where in some sense a sacrifice was offered. A movement toward God is, of course, already indicated in the expression *eucharistia*. And the words pronounced over the bread and wine suggest that these materials have something to do with this God-ward movement.

c) St. Justin Martyr's account

The first concrete description of the Eucharistic celebration comes down to us through Justin Martyr's twofold account, in his First Apology of c. 150 A.D. The first account concerns a Eucharistic celebration at the conclusion of a Baptism ceremony; the second, the Sunday Mass. The texts are all the more important in that the widely traveled author intended merely to report what was firmly established and practiced in all the churches as a whole. For that reason we give the account quoted in full:

> After we have baptized him who professes our belief and associates with us, we lead him into the assembly of those called the Brethren, and we there say prayers in common for ourselves, for the newly-baptized, and for others all over the world. . . . After finishing the prayers we greet each other with a kiss. Then bread and a cup with water and wine mixed are brought to the one presiding over the brethren. He takes it, gives praise and glory to the Father of all in the name of the Son and of the Holy Ghost, and gives thanks at length for the gifts that we were worthy to receive from him. When he has finished the prayers and thanksgiving, the whole crowd standing by cries out in agreement: Amen. Amen is a Hebrew word and means: So may it be. After the presiding official has said thanks and the people have joined in, the deacons, as they are styled by us, distribute as food for all those present, the bread and

wine-and-water mixed, over which the thanks had been offered, and which they carry to those not present (*ch. 65*).

And this food itself is known amongst us as the
Eucharist. No one may partake of it unless he is convinced
of the truth of our teaching and is cleansed in the bath of
Baptism. . . . (*ch. 66*).

. . . And on the day which is called after the sun, all
who are in the towns and in the country gather together for
a communal celebration. And then the memoirs of the
Apostles or the writings of the Prophets are read, as long
as time permits. After the reader has finished his task, the
one presiding gives an address, urgently admonishing his
hearers to practice these beautiful teachings in their lives.
Then together all stand and recite prayers, as has already
been remarked above, the bread and wine mixed with water
are brought, and the president offers up prayers and
thanksgivings, as much as in him lies. The people chime
in with an Amen. Then takes place the distribution, to all
attending, of the things over which the thanksgiving had
been spoken, and the deacons bring a portion to the absent.
Besides, those who are well-to-do give whatever they will.
What is gathered is deposited with the one presiding, who
therewith helps orphans and widows (*ch. 67*).

d) Elements in Justin's account

In this account we learn for the first time of a number of
details that recur in the further history of the Mass and perdure
in great part to this day. Thus, Sunday is the day of the meeting
and the day chosen especially for the Eucharistic celebration. The
celebration proper is preceded by a service consisting of readings
from the Old and New Testaments, which is followed by the celebrant's homily and a prayer in common. This sheds light on a
practice corresponding to the Synagogue service on the morning of
the Sabbath. Reading and sermon are referred to in the Gospels
(Luke 4:16-30) and in the Acts (13:15-16). In Justin's time,
however, this Scripture-reading service was not yet closely identified
with the Eucharistic action; that is why a baptism ceremony could
take its place.

The prayer of the community, too, is rooted in the Synagogue
service. A basic form of the so-called "eighteen prayers" harks
back to the time of the Apostles.[18] Justin refers also in other passages
to the prayer offered by the Christian community for each one and

"for all" (Dialogue with Trypho 96:3; 133:6). Another practice borrowed from Jewish tradition was that the gifts presented to the celebrant included water in addition to the bread and wine. That even by *krama* (65:3) only wine is meant is proved by, among other things, the parallel 67:5. It was customary in the Palestine of Jesus' time to mingle water with wine.[19] The emphasis St. Cyprian later laid on this mingling of water shows that in this usage they saw a Last Supper tradition.

The celebrant's role at the thanksgiving may already be perceived. He alone speaks, unlike at the prayer following the reading; whereas the part of the community is to add the ratifying *Amen*. Hand in hand with his *eucharistia* (thanksgiving) go the *euchai* (intercessory prayers), as Justin also insists in Dialogue 117:2 and 5. It is the celebrant who offers up the prayers and the thanksgiving to God "in the name of the Son and of the Holy Spirit," or, as phrased in another place, "in the name of the crucified Jesus" (Dialogue 117:5). The accent, however, is on the thanksgiving.

The object of the thanksgiving is "that we have been made worthy of those things" (65:3); this could mean simply the vocation to the grace of gospel faith. It is a motif that is elaborated at greater length in Dialogue 41:1. The Eucharistic bread is given to us in order that through it we may thank God "for creating the world and all that is in it for man's sake, for delivering us from the evil in which we were born and for fully destroying the Dominions and the Powers through him who according to his will undertook to suffer." Likewise, Dialogue 117:3 speaks of the memorial celebration of the solid and liquid food with which Christians "recall the sufferings which the Son of God has borne for them"; and in 70:4 the memory of God's incarnation is closely associated with the bread, and the memory of the blood with the chalice of thanksgiving.

Thus, far from constituting a kind of parenthetical statement, the thanksgiving prayer, as in the passage quoted above, is repeatedly and explicitly associated with the bread and wine that the celebrant has earlier "accepted" (65:3). It is "the Eucharist of the bread and of the chalice" (Dialogue 117:1). Hence the bread is called the "bread of the Eucharist" (41:1, 3), and the chalice, the "chalice of the Eucharist" (41:3).

In other words, the God-ward movement in the thanksgiving prayer takes along in its sweep the bread and the chalice. They are offered up to God. It is not surprising, therefore, that Justin, in his Dialogue with the Jew, not only cites several times the prophecy of Malachi fulfilled in the celebration of the Eucharist, but also designates the Eucharist immediately as sacrifice, *thysia* (Dialogue 41:3; 117:1).

e) St. Irenaeus

While St. Justin was concerned chiefly to describe the liturgical form of the Eucharist, St. Irenaeus was interested more in a reflection on the very essence of the Eucharist, even though it is a reflection wholly colored by polemic against the Gnostics. In the fourth book of his treatise "Against the Heresies" (Adv. Haer.; c. 180–90), he hoped to show that the new covenant, far from contradicting the old, was in fact its fulfillment. The same held for the new sacrifices, for Christ told his disciples

> to offer up to God the firstlings of all creation, not because he needs these things, but that they themselves may not appear barren and ungrateful. Therefore he took the bread (which comes from his creation) and gave thanks and said: This is my body; and in like manner he spoke of the chalice . . . as his blood and so taught the new sacrifice of the new covenant, that sacrifice which the Church has received from the apostles and which she offers to God throughout the world (ch. 17:5).

Malachi 1:10f. is cited in this context.

Elaborating the thought further, St. Irenaeus underlined various points of this statement: God does not need these sacrifices (18:1, 6); the sacrifice of the new covenant proceeds from the gifts of the very earth despised by the Gnostics. He laid special emphasis on the symbolism of the sacrifice: thus it must be offered "in purity and innocence . . . for sacrifices cleanse not the man . . . but the offerer's conscience makes the sacrifice hold" (18:3). We must "show ourselves grateful to God our Creator" as we offer his sacrifice "in purity of mind, in faith without delusion, in steadfast hope, in ardent love" (18:4).

St. Irenaeus placed the sacrifice in a broad context, likening it to a gift presented to a king as a token of honor and reverence toward him (18:1). If the gift is accepted, it is at the same time an honor for the man who presents it. God accepts our good will in order to requite us with his benefits (18:6). The sacrifice of the new covenant is now no longer offered by slaves but by free men, men who thereby gladly surrender to the supreme Lord all they possess (18:2).

We have uncovered very little about the ritual itself. Only the word *eucharistia* (thanksgiving, *gratiarum actio*) recurs any number of times. Just once are we told — and then in passing — that the bread receives the invocation of God and is thus no longer ordinary bread but in fact is *eucharistia* (18:5). The fragment of a letter to Pope Victor preserved in Eusebius' Ecclesiastical History (Hist. eccl. 5:24, 27) is revealing, however, for in it Irenaeus points out that when Bishop Polycarp of Smyrna visited Rome in about the year 160, Pope Anicetus yielded to him the right of the *eucharistia* — which evidently means that he invited Polycarp to celebrate in his stead. This reveals clearly the essential conformity between Rome and Asia Minor in the understanding of the Eucharist as well as in its general liturgical form.

f) The Eucharist among the Gnostics

Since Irenaeus' attack was directed against the Gnostics of his time, we must briefly focus our attention on them. Irenaeus gives us to understand that even these heretics believed firmly in the Eucharist, even though being anti-matter in orientation they were obliged to reject it on principle. We have documents originating in Gnostic circles that give us a glimpse of their practice of the Eucharist.

Among numerous apocryphal "Acts of the Apostles," those of John (mid-second century) and of Thomas (third century) accord the Eucharist an important place (Hänggi-Pahl 74–79), and special prayers are attached to it. In the Acta Johannis the "apostle" John while standing over a grave takes bread, breaks it, and pronounces a prayer directed to Christ; the words "We thank you" recur several times. Thereafter he distributes the "Eucharist of the Lord" to all the brethren (chs. 85f. and 86; see ch. 109).

In the Acta Thomae the Eucharist follows the "act of putting the seal" — otherwise Baptism (chs. 27 and 49). A table is covered with a cloth, the "bread of benediction" is laid on it, and the so-called "apostle" stands and begins the prayer invoking Jesus: "You have granted us to share in the *eucharistia* of your body and blood. . . . Come and hold fellowship with us" (ch. 49). Then the apostle makes a sign of the cross over the bread, breaks it, and distributes it. The effect hoped for is forgiveness of sins as well as immortality (ch. 50).

Just as in such a ritual the general Christian and Catholic tradition comes to light, so too the prayers reveal in part thoroughly orthodox doctrinal belief. Thus the prayer in the Acts of Thomas contains an impressive array of motifs from the history of Christ's Passion as well as of graces prayed for. Here, too, is to be found an invocation to Christ that will be cited in the Irish palimpsest sacramentary of the seventh century.

But side by side with these orthodox expressions, strange names and ideas turn up that can be understood only in terms of the Gnostic Aeons theory: "Come, you fellowship of the Masculine . . . Come, secret Mother" (Acts of Thomas, ch. 50). Moreover, the constant custom of addressing the prayer exclusively to Christ corresponds perfectly to the Gnostic theory that the Godhead itself is inaccessible.

A special group of Gnostics, the Encratites, abstained from wine and conducted the Eucharist with bread and water; but they were not the only ones who did so. Clement of Alexandria tells of heretics who used bread and water at the *prosphora*, when they celebrated the Eucharist, a practice contrary to Church regulations (Stromata 1:19-96).[20] The Ebionites, a Hebrew Christian sect, also employed water instead of wine; but they were perhaps related to those groups among the first Christians in which there was opposition to the chalice, as research has established; and this aversion to drinking blood (albeit under the sacramental species) is explained as a carry-over from an old biblical tradition.[21]

Despite the fact that the biblical accounts already yield several indications of this early emphasis on the chalice,[22] in North Africa Cyprian still had occasion to speak words of admonition and warning (in his letter 63, to Caecilius) against the use of mere water in the Eucharist, as some Catholic clerics were doing "out of ignorance or simplicity" (*ignoranter vel simpliciter*). It is difficult to say how they ever got this idea.

The above reports indicating a certain wavering with regard to the chalice on the margin of Church life in the second and third centuries have been quoted by Lietzmann (in *Messe und Herrenmahl*, pp. 238–49), to support his theory that from the very beginning, in addition to the ritual of celebrating Eucharist attested by St. Paul, there was a second ritual in which only bread was used.

This thesis, however, has been almost universally rejected by Protestant exegetes as being contradictory to the unanimous testimony of the Gospels about the twofold form of the Eucharist.[23]

g) St. Clement of Alexandria and Origen

The great Alexandrians Clement and Origen do indeed repeatedly touch upon the mystery of the Eucharist, but their interest is directed primarily toward an allegorical interpretation of Church traditions in terms of their favorite ideas. Hence, for our purpose very little is to be gathered from their remarks, which merely confirm the impression we already have.[24] The key ideas of St. Irenaeus reappear in Origen. Thus, in his treatise "Against Celsus," we offer up the firstlings (Contra Celsum 8:34). Further, the sign of our gratitude toward God is the bread that we call *eucharistia* (8:57).

3. ST. HIPPOLYTUS OF ROME

Among the Latin Fathers, Hippolytus of Rome belongs to the period when even in the West ecclesiastical literature was still composed in Greek. From his exegetical and theological writings we learn practically nothing about the form and content of the Eucharistic celebration. In his Commentary on the Book of Daniel 4:35, he observes that when Antichrist comes, there will be an end to the sacrifice and libation (9:27) "now offered up in all places and by all nations." That is about all. In the *Traditio Apostolica*, on the contrary, there emerges a surprisingly clear picture of the setup of Church life, and it contains the first complete text of a Eucharistic Prayer that has come down to us, one now well known everywhere:

> The Lord be with you.
> And with your spirit.
> Lift up your hearts.
> We have lifted them up to the Lord.
> Let us give thanks to the Lord.
> It is meet and just.

The celebrant then proceeds:

> We render thee thanks, O God, through thy beloved child Jesus Christ, whom in these last times thou hast sent us as Savior, Redeemer, and messenger of thy will; who is thine inseparable Word, through whom thou madest all things, and in whom thou wert well pleased. Thou didst send him

from heaven into the womb of the Virgin, where he was
incarnate and manifested as thy Son, born of the Holy
Spirit and the Virgin; fulfilling thy will and acquiring for
thee a holy people, he extended his hands in his Passion, in
order to deliver from suffering those who have believed
in thee. And when he was betrayed voluntarily to his
Passion, in order to destroy death, break the chains of the
devil, tread hell under his feet, enlighten the just, fix a
term, and manifest the resurrection, taking bread and
giving thanks to thee, he said: "Take, eat, this is my body
which is broken for you." And likewise the chalice, saying,
"This is my blood, which is shed for you: when you do
this, you make a memory of me." We, therefore, remembering his death and resurrection, offer to thee the bread
and the chalice, giving thee thanks that thou hast deigned
to allow us to appear before thee and to serve thee. And
we beg thee to send thy Holy Spirit upon the oblation of
thy holy Church and, gathering all together in one, grant to
all the saints who partake, to be filled with the Holy Spirit
and to be strengthened in the faith in truth, so that we may
praise and glorify thee by thy child Jesus Christ, through
whom be glory and honor to thee, Father and Son with the
Holy Spirit, in thy holy Church, now and for ever and ever.
Amen.

The Sunday meeting of the people is here presupposed (Botte
4). The bishop is surrounded by his presbyterium. There appears
for the first time the introductory dialogue in which the response
is given by the whole congregation. The bishop alone says the
thanksgiving prayer, whose content corresponds exactly to the
Christological part of the Creed — just what we would expect after
all that we have so far seen of a Christian *eucharistia*. The words
of the Institution, as compared with the New Testament texts,
reveal a certain independence. As the prayer is addressed to God
the Father and concludes by petitioning that the Holy Spirit be
sent down, the Trinitarian structure of Christian prayer as well as
of the Catholic faith stands out prominently. That all "receive"
appears as a self-evident presupposition.

Most revealing of all, however, is the short sentence following
the account of the Institution and the mandate to repeat it: "We,
therefore, remembering his death and resurrection, offer to thee
the bread and the chalice." Significantly, this offering is again

linked to giving thanks: now specifically "giving thee thanks that thou hast deigned to allow us [obviously priest and people included] to appear before thee and to serve thee" (see Apoc. 1:6; 5:10). Crystal clear as are the concepts we encounter here, it has still been maintained on the part of a most scholarly author that what is unfolding is simply the liturgical practice going back to the primitive communities. Thus, according to Lietzmann, p. 181, "What we find there could . . . have been spoken also at the time of the Apostle Paul in Corinth or Ephesus."

4. SUMMARY: THE EUCHARIST IN THE FIRST AND SECOND CENTURIES

Now to recapitulate the testimony of the period concerning thanksgiving and sacrifice, and bring the chief points into sharper focus. Clearly, the one idea predominating from the end of the first century is that what the Lord established at the Last Supper and what the Church has since been celebrating is an *eucharistia*. The word was suggested already by the *eucharistesas* of the New Testament accounts. In the linguistic usage of that time it means to consider and conduct oneself as *eucharistos*, that is, as one richly overwhelmed with gifts and graces—an attitude that found expression in words but did not exclude expression in the form of a gift. This linguistic usage has been examined by Schermann,[25] and he demonstrates that the meaning "thank-offering" may be found in Philo and that this sense of the word is not entirely foreign even to pagan Greek usage.

a) Stress on thanksgiving vs. material sacrifice

In any case the emphasis was on the word and sentiment of gratitude. Clement of Alexandria stresses the importance of this element when he observes that the Redeemer, before breaking bread and handing it around, pronounced a thanksgiving prayer so that we might be able to eat of it in a reasonable manner (Strom. 1:46, 1). It is precisely this thanksgiving that marks off the spiritual moment that was meant to be and in fact *was* the sign of sharpest distinction between Catholic worship on the one hand and, on the other, both pagan and Jewish forms of sacrifice. For pagans and the Pharisees of New Testament times the all-important thing was the exterior performance and the right ritual execution, which in the Christian *eucharistia* remained completely secondary.

Hence it should not surprise us to find the Apologists stating that among Christians there is no sacrifice. They had to assert, as opposed to the pagans, that God does not need our gifts. Thus Aristides (c. 140) can say that "He does not need our sacrifice and gifts, nor anything else from the entire visible world" (Apologia 1:5; p. 4 in Goodspeed edition). Justin develops the same thought further (Apol. 13).

Against the reproach that Christians are atheists (*atheoi*) because they do not offer sacrifice to the divinities, Justin replies by pointing out: "By the tradition that has come down to us the only worship worthy of God is this: not to waste in fire what he has created for nourishment," but to use it and thank him for it "in words of solemn prayers and hymns" (Apol. 13; see ch. 10). Similarly Athenagoras (c. 177), in his Supplicatio:

> The Creator and Father of all needs not blood, nor smoke of burnt fat, nor perfume of flowers nor burnt offerings, since he himself is the perfect odor, wanting nothing, and sufficing unto himself. The greatest sacrifice is that we acknowledge him who has made the heavens . . . and that we lift up pure hands unto him (ch. 13; p. 327f. in Goodspeed, *Die ältesten Apologeten*, Göttingen 1914).

The writer of the Letter to Diognetus expresses similar ideas. The full force and significance of these concepts emerge in the declaration of Minucius Felix in the second century:

> We have no temple and no altar [*delubra et altaria non habemus*]. . . . How should I offer as sacrifice to God [*hostias et victimas*] what he has given for my use, and return to him his own gifts? That would be ungrateful. A genuine sacrifice, on the contrary, is a good soul, a pure mind . . .(Octavius 32).

That such expressions do not necessarily conflict with the evidence — in the same period as well as in the preceding age — that the Eucharist is called a sacrifice appears also from the fact that very similar assertions are to be found in even later authors when they address themselves to heathens at a time when the word *sacrifice* had long since enjoyed currency as the accepted word for the Eucharist, e.g., Arnobius, in his treatise Adversus Nationes 6:1-3; or his pupil Lactantius, in *Epitome divinarum institutionum* 53.

b) *The Christian conception of sacrifice*

The reconciliation of the seeming contradiction in terms is implied when Apollonius, martyred under Emperor Commodus (180–92), declares before the judge: "A sacrifice bloodless and pure, I too and all the Christians bring unto almighty God . . . the sacrifice in the form of prayers" (from the Acta Apollonii 8).[26] As the Epistle of Barnabas puts it (2:6): in the Christian Church it is no longer material gifts that are offered to God, not even gifts made by men; sacrifice now appertains to the sphere of prayer, of the spiritual. It is nothing but *eucharistia.*

So long as there was need to urge the distinction between Christian Eucharistic worship on the one hand and the sacrifice of the pagans or even of the Old Testament Hebrews on the other, the thanksgiving element had to be kept prominently in the foreground as *the* action of the spiritual man. Nevertheless, as we have seen, mention of *prosphora* and even of *thysia* does appear now and then. For in the Christian gathering there was something that went beyond the mere words of thanksgiving, something that called for the action of the celebrant, the bishop, who pronounced the prayer over bread and wine, so that the gift itself became the *eucharistia* (this further meaning obtains already in Justin) and was carried up to God in and along with the prayer.

Here already we have the essentials of a purified concept of sacrifice, for a corroboration of which one had only to turn to Malachi's word about the pure offering. In his work *Der vor-irenäische Opferbegriff* Franz Wieland maintained (mistakenly) that no sacrifice can be shown to have existed in Christian worship before Irenaeus. Of course, if one has in mind, as Wieland did, a sacrifice in the ritually narrow and restricted sense of Old Testament and pagan sacrifices (which were bloody for the most part), then naturally one will not find it in the Christian Church of that time.

There is, however, sufficiently clear evidence for the offering that is *mystically* brought before God. Nor is this new stress on the interior or moral aspect by any means a denial of the concept of sacrifice in the best and truest sense. Indeed, such a shift of emphasis achieves much more faithfully the authentic original spirit of sacrifice, a spirit that the prophets themselves had already fought for.

As compared with Protestant critics who see in the references of the Didache a "departure" from the sense and spirit of the Gospels, there are other more consistent critics who maintain that the same "departure" is to be found already in the concept of *eucharistia*, for in that concept, too, the human factor is brought into the foreground and an "anabatic," rising curve is introduced.[27] But this rising curve is already indicated in the Gospel account of the Lord's own *eucharistia*.

At any rate, what is striking in St. Irenaeus is the prominence given to the material component of the gift-offerings. In the context of the exaggerated spiritualism of the Hellenistic Gnosis, it was no longer necessary to stress the spiritual nature of the Christian sacrifice; rather, it was now the material aspect that needed defense. So attention was directed to the facts that the gift-offerings were from the material world, that these became themselves the *eucharistia* in the thanksgiving prayer, that they were thereby honored and sanctified in the highest degree. It is not by chance that the very first reports that the faithful were bringing bread and wine to the altar belong to this time, for in such a gesture the urge is realized to manifest more clearly — even by an external ritual — that earthly creation, too, is incorporated in the offering.

In this concept of sacrifice, however, attention is focused almost exclusively on the offering of the Church. It has not been explicitly stated that ultimately this is the sacrifice Christ has offered and still offers. Only in Hippolytus do we find an unequivocal statement that the sacrifice of the Church was the fulfillment of the memorial with which Christ's redemptive Passion is recalled, though the matter is treated clearly in Justin as well. And basically the thanksgiving itself is nothing more than just such a recalling, marked at the same time with a God-ward movement. The thanksgiving in fact involves both the recalling and the movement resulting from it and signifying that the gift-offering is taken up before God.

c) Conclusion

During the entire second and third centuries, then, *eucharistia* remains the basic concept through which the Institution of Jesus is grasped and conveyed. With the gradual unfolding of the sacrifice concept contained in it, this *eucharistia* is really nothing more than a memorial offering. At the end of his comprehensive presentation of the early history of the Mass, Ruch rightly proposes a tentative "theory" of what the Mass essentially meant at this period, and it is the "theory" contained in the actual words of the post-Consecration prayer in the Roman Canon which coincides with that of Hippolytus: "We therefore, calling to mind the blessed Passion . . . and also his glorious ascension into heaven, offer unto thy most excellent Majesty . . . a pure host. . . ."

III. THE THIRD CENTURY

1. TERTULLIAN

a) His testimony in general

As we pass to the third century we immediately notice a change of viewpoint in its leading theologians, the Africans Tertullian and St. Cyprian. Neither the word nor the concept of *eucharistia* now occupies the dominant position. True, Tertullian uses the word *Eucharist,* but it is no longer applied to the action but only to the gift proceeding from it. In his argument with Marcion he does use the equivalent expression *gratiarum actiones* to denote the thanksgiving prayer, but only in the more restricted sense, that is, the prayer pronounced over the bread (Adv. Marc. 1:23).

In the form of *oratio et actio gratiarum* (prayer and thanksgiving — which incidentally is reminiscent of Justin's *euchai kai eucharistiai*), the prayer is juxtaposed to the offering a cured leper had to bring to the Temple in the Old Testament (ibid. 4:9); and in this case an offering is implied. But the expression does not serve as a designation for the whole action, as *eucharistia* does in Irenaeus; it would be too complex and unwieldy for that. Tertullian has no fixed name for that action at all. He uses various paraphrases, and among them the most frequent are *offerre* and *oblatio,* and, only less often, *sacrificium.*[28]

In Tertullian the sacrificial nature of the Eucharist is brought out unequivocally. The sacred action takes place with the commu-

nity gathered *ad aram Dei* (at the altar of God), taking part in it
(De Oratione 19), and the *sanctus minister* (holy minister) performing it (De Exhortatione Castitatis 10). The offering is made
through the ministry of a priest (*per sacerdotem*; ibid. 11). From
his hand or from the hand of the presbyters who preside (*praesi-
dentes*), the faithful receive the Sacrament, *eucharistiae sacramentum* (De Corona Militum 3). Yet at same time Tertullian himself
stresses the priestly dignity of all the faithful (De Oratione 28).[29]

  The celebration is held at an early morning hour (*antelu-
canis coelibus*; De Corona Militum 3). As for the day of the week,
Sunday is mentioned just once, and casually (*inter dominica sollemnia*; De Anima 9). Tertullian makes explicit mention of the
Eucharistic celebration on the "station days," Wednesday and Friday (De Oratione 19); so too, at the annual remembrance of the
dead (De Corona Militum 3; De Monogamia 10). All those present
receive Communion as a matter of course; so much so that if one
does not intend to communicate, one must stay away from the celebration itself (De Oratione 19). Communion is distributed under
both species (De Resurrectione Carnis 8); in fact one may even
take the Lord's body home and eat it before all other food (*ante
omnem cibum*; Ad Uxorem 2:5). Tertullian insists upon the greatest reverence before the sacred gift (De Corona Militum 3) and
underlines its holy and salutary effects.

b) His understanding of the Eucharist as sacrifice

  Now, what may we conclude of Tertullian's understanding of
the Eucharistic action from the expressions *offerre* (offer) and
oblatio (offering)? In certain passages the words designate the
whole of the celebration as, for example, when *offerre* is coupled
with *docere* (to teach) and *tingere* (to baptize) to connote the
Church ceremonial denied to women (De Virginibus Velandis
9:2), or when oblations for the dead are referred to as the annual
remembrance of the dead (De Corona Militum 3). But these forms
are applied also to the characteristic action of an individual Christian. Objecting on one occasion to the defender of a second mar-
riage who performs the annual commemoration for his first wife
(*pro qua oblationes annuas reddis*), Tertullian argues, "Will you
offer the sacrifice for both wives and have the priest recommend
them both?" (*Offeres pro duabus et commendabis illas duas per
sacerdotem?*; De Exhortatione Castitatis 11); he obviously allud-

ing to the layman's action, which is of a different kind from that of the priest.

When a thorough investigation of Tertullian's linguistic usage was undertaken by R. Berger, it developed that for Tertullian *offerre* is not a sacrificial term in the full sense.[30] The word is derived from secular speech and retains in later as in older Latin its primary secular meaning: to present, to offer, even when the offering is made to God. In the course of the Mass the faithful present their gifts. But this very action is now valued the more highly precisely because of the Gnostic contempt for matter: it becomes integrated into the sacred action instituted by Christ; it becomes ritualized. And simply for the reason that the gifts offered are palpable and concrete, the words *offerre* and *oblatio* are appropriately extended to encompass the whole reality.

On the other hand, Tertullian does not have the slightest doubt that the object of the Christian sacrifice is not creaturely gifts. In his Apologeticum we encounter statements as emphatic as those of the second-century Apologists. Thus, in opposing the massive pagan sacrifices he emphatically declares: "I offer to God a precious sacrifice, as he requires me to do: it is the prayer proceeding from a chaste body and a pure soul, from a holy spirit" (30:5). In his apologetical letter to the pagan governor Scapula (2), he repeats the daring antithesis of the Apologists: "We offer sacrifice for the welfare of the Emperor, but in the form of genuine prayer [*pura prece*]; for God, the Creator of the whole world, needs not sweet odors nor any blood."

In Tertullian's usage the word *oratio* means also and above all else the Eucharist. Indeed, as Berger observes, "Some texts become intelligible only if the Eucharist is meant by *oratio*" (p. 51). In these texts the word corresponds almost identically to the Greek *eucharistia*. That this prayer implies a sacrifice, a new, a Christian, sacrifice, Tertullian makes clear in another place, where he repeats that the worship in which Christians take part consists of prayers, but prayers that include a sacrifice (*sacrificiorum orationibus interveniendum*; De Oratione 19).

Occasionally a similitude throws clearer light on the essence of this sacrifice. Thus, just as the fatted calf was killed to welcome the returning prodigal son, so too a special feast awaits the apostate returning to the fold; for him Christ will again be sacrificed (*rursus illi mactabitur Christus*; De Pudicitia 9). Christ himself is thus the object of the offering. In remembrance of the blood he would shed (*in sanguinis sui memoriam*; De Anima 17), and thus in remembrance of his death on the Cross, Christ consecrated (*consecravit*) wine at the Last Supper. Christ is also the Priest who ultimately performs the offering in his Church. For the sacrifice, which must be offered in the Temple by a man freed from sin, is prayer and thanksgiving offered in the Church through Jesus Christ, universal priest of the Father (*apud ecclesiam per Christum Jesum catholicum Patris sacerdotem*; Adv. Marc. 4:9).

2. St. Cyprian

a) The Eucharist is a sacrifice

As for St. Cyprian's conception of the Eucharistic celebration, we get to know it in his Letter 63, to Caecilius. In the course of counteracting an abuse that was gaining ground at the time, he argued decisively that at the proper celebration of the Eucharist one must not use water but wine. *Offerre* and *oblatio*, like *sacrificium*, have now come to stay as the accepted predicates for the Eucharistic celebration; in fact as Berger holds (pp. 63f.), they are predicated by Cyprian only of the Christian sacrifice, and not of pagan or Old Testament sacrifices. Drawing a parallel between what was prefigured in Melchisedek and what was instituted by Christ, Cyprian affirms that Jesus "offered that very same thing that Melchisedek offered, that is, bread and wine, to wit, his body and blood" (*obtulit hoc idem quod Melchisedech obtulerat, id est panem et vinum, suum scilicet corpus et sanguinem*; Ep. 63:4; CSEL numbering). What had been only an image in Melchisedek has become the reality in Christ. What Christ did then is also done now and must be performed in exactly the same way. It is the "Lord's sacrifice" (*sacrificium dominicum*), the sacrifice of God the Father and of the Christ (Ep. 63:9). Further, all the material pertaining to this new sacrifice has already been foretold and enumerated in the Book of Proverbs (9:1-5): the slain sacrificial victim, bread and wine, the altar, the apostles (Ep. 5).

b) Christ is its priest

The priesthood of Christ receives very strong emphasis in Cyprian's Letters. Christ is the High Priest of God the Father (*summus sacerdos Dei Patris*); he has offered himself to the Father as a sacrificed victim, and has commanded that this be done in his memory (Ep. 14). Clearly this priesthood of Christ is understood here not merely in the general sense of the Letter to the Hebrews or that of the traditional doxologies in which Christ is seen as the mediator of our prayer, but even more specifically: in living relation to the fullness of the present Eucharistic sacrifice. Of course the priesthood is predicated also of the creaturely office-bearers: they too are *sacerdos*; the "presbyters" too can "offer" and can distribute the Lord's body (Ep. 15:1). But they do so only in the place of Christ (*vice Christi*; Ep. 63:14). In this passage Cyprian also expresses the opinion (which corresponds to his erroneous position on the Baptism of heretics) that the Eucharist of heretics is null and void, since they had cut themselves off from the Church; for the paschal lamb can be eaten only at home (De Ecclesiae Catholicae Unitate 8).

Since the real priest is Jesus Christ, the Eucharistic celebration is also called *sacrificium dominicum* (the Lord's sacrifice), or simply *dominicum* (the Lord's). But, remarkably, its relation to sacrifice of the Cross almost never surfaces. It is called *sacrifice*, not because the sacrifice of the Cross is made present but because at the Last Supper Christ made the offering and even now continues to make it through the priest, then as now certainly with eyes turned toward the sacrificial death on the Cross. It is in this sense that St. Cyprian remarks that at every sacrifice we make mention of Christ's Passion, that Christ's Passion is its raison d'être "because the Passion of the Lord is the sacrifice we offer" (*passio est enim Domini sacrificium quod offerimus*; Ep. 63:17).

Hence wine is required for the purpose of representing his blood. And indeed the greatness of the Eucharist lies in this: it belongs to "the very mystery of our Lord's Passion and our redemption" (*ad ipsum dominicae passionis et nostrae redemptionis sacramentum*; 63:14). But without separating priesthood and sacrifice from the death on the Cross, and despite the fact that the Eucharist is looked upon as a re-presentation of Christ's Passion, the terms *priest* and *sacrifice* point simply to the event taking place in the celebration itself.

c) The Christian people share in the sacrifice

This sacrifice embraces the Christian people, too, says Cyprian; that is why water is mingled with wine. As Christ has borne our sins by his sufferings, so too in this sacrifice the people are joined to Christ just as inseparably as the water to the wine (Ep. 63:13), and thus are included in the gifts offered up. But the people also have an active part to play. The celebration is community worship; it presupposes the assembly of the faithful, so much so that the *lapsi*, whose faith had grown weak in the face of persecution, cannot be admitted to it before they have become reconciled (Ep. 16:3). It is also an established custom for the faithful to contribute bread and wine for the celebration. This appears from Cyprian's censure, in his treatise on almsgiving, of a certain rich widow who comes empty-handed to the *dominicum* or Eucharistic service and receives Communion, thereby taking "a portion of the sacrifice offered by the poor" (De Opere et Eleemosynis 15).

Participation in the sacrifice is not, however, restricted to those who are physically present. The brethren and the benefactor are remembered "in sacrifices and in prayers" (Ep. 62:5), with confidence that this remembrance will benefit the persons concerned. Sacrifice is offered also for the dead, provided they had not become unworthy; and their names are mentioned (*pro eo, pro dormitione ejus*; Ep. 1:2).

Thus Cyprian lays stress on the blessing the Eucharist brings to those for whom it is performed. Yet it would be unwarranted on the part of liberal criticism to read in this an innovation vis-à-vis the earlier times, on the ground that now the Eucharist is no longer regarded as the sacrifice of thanksgiving but only as a work of reparation,[31] when as a matter of fact this idea had appeared already in Tertullian, to whom the offering for the dead was quite familiar. In any case Cyprian brings out more clearly the point that the hierarchy officiates at the celebration: a priest and a deacon, he says, were wrong "in communicating with the lapsed and offering their oblations" (*communicando cum lapsis et offerendo oblationes eorum*; Ep. 34:1).

d) The celebration

Of the celebration itself St. Cyprian gives but few details. It seems that Mass is celebrated daily (Ep. 63:16; De Or. Dom. 18). In order to face the coming persecution one must drink the chalice daily and so to be ready to shed one's own blood for Christ (Ep. 58:1). Importantly, it seems that the daily celebration took place within little groups in the evening and in connection with supper

(Ep. 63:16). Readings too were combined with the celebration; scriptural passages were read out from the pulpit by a lector (Epp. 38:2; 39:4).

3. Evidence of the Syrian Didascalia

We gain valuable insights also from the so-called Syrian Didascalia, a treatise on Church discipline composed in Greek and dating from the first half of the third century. This work revives the Eucharistic concept upholding the spiritual aspect of Christian sacrifice as opposed to the material. Comparing the law of the new covenant with that of the old, the author says, "Instead of the sacrifices which then were, offer now prayers and petitions and thanksgivings," and then proceeds to contrast "the oblations which are offered through the bishops to the Lord God" with the tithes of the old covenant (p. 86 in the R. H. Connolly edition). It is only the reference to the various tithes of the old law that prompts the author to advert also to the material side of the Eucharist and, in that connection, to the priest's function.

In the Didascalia all are exhorted to assemble in church on the day of the Lord and not cause the body of Christ to be short one member (p. 124). At the same time, without the Old Testament dread of uncleanness, they should gather together "even in the cemeteries, and read the holy Scriptures . . . and offer an acceptable Eucharist . . . and pray and offer for them that are fallen asleep" (p. 252). Thus the same understanding of the Eucharist's function vis-à-vis the remembrance of the dead prevails in northern Syria as in North Africa.

Also of interest is the courteous gesture with which a visiting bishop was to be received. The local Ordinary should invite him not only to speak to the community but also to celebrate the Eucharist. "And when you offer the oblation, let him speak. But if he is wise and gives the honor to thee, and is unwilling to offer, at least let him speak over the cup" (p. 122). The most faithful and straightforward interpretation of this instruction is that he should be permitted the honor of uttering the words of Consecration over the chalice. Not so for the editor, Dom Connolly; for him it is only the cup "offered at the Agape" (p.liii).

IV. THE GREEK FATHERS
THE EASTERN LITURGIES

1. THE GREEK FATHERS

When the Greek Fathers of the fourth century touch upon the Eucharist in their writings, they are chiefly concerned with its divine significance and spiritual efficacy — and understandably so, in the context of those controversial times. But when they advert to the actual celebration, they speak of it quite simply as sacrifice, *prosphora, thysia*. And with this there moves to the foreground an aspect that had been neglected before that time. The Eucharist is a sacrifice, not so much because it is an action in which the community offers, but above all else because through it the sacrifice of Christ, his sacrificial death on the Cross, is made available to us.

a) Eusebius of Caesarea and St. John Chrysostom

Thus, for Eusebius of Caesarea (d. 339), Christ has offered the wonderful sacrifice to the Father for the salvation of us all, "having at the same time handed down to us a memorial (*mneme*) that we can continually offer to God as a sacrifice" (Demonstratio Evangelica 1:10; PG 22:88). It is an idea he returns to several times and in different forms. This is why, as he explains on another occasion (i.e., in his panegyric of Constantine), "altars and sacred meeting places have been set up over the entire face of the earth," even though the sacrifices in question are "unbloody and spiritual sacrifices [this last is a favorite idea of the old Apologists], sacrifices such as are performed through prayer and through the word of God" (De Laudibus Constantini 16; PG 20:1425f.). Incidentally, the suggestion of "reasonable sacrifice" (*logike thysia*) had already been put forward by the pre-Christian philosophers, and the Apologists eagerly appropriated it to apply to the Eucharist.[32]

St. John Chrysostom develops this same idea to the fullest. According to his Homily on Hebrews, Christ has once and for all offered himself as sacrificial victim.

> But do we not offer sacrifice every day? Yes, we do, but we do it in performing the memorial (*anamnesin*) of his death. . . . We do not perform [every time] a different sacrifice as did the High Priest in the Old Testament, but always the same, or rather, we perform the memorial of the sacrifice (In Hebr. Hom. 17:4; PG 63:131).

This idea seems to be shared by the Greek Fathers. Theodoret in his Commentary on Hebrews repeats it in almost identical words (In Heb. 9; PG 82:736). Chrysostom speaks of the manner in which the sacrifice comes about in the Eucharist: "It is not man that causes the offerings to become the body and blood of Christ, but Christ himself . . . acting through us." The priest pronounces the words "This is my body"; and "These words transform the offerings . . . they effect the perfect sacrifice" (In Proditione Judae Hom. 1:6; PG 49:380). In another passage he speaks of the invocation to the Holy Spirit upon the offerings, but offers no further explanation as to how this invocation is to be harmonized with the words of Institution, with regard to their respective effects.

Further, according to Chrysostom, the efficacy of the words of consecration do not signify the only way in which Christ is present in the Mass. His invisible presence pervades the entire celebration; he is the "Lord of the Banquet," as Betz construes it (*Die Eucharistie* 1.1:131). Even when the priest gives Communion, it is the Lord's hand that invisibly gives it (In Matthew Hom. 50:3; PG 58:507).[33] Christ, who is priest, is also himself the sacrificed victim. Christ is the lamb that is laid on the altar. Thus, for Chrysostom in his treatise on the priesthood, you are no longer looking at an earthly thing "when you see the Lord sacrificed and laid there, and the priest standing before the victim and praying" (De Sacerdotio 3:4; PG 48:642).

b) The Cappadocians and St. Cyril of Jerusalem

The Greek Fathers as well as St. Ephrem the Syrian return again and again to a favorite concept of theirs, that is, Christ had already offered this sacrifice at the Last Supper.[34] St. Gregory of Nyssa advances it unequivocally in his sermon on Christ's resurrection to show that Christ freely gave himself up as a victim for us and that the malice of the Jews would have been powerless without his own will: "He forestalled them by an act of his wisdom . . . and gave himself up as an offering and a victim for us." In this way Jesus showed that the sacrifice had already been accomplished "in a mystical and invisible manner" (In Christi Resurr. Serm. 1; PG 46:612).

Of the mystical slaying that now takes place continually, St. Gregory of Nazianz, too, speaks in his Letter to Amphilochius. Here he asks his fellow bishop to pray for him "when with thy word thou bringest down the Word, when thou dost separate the body and blood of the Lord with an unbloody cut, using thy voice as sword" (Ep. 171; PG 37:281).

Another point to notice here is that intercessory prayer is coupled with the sacrifice as being particularly efficacious. Its value is underscored especially in the fifth Mystagogical Catechesis in which St. Cyril of Jerusalem (c. 383–86) explains the Mass to the newly baptized. When the Holy Spirit is called down and the sacrifice is consummated, he writes, "then we invoke God over this sacrifice of reconciliation for the universal peace of the Church, for the welfare of the world, for kings, soldiers, and confederates, for the sick, the oppressed, and all who stand in need of help . . . for we believe that it will benefit immensely the souls for whom we pray when the holy and awe-inspiring Victim lies before us" (5:8f).

2. THE EASTERN LITURGIES

The most enlightening sources of information on the way the Mass was construed and celebrated in the Eastern Churches during patristic times are the texts of the liturgies themselves, for which there is already ample documentation in the fourth century. The question here is not one of minute details of wording and rubric but rather a matter of structural elements that tell us something about the conception of the celebration as a whole.

a) Egypt

For Egypt, we have the Euchologion of Serapion, whom we may reasonably identify with Athanasius' friend, Bishop Serapion of Thmuis (d. after 362), despite certain doubts raised by Botte. The significant passage for our purpose here is known as the *Euche Prosphorou* (Hänggi-Pahl 128-33); its very title stresses the sacrificial character of the action. The opening is typical of the East, even of later periods: "It is becoming and just . . ."; and as it unfolds it appears less as a thanksgiving prayer than as a prayer of adoration culminating in the Sanctus.

The offering is pronounced three times: first in the transition from the Sanctus to the Institution narrative; then after the words over the bread: "Therefore we too, re-enacting the re-presentation of [his] death, have offered bread"; and again after the words over the chalice. Moreover, an epiclesis occurs twice: first immediately after the Sanctus: "Also fill this sacrifice with thy power"; and once more after the offering of the chalice, this time as a prayer for the descent "of the holy Logos" (no explicit mention is made of the Holy Spirit on either occasion). In the final prayer for a fruitful Communion and for every blessing upon the assembly, the people are referred to as those who offer oblation together with thanksgiving (*ta prosphora kai tas eucharistias*). Offering and thanksgiving are thus looked upon as being at least very closely associated if not indeed identical.

b) Antioch

The lengthy Eucharistic Prayer that has come down from the region of Antioch (Hänggi-Pahl 82-95) as part of the so-called Clementine liturgy of the Apostolic Constitutions (VIII.12:6-49), may be traced to the end of the fourth century. Here the thanksgiving prayer swells into a song of gratitude for the gift of creation and especially that of redemption. After the Institution narrative there follows a sentence that echoes the wording of Hippolytus' Eucharistic Prayer (reproduced in ch. 2 above), a sentence whose twofold theme appears from now on in all the liturgies of the Greek-speaking area: "We recall and we offer" (*memnemenoi toinun . . . prospheromen*); and this is followed by the epiclesis, the Communion Prayer, and a long litany of intercessions. Another passage in the same collection (II.59:4) contains the term *anaphora,* which from then on gained currency almost everywhere in the East as the designation for the entire Eucharistic part of the Mass including Communion as well as for the formularies composed for this part: what comes after the readings is described as "offering of the sacrifice and gift of the sacred nourishment" (*thysias anaphora kai trophes hieras dorea*). This reveals the new shift of emphasis from the mode of thanksgiving, which had found expression in the heretofore prevailing thanksgiving theme (*eucharistein*), to that of presenting, offering (*anapherein*).

To the fourth century belong also the two basic formularies that came to be widely accepted as standard or ideal prototypes for the further evolution of the anaphora in the East: the Anaphora of James for the West Syrian and Byzantine regions with Antioch as metropolis (Hänggi-Pahl 244–61), and the Anaphora of Mark for the Egyptian region around Alexandria (101–23). The two types differ to some extent in their structural arrangements. In the Anaphora of James, the prayer between the Sanctus and Consecration is centered upon the notion of gratitude for God's work of redemption, and it is only in the second part of the Mass, i.e., after the anamnesis, offertory, and epiclesis, that the intercessions are introduced. Whereas in the Anaphora of Mark the thanksgiving as well as the first expression of offering and the intercessions precede the Sanctus.

c) Other formularies

In the East there are also some individual formularies that must be at least as old as those mentioned above, if not older. Among these is the basic form of the Anaphora of Basil that has been retained in the Egyptian tradition (Hänggi-Pahl 347–57). It is the thanksgiving prayer text that Basil the Great (d. 379) had in hand and expanded, by introducing many biblical turns of thought and phrase, into the form used even today in the whole sphere of the Byzantine rite, as the Liturgy of St. Basil. Even the well-known St. John Chrysostom liturgy of the Byzantine rite, in an embryonic form suggesting the fourth century, seems to be retained in the West Syrian Anaphora of the Twelve Apostles (Hänggi-Pahl 265–68).[35] But these texts do not differ essentially from the Anaphora of James in their structure or, consequently, in their handling of the concept of sacrifice.

d) Anaphora of the Apostles Addai and Mari

The situation is different in the case of the Anaphora of the Apostles Addai and Mari (Hänggi-Pahl 374–80), the oldest and most important formulary of East Syrian liturgical prayer. According to some authors, this formulary contains a kernel of native growth rooted in the Syriac-speaking region, despite strong Greek influence. The most striking thing about it is that the oldest manuscript versions do not contain the Institution narrative. Several explanations have been proposed: that the "discipline of the secret" required the text to be kept concealed; that the text was too well known to have had to be written down; or that a general allusion to the work of redemption may have been considered sufficient.

Whatever, this anaphora combines a series of praises of God with a confession of one's own lowliness as well as intercessions. There does appear an anamnesis mentioning the suffering, death, burial, and resurrection of Christ, followed by the epiclesis as prayer for the coming of the Holy Spirit "upon this oblation"; so that we do get merely a casual mention of sacrifice. And, of course, the concept of the Mass as sacrifice is certainly implicit as a venerable tradition particularly in the sphere of the East Syrian liturgy, since it is precisely here that the invocation *Let us give thanks* — common to all other liturgies — has been replaced even in the oldest documents by the formula, "The oblation is being offered unto God the Lord of all." Then follows the usual response: *It is right and just* (Brightman 283). The invitation is not to give thanks but to offer sacrifice.

e) The fraction

In the Eastern liturgies of Greek origin the continuation of the anamnesis is not the only point at which the sacrificial aspect is articulated. A second point is the fraction (breaking of bread), and a third, the Great Entrance. And here again, we discover the same tendencies that we have already noticed in the Greek Fathers.

Originally the fraction had no other meaning than to divide the one bread for the purpose of distributing a share to the whole assembly. But already Chrysostom, in his Homily on First Corinthians, saw the Passion of Christ symbolized in the fraction: "What Christ did not suffer on the Cross, he suffers in the sacrifice for thee" (In 1 Cor. Hom. 24:2; PG 61:200). Later, Patriarch Eutychius (d. 582) brought out this idea clearly: for him the fraction represents the slaying of the victim (De Pascha 3; PG 86:2396).

In the next period this interpretation of the fraction found still clearer expression in the Byzantine rite and in other rites as well — so much so, indeed, that finally the "slaying of the lamb" was introduced at the beginning of the Mass as a separate ritual; and a special instrument, "the holy spear," was fashioned for the purpose. The idea itself, however, must have been even older. Indeed, it seems to be implied even in the variant "body broken" (*soma klomenon*) interpolated into Paul's First Corinthians 11:24 and handed down in the entire Syrian tradition in this type of wording: As the Lord's blood was shed, so the Lord's body was "broken" with the breaking of the one bread.

The term *lamb* as used to designate the body of Christ lying
on the altar (already Chrysostom was fond of this figure) belongs
to the same tradition. The apocryphal Acts of Andrew had this
apostle say: "Every day I offer to the almighty one and true God
. . . a spotless Lamb."[36] Finally, in the Byzantine liturgy lamb
(*amnas*) became the common current expression for the bread
even before its consecration, as with host (*hostia*) in the Roman
liturgy.

f) The offering of the gifts

In the Eastern rite the practice of bringing gifts to the altar
took the form of the so-called Great Entrance. It was but natural
to associate this gift-giving with sacrifice, for in it the *anapherein*,
the anaphora, literally came true. Theodore of Mopsuestia, in his
Catechetical Homilies (written *c.* 390), sees in this act a starkly
realistic re-presentation of Christ being led to his suffering and
stretched on the altar to be sacrificed for us.[37] But even though the
Eastern liturgies stress strongly that Christ is sacrificed, and though
their ritual function is to revive Christ's sacrificial suffering, they
still make it quite clear that we are dealing here with an *unbloody*,
spiritual sacrifice.

The gesture of offering in the specific sense of bringing or
presenting gifts has affected the ritual in still another way, i.e., in
the position and arrangement of the altar. As far as we can make
out from the fragmentary information that has come down to us,
in early times no hard-and-fast rule determined at which side of the
altar the priest was to stand. In Egypt he usually stood facing the
people; in Syria, as early as the fourth century, the altar was usually
placed against the eastern wall of the church, so that both priest
and people faced east. This was characteristic of those parts of
Christendom (e.g., eastern Syria) where the call to give thanks had
become a call to offer sacrifice.

In other Eastern as well as Western rites both arrangements
were still in common use during the fourth century. Yet it could
not have been by chance that during the following centuries in all
the Eastern countries the practice of having the priest face the people was abandoned, so that today the only accepted positioning of
the altar in the East is that in which the priest faces the same direc-

tion as the people — a usage that corresponds to the action of laying gifts before God.[38]

g) The liturgy as "mystery"

In the Eastern liturgies the concept of sacrifice not only received special emphasis but was characterized by a distinctive approach as well. The Christian sacrifice is a mystery, a mystical event. The "discipline of the secret" was not engendered by association with the sacrifice concept, and was in fact never restricted to the Eucharist alone; it merely found the most visible application in this area. The act of dismissing those not permitted to participate (specifically the catechumens), accepted as a matter of course as early as Tertullian (De Praescript. 41), develops into a substantial ritual in the Apostolic Constitutions (VIII.6-9). In the Byzantine liturgy the dismissal of catechumens is retained as a ritual even to this day (Brightman 375).

But then in this rite still another element of secrecy (*arcanum*) has been introduced within the celebration; the sacred parts are not to be performed in the presence of even the faithful permitted to gather there. As early as during the sixth century the sanctuary of Hagia Sophia was separated from the congregation by a series of columns and railings. During the seventh century in some Eastern countries, this actually amounted to a wall completely cutting off the sanctuary from the people.[39] Although the disposition to preserve contact with the people is evident, especially by way of the litany (*ektene*) of the deacon, the "Canon" of the Byzantine Mass remains closed to the congregation's view except for certain moments.

The presence of mystery seems to have been regarded as awesome quite early in the evolution of the Eastern liturgies. From the last decade of the fourth century onward, when several Fathers of the Syro-Antiochian region spoke of the Eucharist, the accent invariably fell on the ineffable, the fearful, the *awe*-ful. Chrysostom in particular used the strongest available expressions in several passages. The mysteries are called *phrikta, phriktodestata*. These predicates are applied to the altar, the chalice, the blood, even to the hour of celebration — as has been pointed out especially by Edmond Bishop in his study "Fear and Awe Attaching to the Eucharistic Service."[40] In the liturgies themselves expressions of this kind likewise recur often enough.

h) Shift of attitude toward Christ

Several factors may have been at work here. Accent on the realism of the sacrifice was probably one of them. Moreover, in time of peace the people had begun to transfer to Christ epithets usually applied to emperors. In the Great Entrance the coming of Christ becomes the King's entry; hence, a rich, courtly ceremonial is indicated. Again, during the controversy over Arianism the need was felt to underline Christ's divine majesty, his equality of substance with the Father. All this operated to exaggerate his distance from humankind.

From another angle, too, the struggle against the Arian heresy caused a considerable change of outlook in the Eastern Churches. In order to avoid the accusation of subordinationism, the Church began to drop the reference in the doxologies to Christ as Mediator, the High Priest through whom God is glorified, in favor of emphasizing his divinity.[41] Only the Egyptian liturgies were content with complementing "through him" by "with him." The Byzantine liturgy on the other hand recognizes only the form of doxology in which Christ is glorified *with* the Father and *together with* the Holy Spirit, or even that in which the three divine Persons are simply mentioned together on an equal level in the manner of the mandate to baptize in Matthew 28:19, "And we praise thy glorious name 'of the Father, and of the Son, and of the Holy Spirit'."

A further consequence of this emphasis was that not only the hymns and litanies (*ektenes*) but also the priest's prayer (until then regularly addressed to God the Father) were now occasionally or even regularly addressed to the Son. The West Syrian-Jacobite liturgy applies this change, at the very heart of the Anaphora, to the prayer of the anamnesis and of the offering: "As we now, Lord, recall *thy* death . . . we offer *thee* this awe-ful and unbloody sacrifice" (Hänggi-Pahl 271). In this change the West Syrian-Jacobite liturgy was preceded in the fifth century by the so-called Testamentum Domini (ibid. 221). In the Syrian Anaphora of Gregory carried over to Egypt, the same change is further extended to embrace the whole range of the Anaphora: all the prayers are addressed to Christ (ibid. 360–73).

It is clear that such an unbalanced approach not only caused the faithful to neglect the humanity of the God-Man at the right hand of the Father; in addition, and emphatically, it rendered their understanding of the sacrifice more difficult. The question did not bring about a serious crisis until somewhat later. Soterichus, elected Patriarch of Antioch, took exception to one such prayer in which sacrifice is offered to Christ: the well-known "Worthy is No One" (*oudeis axios*), which was recited at the Great Entrance and closed with the address: "For Thou Thyself dost offer and art offered, dost receive and art received, O Christ, our God . . ." (in the translation of the Monks of St. Procopius Abbey, Lisle, Illinois).

A synod in Constantinople decided against Soterichus, pointing out the two natures in Christ: as man offering the sacrifice, as God receiving it. Considered purely theologically, the decision could not have been different; yet in the process, the viewpoint of the economy of salvation and a balanced spirituality corresponding to it were not taken into consideration.[42]

The change of attitude was echoed also in the new concept of the High-Priesthood of Christ, as may be seen already in Chrysostom.[43] The epithet *High Priest* is now taken to mean not so much the mediation that Christ exercises in his humanity, but far more the power of his divinity with which he accomplishes through the priest's words the transformation of the earthly gifts. *High Priest* now signifies consecrator exclusively (as the present author has pointed out[44]). To this interpretation belongs also the representation known as "Liturgy" in older Byzantine iconography and depicting Christ as High Priest surrounded by angels bearing sacrificial vessels; it is a representation closely related to that of Christ as Pantocrator.

i) Allegorization of the anamnesis

Despite all the emphasis laid on the concept of sacrifice in the Eastern liturgies, it should not be overlooked that in the course of time the second principle involved from the beginning in the liturgy's formation gradually asserted itself more and more, i.e., the principle of the anamnesis. People were not content with seeing in the sacred action instituted by Christ a memorial of his Passion and resurrection in the abstract; as is clear from Schulz' work (p. 67), the individual customs and rituals introduced by the Church had also to be put at the service of this theme and its unfolding. The new drift is already discernible in the Catechetical Homilies of Theodore of Mopsuestia, who sees re-presented in the Great Entrance the beginning of the Passion, and in the breaking and distribution of the bread the various appearances of the risen Lord (Mingana ed., 106f.).

The allegorical expositions during the following centuries laboriously interpret the entire progress of the liturgy as a representation of Christ's life from his incarnation to his ascent to heaven. These various interpretations frequently conflict with one another; thus, when the bread is laid upon the altar it is now the birth of the Child, now the slaying of the Lamb, and so on. Images from the sacred liturgy were scrambled with those of the earthly life of Christ. Only later did liturgists such as Theodore of Andida (eleventh century) and Nicholas Cabasilas (fourteenth century) endeavor to contain allegorical interpretation within clear bounds once more.

While there are few traces of parallel glossing of the ceremonies in the Western Mass, such "conceits" exercised a strong influence on the Byzantine liturgy. The basic form flowing from the *eucharistia* was clothed in layer upon layer of allegory. As such, the Byzantine liturgy became like a play on two stages. The feeling of the mystical and of the other-worldly was thereby strengthened, but at the same time the Mass was made more difficult to understand. In any event, however, in adopting wholeheartedly the language of the people of the day, the Eastern liturgies found an important counterweight to maintain a balance between the intelligible and the ineffable.

V. THE LATIN FATHERS THE LITURGIES OF THE WEST

1. St. Ambrose

Among the Latin Fathers, St. Ambrose is distinguished for the clarity with which he explains the consecrating power of Christ's words in the Eucharist. He is also a witness of the traditional teaching concerning its significance, for in the Eucharist, he says in his defense of Christ's divinity, the Christian recognizes "the sacrament of the Lord's death" (De Fide 4:10; CSEL 78:201); and, in writing on Luke's Gospel, he says that in the Eucharist Christ is sacrificed (*immolatur*; In Lc 1:28; CSEL 32:4, 28).

Christ has offered his blood for us once; but now it is the same Christ who offers through us as well ("he evidently offers through us, for it is his word that consecrates the sacrifice"; *ipse offerre manifestatur in nobis, cujus sermo sanctificat sacrificium;* In Ps. 38:25; CSEL 63:204). Thus, while the relation of the Eucharist to the death on the Cross is kept well to the fore, the sacrificial character is seen as flowing from the event taking place here and now in the Eucharist, not from a re-presentation of the sacrifice of the Cross.

2. St. Augustine

a) The daily sacrifice

St. Augustine's thinking on the Eucharist is similar in the essentials. At the center of his thought and of his spirituality stands Christ crucified, and the sacrifice in which he has offered himself ("he is both priest and sacrifice"; *ipse sacerdos, ipse sacrificium*; Sermo 374:3; PL 39:1668). But the offering takes place each time in the Eucharist as well. As one letter states it, Christ has been sacrificed once in his own person (*in se ipso*); but in the sacrament he is sacrificed daily for the nations of the world (*in sacramento omni die populis immolatur*; Ep. 98:9; CSEL 34:530-31).

Now, says St. Augustine in his debate with Faustus, this daily sacrifice is seen in total relation to that one sacrifice; it is the memorial of that one sacrifice that Christians perform: "They celebrate the memory of the identical sacrifice once offered, and do so by a holy offering of it and by sharing in Christ's body and blood" (*per acti ejusdem sacrificii memoriam celebrant sacrosancta oblatione et participatione corporis at sanguinis Christi*; Contra Faustum 20:18; CSEL 25:559). Time and again, moreover, he invokes the whole tradition, reasserting that what was foreshadowed in Melchisedek and prophesied by Malachi is here fulfilled.

Augustine's Eucharistic theology embraces a broad vision and ranges over a wide horizon; and for that reason he is not so much concerned with the technical details of the liturgy. Still, he speaks in another letter of prayers (*orationes*) pronounced when the gifts laid on the Lord's table are sanctified (the bread "is blessed and consecrated and broken for distribution"; *benedicitur et sanctificatur et ad distribuendum comminuitur*) after which the Lord's Prayer is said (Ep. 149:16; CSEL 44:362).

To him it is self-evident that the sacrifice of the Mediator (*sacrificium mediatoris*) may be offered for the dead (Enchiridion 110; PL 40:283), as well as for other intentions, even those involving earthly things. Thus, as we read in *The City of God*, one of his presbyters is sent to the court of Hesperius (Emperor Valentinian's Prefect of the West) where people suffer from diabolic molestation, and the molestation ceases when the presbyter offers the "sacrifice of the body of Christ" (*sacrificium corporis Christi;* Civ. 22:8; CSEL 40:2, 602).

b) The interior sacrifice

For St. Augustine, however, the special power of the Eucharist consists in this: our union with the sacrifice that Christ has offered and still offers. Augustine's special achievement is that, beyond mere ritualism, he stressed so strongly the symbolic meaning underlying every sacrifice. While Ambrose stands at the beginning of a "metabolic" tendency to put greater emphasis on the Real Presence, Augustine is considered the pre-eminent representative of a later current in favor of symbolism above all else. In two passages in *The City of God* (10:5f., 19f; CSEL 40:1, 452-56, 479-81), he goes very thoroughly into this matter. The true sacrifice, he maintains, consists in the interior surrender to God and in every deed flowing from this surrender. Even the Old Testament sacrifices had their meaning only in such an interior act: "A visible sacrifice, therefore, is a sacrament or sacred sign of an invisible sacrifice" (*sacrificium ergo visibile invisibilis sacrificii sacramentum, id est, sacrum signum est*; ch. 5).

For Augustine this invisible sacrifice is so important that finally he rejects the distinction between the sign and the thing signified, declaring simply: "There is a true sacrifice in every work which unites us in a holy communion with God" (*verum sacrificium est omne opus quod agitur ut sancta societate inhaereamus Deo*; ch. 6). The true sacrifice is the man "who dies to the world and lives for God." Our body becomes a sacrifice if we bring it under subjection, provided we do this for the sake of God. All the more so does the soul, if afire with God's love, form itself in God's likeness. True sacrifices are all the works of mercy when they are oriented toward God. That is why redeemed humanity, the community of saints, is a "universal sacrifice," offered to God through the High Priest who has offered himself for us by his suffering "so that we might be the body of such a Head."

In this sacrifice Christ is at one and the same time Priest and Victim (*ipse offerens, ipse et oblatio*). As a sacramental re-presentation of this fact, as its daily sacrament (*sacramentum cottidianum*), he has willed the sacrifice of the Church, which, because the Church is the body of him who is Head, learns to offer itself through him (*se ipsam per ipsum discit offerre*; ch. 20); this phraseology has been incorporated in the Constitution on the Sacred Liturgy by Vatican Council II (§48). In this sense Augustine speaks emphatically of the priesthood of the faithful as well. According to him, however, "it is only because Christians are members of Christ that they share in this priesthood" (as Ryan points out in his article cited in note 29, "Patristic Teaching on the Priesthood of the Faithful," p. 281).

3. St. Fulgentius of Ruspe

As for doctrinal development on the Eucharist and the Eucharistic celebration, the time after Augustine is an interval of quiet, without controversy and without much reflection. That spokesman for the church in North Africa, Fulgentius of Ruspe (d. 532), developing in his Commentary on Faith a key concept of Augustine's, juxtaposes the fulfillment of the new covenant to the promise of the old and insists that the sacrifice of bread and wine offered by the Church over the entire face of the earth is centered upon "thanksgiving and the consecration of that flesh which Christ offered for our sake" (*gratiarum actio atque commemoratio carnis Christi quam pro nobis obtulit*), as against the "fleshly sacrifices" (*victimae carnales*) of the old covenant with which the sacrifice of Christ was foretold (De Fide 1:60; PL 65:699). For him the memorial aspect brought thus to prominence is implied in the thanksgiving aspect of the Eucharist. That is why at this sacrifice we begin with thanksgiving (*gratiarum actione*); which is, as he writes, just another way of saying that "Christ is not still to be given to us but has already been given" (*Christum non dandum sed datum nobis*; Ep. 14:44; PL 65:432).

In Fulgentius the recognition of Christ's priesthood also finds clear expression. For in the prayers of the Church it is customary to address the prayer not only to God the Father "through Jesus Christ," but sometimes explicitly also "through the eternal Priest, your Son, our Lord Jesus Christ" (*per sacerdotem aeternum Filium tuum Dominum nostrum Jesum Christum*), a formula whose meaning he explains at great length in the same Letter (14:36-37; PL 65:424-26). In another connection (in discussing the Semi-Pelagians) he mentions also the working of the Holy Spirit, with regard both to the sanctification of the faithful gathered together and to the transformation of the gifts (Ad. Monimum 2:6, 10; PL 65:184, 188).

4. St. Gregory the Great

St. Gregory the Great discusses the Eucharist and the "celebration of Mass" (*missarum solemnia,* as he is fond of calling it) in many passages, especially in his Dialogues. Here the focus is on its sacrificial character, as is clear from recurring phrases such as "to sacrifice the saving host" (*hostiam salutarem immolare*) and "to offer the sacrifice of the saving Victim" (*offerre sacrificium victimae salutaris*). Thus the sacrifice of the Cross is never lost sight of; as he states in a homily on the Gospels, we "renew his Passion" (*passionem illius reparamus*; In Evang. Hom. 2:37.7; PL 76:1279). This victim (*victima*) "in mystical fashion renews the death of the only-begotten Son and imitates his Passion" (*mortem Unigeniti per mysterium reparat . . . passionem Unigeniti Filii semper imitatur*; Dialogue 4:58; PL 77:425). For here (Gregory continues) his blood is shed, no longer at the hands of unbelievers but now "into the mouths of believers" (*in ora fidelium*).

In his idiom, however, the term *sacrifice* derives not from the sacrifice of Calvary but directly from what takes place on the altar. It is the priest's word that brings about the mystery. No one can doubt that, as Gregory writes, "heaven opens at the word of the priest, choirs of angels appear at the mystery of Jesus Christ; the highest and the lowest, the earthly and the heavenly meet."

These words with which Pope St. Gregory brings the mystery down to our level of understanding were to be repeated innumerable times in the Middle Ages; so too the passage following them, where Gregory drew the moral conclusion that if we perform the mystery, we must live it in our lives (*imitari quod agimus*): "For the sacrifice is truly offered to God for us only then when we make ourselves victims" (4:59); PL 76:428).[45] It is the same idea that Augustine stressed, but with this sharp difference: Gregory specifies as a moral requirement what Augustine took for granted as the self-evident corollary of the mystery itself.

As one actively engaged in practical pastoral work, Gregory also emphasized and recommended the fruits of the Mass. The Mass for the Dead occupied an especially important place in his teaching. He referred to and repeatedly offered the sacrifice for the dead, apparently without taking into consideration the participation of the faithful. In his own monastery, after he had ordered Mass to be offered on thirty successive days for the soul of a monk who had died after falling away, he received signs that the intercession was heard (Dial. 4:55; PL 77:416-21). And thus was initiated a precedent that has been followed down to our own day.

5. THE LATER FATHERS

Nor do we find much controversy or speculation over the Eucharist during the subsequent period. When St. Isidore of Seville and later Venerable Bede happened to mention the matter, they merely repeated what they inherited from the past. In St. Isidore we get a certain well-rounded approach, but also an unmistakable shift of emphasis. In the sacrifice Isidore saw above all the consecrating action of the priest: "'Sacrifice' means 'that which is made holy,' for it is consecrated by the mystical prayer" (*sacrificium dictum quasi sacrum factum, quia prece mystica consecratur*; Etymologies 6:19, 38; PL 82:255). The "mystical prayer" (*prex mystica*) is for him the section of his Spanish-rite Mass that he calls "the sixth prayer" (*oratio sexta*) — the part between the Sanctus and the Lord's Prayer, where the "confection" (*conformatio*) of the sacrament takes place (De Ecclesiasticis Officiis 1:15:3; PL 83:753); the thanksgiving prayer of the Preface was thus cut off from this main section. By the same token, as we read in the Etymologies, the word *eucharistia* was no longer taken in its original sense, but was interpreted as "good grace" (*bona gratia*), thus introducing a phrase that remained current right through the Middle Ages.

Mention must here be made of the strikingly realistic conception of the Eucharistic sacrifice that appears in the old "Exposition" of the Gallic liturgy ascribed to Bishop Germanus of Paris (d. 576)

and recently reasserted to be genuine.[46] At the breaking of the
Host, an angel was seen cutting apart the limbs of a child from
whom rays of bright light emanated, and holding the chalice to
catch the blood. The story had in fact traveled to the West from a
monk's version narrated in the Vitae Patrum (1. 5, 18-3; PL
73:979).

6. THE GALLIC LITURGIES

Meanwhile the liturgies of the West had been taking definite
shape. Two types stand out above the rest: the Roman liturgy,
closely related to the African; and the liturgies of the Gallic type,
which evolved in various directions, taking Spanish (Mozarabic),
Gallican, Milanese, and Celtic forms. Common to all these, as compared with the liturgies of the Greek Orient, is the uniform Latin
language and the principle of a wide repertory of prayers and
hymns corresponding to the feasts of the Church calendar, grounded
on a single and almost invariable "Canon" — until 1968, that is.
This Canon begins with what later came to be known as the Common Preface and continues to the Lord's Prayer.

The liturgies of the Gallic type, in the course of time, frag-
mented the entire course of the Mass into autonomous prayers that
are subject to change, and only the triple Sanctus, the Institution
account, and the Lord's Prayer remained invariable. After the preparatory acts and the dialogue inherited from ancient Christian
tradition, the principal prayer begins with the Preface (*illatio* —
offering, *contestatio* — supplication, *immolatio* — immolation).
There follow the three parts of the prayer corresponding to Isidore's
"sixth prayer" (*oratio sexta*): "after the Sanctus" (*Post Sanctus*);
"after the 'On the day before'" (after the silent prayer [of Consecra-
tion])" (*Post Pridie; Post Secreta*); and "before the Lord's Prayer"
(*Ante Orationem Dominicam*; Hänggi-Pahl 461-513).

Naturally the tendency to re-word the prayers of the Mass
each time in a different way brought with it the danger of losing
sight of the central thing and of wandering into a maze of secondary, nonessential considerations. In the Gallic liturgies this went
to extremes. The Preface, which should have been a prayer of
thanks and praise for God's gracious interventions in salvation
history, often became on saints' feasts a panegyric on the saint or
a description of his suffering and death (*passio*).

The "Post Pridie" was meant to be above all an expression
of what takes place in the celebration of the Eucharist, i.e., the

Lord's memorial and the offering unto God; but now, especially in the Spanish rite, this became chiefly a very loose form of epiclesis: asking God or Christ for grace and blessing or for the descent of the Holy Spirit; mentioning sometimes the gifts on the altar; even joining the prayer occasionally to Christ's mandate to repeat ("we recall, we believe, we do, in doing this"; *recolimus, credimus, facimus, haec facientes*); while on saints' days recalling at this point in particular the saint's victorious struggle.

It would, however, be incorrect to conclude that the concept of sacrifice had lost its meaning in these liturgies; it had rather become so self-evident a theme that it did not have to be constantly insisted upon. This seems to be implied in the terms used to describe the introductory section of the Eucharistic Prayer: the expression "offering" (*illatio*), which always stands at the head of the Spanish Preface, corresponds in fact to the Eastern anaphora (offering); and the heading *immolatio* (lit.: "immolation"), written over many Prefaces in the Gallic Missale Gothicum, is certainly an unmistakable designation for sacrifice.

Again, it must have been a very lively recognition of the sacrifice that prompted the significant change we find in an Irish sacramentary fragment of the ninth century, in which the invitatory "Let us give thanks" (*Gratias agamus*) found in all the liturgies except the Eastern Syrian takes the form "Let us offer to our Lord sacred, spiritual gifts" (*Offeramus Domino nostro sacrosancta munera spiritualia*).[47]

On one point the liturgies of the Gallic type have resisted later tendencies. They too contain in their original place the intercessions that the other liturgies have incorporated into their Eucharistic Prayer since the fourth century, that is, they occur between the Readings and the Eucharistic action proper. Thus the gifts are brought to the altar, then the names are read out with the announcement that they are the names of those who "offer the sacrifice" (*Nomina offerentium*), even though it might be the name of a dead person: and the priest recites the prayer "after the names" (*Post nomina*). Only then is the Pax given and the Preface begun.

7. THE ROMAN LITURGIES

a) Change and increasing pomp

At this juncture the Roman liturgy took another course. As in the Egyptian liturgies, in the Roman Canon the intercessions are already incorporated before the Consecration as prayers for the Church and for the offering congregation (*offerentes*); and these prayers for the Church are joined to the commemoration of the saints invoked in a symbolically meaningful number. Other prayers for special intentions could then follow the "this our offering" (*Hanc igitur*). Then the Roman liturgy made a definite shift of emphasis. First, according to the law of change obtaining at the time, the thanksgiving prayer corresponding to the invitation "Let us give thanks" (*Gratias agamus*) proliferated in numerous formulas (as the Sacramentarium Leonianum shows) and was encumbered with a number of unsuitable texts.

This state of affairs led to a sharp reaction during the sixth century with the result that, except on certain feast days and during festive seasons, the pendulum swung from the one extreme of abundance to the other of poverty. For example, the Common Preface, which at the time came to be used most often, had hardly any of the unction of a deliberate and enthusiastic thanksgiving prayer left in it. On the other hand, the Roman Canon, as it took definite shape early in the fourth century, went far beyond the mere *memores offerimus* of the classical type, for in this Canon the idea of offering and sacrifice (the sacrifice, i.e., of the Church) was expressed directly after the Sanctus and worded in a threefold form (the "Look upon these gifts" [*Supra quae*] and "We beseech thee" [*Supplices te rogamus*] as well as the "Mindful therefore" [*Unde et memores*]) after the Consecration, so that this theme was accorded extraordinary prominence.

After the Peace of Constantine the liturgy in Rome must soon have received great impetus to develop as the magnificent new churches of the fourth century bear witness. Moreover, with the promotion of the bishops to the highest official ranks in the Roman Empire, the liturgy began to take on corresponding forms of courtly ceremonial such as lights, incense, prostration, supporting the celebrant, insignia; such ceremonial became quite conspicuous in the festive and solemn liturgical services prescribed in the Ordines Romani since the end of the seventh century.

From all the evidence the liturgical service was the concern of the whole congregation. For the Ordo Romanus I it was even the concern of the entire city and not merely of the community belonging to one specific basilica. On certain feast days and during festive seasons delegations from every region converged on the bishop at the "station" (*statio*), and this practice was customary also in other episcopal cities during the early Middle Ages. Beside a large congregation of clerics and papal court representatives, there now emerges a special choir, the "school [i.e., corporate body or group] of singers" (*schola cantorum*), to introduce a new element in the liturgy: hymns of a decorative, embellishing kind, corresponding to the changing seasons of the Church calendar and sung at moments when external "business" had to be taken care of, e.g., the procession of the clerics, the collection and preparation of the gifts, the people's Communion. Already one may sense negative implications in all this new pomp and circumstance: even the people's responses and acclamations came to be monopolized by a group of clerics. Still, on the positive side, it had now become the regular thing for all the participants to receive Communion, just as they all brought their gifts of bread and wine.

b) The votive Mass and the private Mass

Along with all this new splendor there is a collateral development, in quite the opposite direction, between the fourth and sixth centuries: the votive Mass (from the expression *missa votiva* occurring for the first time in Letter 3 [PL 87:412] of Eugene of Toledo, d. 657) and with it the private Mass. The principle was not new. Side by side with the regular Sunday Eucharistic service of the community as a whole, the practice of celebrating Mass in smaller groups had existed from quite early times, if not from the very beginning. And as far back as Tertullian the sacrifice offered as intercession *for* someone, for the dead, or some other intention, was not unknown. Only its application on a large scale was new.

Eloquent documentation for the new trend is found in the Sacramentarium Gelasianum (Vat. Reg. 316), the third part of which comprises a collection of about sixty formularies of the priest's Collect at Masses for various occasions: on the day of the wedding and its anniversary; at the time of affliction and illness; or the time of epidemic or of war; for good weather; for one undertaking a journey; for the sick and the dead. Much of what has been preserved from this seventh-century collection doubtless dates back to an earlier time.

The repertory expanded further in the sacramentaries of the following centuries; thus the Sacramentary of Fulda (tenth century) numbers one hundred and eighty votive Mass formularies. Some of these formularies presuppose the participation of a group of the faithful, but that does not mean that everyone also received Communion. In others participation of the faithful was not a requisite, and with this relaxation the private Mass came to stay.

Another development closely associated with this is the increasing incidence of the Mass celebration after the sixth century. There is a letter (*c.* 590) of Bishop Palladius of Saintes in Gaul informing Pope St. Gregory the Great that he has set up thirteen altars in his new church and requesting the Pope to send relics of martyrs for some of these altars (Reg. Ep. 6:48; MGH Epistolae 1:423). From this it would appear that one reason for the increased frequency of Mass was the honor paid to martyrs by dedicating to each an altar at which Mass was obviously going to be celebrated regularly. The same principle was at work in monasteries and monastic churches.

Hand in hand with this went the problem of the faithful who in return for their donations demanded the benefit of the prayer and of the sacrifice for their intentions; and for this the formularies of votive Masses came in handy. At any rate, as we read in Otto Nussbaum, from the seventh century on, the number of ordained monks in monasteries was on the increase.[48] There is also explicit evidence for the increasing incidence of private Masses at this time (pp. 137-52); and toward the end of the eighth century it was the normal thing in monasteries for Mass to be celebrated several times a day by the same priest, even as a *missa solitaria* (Mass said alone, without a server; Ordo Rom. 15; Andrieu OR 3:120); but bishops' synods in the ninth century came out strongly against this practice.[49]

Clearly this cultivation of one aspect of the Mass that had always been recognized was one-sided to a certain extent. Actually the new emphasis coincided with the incorporation of intercessions into the body of the Eucharistic Prayer (in most liturgies this was already being done in the fourth century). The Eastern rites do not seem to have ventured very far in this direction, and in the West it was obviously the irrepressible devotion of the faithful that moved it forward. The votive Mass became the dominant type of the Latin Mass.

How forceful this movement was may be seen in the new designation given to a Eucharistic celebration, namely, *missa* (the Mass). Just as in the third century *eucharistia* was replaced by *oblatio* (offering), so after the fifth century *missa* took the place of *oblatio*. The meaning of *missa* had already undergone a process of evolution in Christian linguistic usage: from *dismissal* to *concluding prayer*, thence to *service* and to *blessing*. Of all the forms of blessing the one imbedded in the offering of the sacrifice was considered the most important from very early times.[50] The new term first became current not in liturgical usage but in colloquial speech. In liturgical documents it turned up for the first time in the above-mentioned Gelasian collection of votive Masses as the heading for individual formularies (e.g., *Missa pro . . .*, i.e., "Mass for . . .").

c) Reactions to this development

At the same time there was an awareness that a blessing was implicit in every Mass; indeed, the Mass itself constituted the great blessing and sanctification of the cosmos. It was from this time too that *eucharistia* was taken to mean *bona gratia* or "good grace." Still, at first it was apparently felt that the term *missa* connoted the reality in a very incomplete manner, and thus the word was used most often in the plural and coupled with a distinguishing complement; thus the phrase "holy Mass" (*sacra missa*) or "celebation of Mass" (*missarum sollemnia*).

There were also those who cautioned greater reserve in the matter of multiplying Masses. The Synod of Auxerre in 578 forbade the celebration of two Masses at the same altar on the same day (Can. 10; Mansi 9:913). A Roman synod in 853 warns priests not to exclude in favor of one single person the oblations of the faithful who have come to Mass, since the Redeemer is rich enough to accept the *vota* (prayers of petition) of all (Can. 17; Mansi 14:1005). St. Peter Damian also, in a blast at the ignorance and indifference of the clergy, complained that the sacrifice the Lord offered for the salvation of the world was now offered "for the benefit of one limited individual" (*pro unius homuncionis utilitate*; Contra Inscitiam et Incuriam Clericorum 2; PL 145:501). Abbot Odo of Cluny (d. 942) pointed to the early Church, when the Eucharist was celebrated less often and precisely for that reason more devoutly (*quanto rarius tanto religiosius*; Collationes 2:28; PL 133:572); and during the early years of the Carthusian Order (*c.* 1100) priests were not allowed to celebrate private Mass every day.

VI. THE EARLY MIDDLE AGES

During the first centuries of the Middle Ages, theologians of the Eucharist seemed content to reflect on what had been inherited from the teaching of the Church Fathers. Interest and attention were now concentrated all the more on the practical side of the liturgy and on the form of the celebration. It was a time when the evolution of liturgies had reached its final stage and gradually each of them assumed its final, distinct and definitive shape. We have already seen the outcome of the process with regard to the central part of the Mass.

In the Roman liturgy the priest's prayers for the various feasts of the liturgical calendar were first embodied in the several tentative forms that have come down to us in the Leonine and Gelasian sacramentaries; finally they were frozen in their definitive form under Gregory the Great in the Sacramentarium Gregorianum. Then in the seventh century a fixed order took hold for the readings (*capitulare evangeliorum*, the listing of Gospel readings; also known as *lectionare*, lectionary) and the variable antiphons (*antiphonale*, book of antiphons); while from the end of the seventh century the Ordines Romani (or: rituals for ceremonies of the Roman rite) become the norm for the more complicated and solemn ceremonies.

In the case of the Gallic type of liturgies a still more dynamic though less orderly development may be noticed. The best-preserved documents, those of the Spanish liturgy, reveal a real abundance of ever freshly formulated Mass prayers. While these prayers do contain the essential dogmatic concepts, their turns of expression suggest in general a trend toward deterioration. Here, unlike in other liturgies, a misty formlessness replaced the sharp and clear ideas we have seen at work in the construction of the central part of the Mass.

1. INTRODUCTION OF THE ROMAN LITURGY INTO GAUL

In Gaul this decadence was compounded by the absence of an ecclesiastical center. In fact, conditions in the Gaul of the seventh century and after led bishops and monasteries to look more and more to the well-ordered Roman liturgy for guidelines, and even to acquire Roman texts. Finally King Pepin and Emperor Charlemagne rectified this situation by ordering the introduction of the Roman liturgy in their territory. The Sacramentarium Gregorianum, which Charlemagne imposed at Aachen as the model, became the foundation of the new order.

In this new order the chief consultant to the Emperor was the Englishman Alcuin (d. 804). As the representative man of his age, he is the best witness to the state of affairs at the end of the eighth century. Wherever in his theological writing he touched upon the Eucharist, he simply resorted to the traditional theology, citing above all the words of Augustine and Chrysostom. As he maintained in his Commentary on Hebrews, Christ is not sacrificed anew when we offer; for we offer "in order to make remembrance of his death" (*ad recordationem faciendam mortis ejus*; PL 100:1077).

But there is also a new emphasis in Alcuin, for he stressed that the sacrifice of the Cross has efficacy because it becomes truly present in this offering. That is why Alcuin himself composed a number of votive Masses centered upon the individual mysteries of faith as these were interpreted by the piety of that time (the Trinity, the Holy Cross, Mary). Above all else, his votive Masses bring out the idea of a spiritual struggle or include intercessions for the living and the dead (PL 101:445-61).[51]

Wherever gaps showed up in the Sacramentary borrowed from Rome, Alcuin filled them, as far as was possible, with equivalent Roman material and thus compiled what is known as the Alcuinian Supplement. But it is not in his votive Masses alone that Alcuin betrays a new spirit, for this attitude appears also in his having permitted a significant change in the Roman Canon itself. In the Memento for the Living, the living had been described merely as those "who offer up to you this sacrifice of praise" (*qui tibi offerunt hoc sacrificium laudis*); whereas in Alcuin's new version these words are preceded by "for whom we offer or . . ." (*pro quibus tibi offerimus vel*). The words reveal a changed outlook, at least insofar as the function of the priest is explicitly distinguished from that of the community.

That is not the only change the Roman liturgy underwent during the ninth century in the new climate of the northern European countries. In part, the changes went hand in hand with adherence to the Latin language; for, since in the meantime with the evolution of the vernacular, Latin had become unintelligible even to the Romanic peoples, the liturgy, by necessity, had become essentially a monopoly of the clergy. Although on the whole the traditional texts were faithfully transmitted, they were supplemented with prayers to be recited inaudibly by the celebrating priest alone: at the beginning of the Mass; during the preparation of the sacrificial gifts; before Communion; at the end.

On the other hand, the external ritual was the richer for new elements accessible to the senses and hence to the people; such were the changing positions of the priest at the altar, the incensing according to fixed rubrics, the alternation of softly or loudly recited prayers. In other words, what St. Isidore had said about the *oratio sexta* was now carried over into the Roman Mass. As we saw above, the section beginning with the Sanctus was now held to be the part in which the essential sacramental action (*conformatio sacramenti*) took place, and it was marked by silent prayer at the very heart of the sacred mystery. In other ways, too, there was now a heightened reverence before the Blessed Sacrament: for at about this time also came the shift to unleavened bread.[52] Obviously in this ambience even the unfamiliar language, throwing as it did a veil upon the mystery, was seen as a gain rather than a loss.

2. The "Explanations of the Mass"

Nevertheless, during the Carolingian renaissance there was no lack of effort to encourage the people to relate to the liturgy. There appeared several "Explanations of the Mass" (*Expositiones Missae*), though of course most of them did not go beyond a mere paraphrase of the Mass prayers. They were intended chiefly to help the priest to understand the Mass better, but they were also meant for the instruction of the people, as may be clearly seen in a certain commentary (*Quotiens contra se*, PL 96:1481-1502), which explains only the prayers recited aloud, skipping the Canon (prayed inaudibly at this time), and resuming with the Lord's Prayer.

Amalarius of Metz (d. 850) sought to meet the changed situation and the "new look" with a radical approach inspired both by traditions from the Gallican liturgy and by influences from the East. Amalarius proceeded from the assumption that whatever can be seen and heard in the Mass must have a deeper meaning. This meaning he hoped to supply from tradition, so far as such traditions were still available. Wherever tradition was lacking, he himself interpreted the forms by making them "say something else" (allegory: *alla agoreuein*) that could contribute to edification. And as he realized, like his master Alcuin, that the Mass is above all the remembrance (*recordatio*) of Christ's redemptive Passion, he took it that its every part was intended to dwell above all else on the Lord's life and sufferings.

Thus the Mass began with the Introit, wherein the chorus of prophets announces the coming of Christ, and with the Gloria, the song of the angels at his birth. And it ended with the blessing Christ imparted to the Apostles before his ascension into heaven. While in this retrospective allegorization there were quite a number of forced and farfetched interpretations, one must concede that it caught the essential character of the Institution, i.e., the remembrance of the Lord — but of course in a very superficial and peripheral manner that brought sharp criticism.

Amalarius' chief opponent was the deacon Florus of Lyons, himself the author (c. 835) of an explanation of the Mass (PL 119:15-72) in which he fashioned his entire structure on St. Augustine's configurations and started from the premise that in the Mass Jesus has given us the mystery of his death (*mysterium suae mortis*) in order thus to make available its merits and efficacy. While Amalarius saw in every detail of the liturgical structure of the Mass "mysteries" reminiscent of some aspect or another of the life of Jesus or even of the Old Testament or of an external nature, Florus held fast to the one mystery that not only recalls the salvific plan but itself contains it.[53]

For Florus the Mass is not a mere theater piece in which the faithful take part only as spectators; for him, as for the older tradition, it is an action of the Church, that is, of the totality of the faithful and, above all, of the community gathered together. For what is performed through the offices of the priest (*ministerio sacerdotum*) is performed in a general way (*generaliter*) by all the faithful (ch. 52).[54] Although Amalarius' doctrine was condemned by the Synod of Quiercy in 838, during subsequent centuries liturgical theology proceeded along his line and not that of Florus.

3. CONTROVERSY OVER THE REAL PRESENCE

Besides the remembrance of the Lord that received singular stress through Amalarius' work, the offering (*oblatio*) was also given prominence at this time. As appears from what we have said so far, this *oblatio* was seen above all in the Consecration, in the function proper to the priest, who acomplishes the transformation of the Eucharistic species "by the power and words of Christ" (*Christi virtute et verbis*; Florus, Expositio 60). Then with the ninth century's very first work devoted to the mystery of the Eucharist — Abbot Paschasius Radbert's (d. *c.* 860) "A Treatise on the Lord's Body and Blood" (*Liber de Corpore et Sanguine Domini*) — the prolonged controversy over the effect of Consecration arose; and this was to subside only with the condemnation of Berengarius of Tours in a number of synods between 1050 and 1079.

The quarrel was not precisely about what happened in the Mass, but rather about its effect, i.e., the Real Presence of the Lord in the Eucharist. The question was whether the actual, historical body of Christ was present in the Eucharist, or whether bread and wine were only its symbol with which some power of God was associated, as had in fact been maintained already by Radbert's first opponent, the monk Ratramnus (d. 868), on the basis of his distorted interpretation of Augustine's utterances. On the assumption of Ratramnus the Mass itself would naturally be deprived of its innermost content.

Of course, this might well be meant to restore the bond with Christ, but, as the argument of John Scotus Erigena shows, it would then be no different from what Baptism effects. Communion, as construed by Abbot Aelfric (d. *c.* 1020), would have no other significance but that of the manna in the desert or the water from the rock. Drawing the natural conclusion from this line of thought, Berengarius demoted the sacrifice that takes place in the Mass to the same level as the sacrifices of the Old Testament. The difference, according to his treatise on the Mass (*De Sacra Coena*), consists only in this: the sacrifices of the Old Testament were a heralding of something in the future, while that of the New would be a "vivid reminder, in symbolic form, of something already existing" (*figura rei existentis commonefactoria*).[55]

Such a devaluation of the Eucharistic mystery had already been challenged by Radbert's endorsement of the traditional faith of the Church and the distinction between symbol and truth (*figura et veritas*). The Consecration means not only to communicate some kind of higher power to the gifts of bread and wine; as he writes in his treatise on the Body and Blood of the Lord, it must rather be compared to creation or the Incarnation (De Corp. et Sang. Dom. 4:1; PL 120: 1277f.); and what becomes present at the Consecration is not merely the natural body of Christ, which was born of Mary.

Radbert uses very forceful terms to express the identity of the sacrifice with the sacrifice of the Cross: thus, Christ suffers anew (*iterum patitur*, 9:11; PL 120:1302); his Passion is repeated (*iteratur*) in a genuine immolation or slaying (*mactatio*), even though without death and without a new redemption.[56] It need not surprise us that the legend of Germanus' Expositio (originating in the East), concerning the Child slain on the altar, should turn up again in Radbert (see 14:4; PL 120:1318-19). Radbert's fellow controversialists, however, were not misled by such exaggerations.

4. REPRESENTATION OF THE "IMMOLATION"

Characteristic of the period following the controversy over the theology of the Eucharist is the certainty with which the Consecration is affirmed as the decisive event in the Mass, and the Mass affirmed as sacrifice, as well as the uncertainty on the question of how the sacrifice takes place. The two expressions used are *oblatio* and *immolatio*, sometimes as synonyms, sometimes with immolation being understood in the sense in which Radbert had used it, i.e., with emphasis on the aspect of the slaying that took place on the Cross and must take place on the altar as well — though of course in an unbloody manner.[57] People wanted to see this immolation re-presented in the Mass. The separation of the species of bread and wine did not impress anyone as a substitute, since these were looked upon much more as food and drink for the recipient, as they were even later, e.g., in the case of the Corpus Christi hymn: "that he might feed the whole man with his twofold nature" (*ut duplicis substantiae totum cibaret hominem*).

Accordingly, a re-presentation of the immolation was found in the fraction, or in the fraction and the Communion following it immediately, for there the body of Jesus is ground with the teeth and the blood is poured into the mouth of the faithful; or again in the handing of the sacred Host into the hands of the faithful (Lepin 112–18). But the re-presentation was found especially in the entire section following the Consecration, during which the priest prays with outstretched arms (in the manner of the Crucified) and then at the "Supplices" makes a low bow that signified death (Lepin 118–21). It should not surprise us that even in the Mass ritual the people ventured to contribute small alterations to dramatize their reflections on the Passion. Such were the bow at the end of the Memento for the Dead, and the five signs of the cross to recall the five wounds in connection with the final doxology.

The liturgists directed their attention above all to the "Supplices," the prayer in which we ask that our sacrifice may be carried to the altar in heaven. As Remigius of Auxerre (d. 908) held in his Expositio, the Lord's body made present in the Consecration must at this point be united to his glorified body (PL 101:1262f); or as Isaac of Stella (c. 1169) later on developed the same thought in his Letter on the Offering of Mass: after we have (as it were) offered bread and wine upon the altar of holocaust and the Lord's body and blood upon the golden altar of incense, our sacrifice is borne up by the angel's hand and becomes united with the glorified Christ in heaven (Ep. de Off. Missae; PL 194:1889–96).

5. THE CONSECRATION AS MEMORIAL SACRIFICE

Still others, aware that such speculation is far from adequate, underlined the idea that the sacrifice is completed with the Consecration: "For with this utterance the whole sacrifice is immolated and sanctified" (*hac enim voce totum sacrificium immolatur et sanctificatur*), as Bruno of Segni (d. 1123) declared in his Expositio on Leviticus (8; PL 164:407). The Consecration is decisive even though the symbolic re-presentation of the *immolatio* can reach out beyond the moment of transformation (Lepin 130–32). This development, in which for centuries attention had been focused on the manner and the moment of the Lord's first presence in the sacrament, came to an end when, around the year 1200, the ideas clarified thus far began to find expression in the very ritual of the Mass. Accordingly, it became the custom or even the rule to raise the Host at or immediately after the words of Consecration in order to present it for the veneration of the faithful.

Sources for the Eucharistic speculation originating in the Carolingian period consisted in Sacred Scripture and in a rather limited selection of patristic texts, the most important of which we have already indicated above: chiefly Augustine, Gregory the Great, and (under the name of Ambrose) Chrysostom.[58] During the later centuries until the onset of Scholasticism, the basic texts for the Eucharistic discussion, which extended beyond the manner of the presence in the sacrament, were taken largely from Augustine, whose ideas were revived at this time. Peter the Venerable, Abbot of Cluny (d. 1156), who had to defend the Eucharist against the Petrobrusian heretics, revived in his Tract against them the half-forgotten basic ideas of the Doctors of the Church and emphasized that the meaning of every sacrifice lies in acknowledging God as the origin and end of all, and subjecting oneself to his will (Contra Petrobrus.; PL 189:791). The exterior ritual has only the function of expressing the interior sentiment, so that even when we say that Christ offered himself, we mean that he freely, of his own accord, surrendered his life (797).

The great Cluniac examined also the concept of *immolatio*. But while until then the question almost always put was how far this immolation was realized in the Mass, Peter declared in unmistakable terms that when we predicate this *immolari* of Christ, it simply means that through the various signs of breaking, dividing, eating, and so on, his death must be re-presented. With this, said the abbot, we announce the death of the Lord, in accordance with the command of the apostle Paul (812f.).

A further and important step toward the clarification of ideas is found in Peter Lombard (d. 1164). Like other theologians of his time who devoted a tract to the Eucharist (Hugh of St. Victor, for example), Peter too dealt with the Mass only in passing. But here we find at least an implicit indication of the distinction between *oblatio* and *immolatio*. The Master of Sentences speaks of "that which is offered and consecrated by the priest" (*quod offeratur et consecratur a sacerdote*), and declares it to be "the memorial and re-presentation of the true sacrifice and sacred immolation" (*memoria est et representatio veri sacrificii et sanctae immolationis*) that was consummated by Christ on the Cross (Sent. 4:12.7; PL 192:866).

Hence, if the Mass was called, even in an extended sense and according to general linguistic usage, not only *sacrificium* but also *immolatio*, what actually was meant was an *offerri*, and *oblatio*.[59] Peter Lombard had no objection to the idea that the fraction, which takes place just before the Agnus Dei, might be seen as a re-presentation of Christ's Passion and death (4:12:6); but he insisted that the sacrifice is already completed in the Consecration (Lepin 154–56). That in fact is the distinction formulated by Pope Innocent III in his treatise on the Mass: that the words in the Canon belong primarily to the Consecration, the gesture to the history of the Passion (De Sacro Altaris Mysterio 5:2; PL 217:888).

And this brings us directly to the beginnings of Scholasticism.

VII. FROM HIGH SCHOLASTICISM TO THE REFORMATION

Like their forerunners of the early medieval period, the great schoolmen of the thirteenth century seem satisfied, as far as the Mass is concerned, to sum up and hand on the tradition they had inherited.

1. ALEXANDER OF HALES AND ST. ALBERT THE GREAT

After Alexander of Hales (d. 1245) we have no treatment of the Eucharist that can be ascribed with certainty to his times. Relevant texts attributed to Alexander[60] belong to the section of his Summa Theologiae that seems to have been compiled by his disciple William of Melitona (see Prolegomena to Alexander of Hales, vol. 4 [Quaracchi], p. lxxx). Here once again we confront the distinction between *immolatio* and *oblatio* in the Mass — and precisely in Peter Lombard's sense. Thus the immolation was made upon the Cross and can only be re-presented in the Mass, as is done at the Consecration of the chalice, or even in the fraction and in the Communion, when the sacred blood, as Gregory the Great expresses it, is poured into the mouths of the faithful.

Unlike the immolation, the oblation is actually enacted in the Mass. In his Commentary on the Sentences, St. Albert the Great defines it more precisely as the offering of the thing immolated (*rei immolatae oblatio*; 4 Sent. 13:23; Borgnet 29:370f.). As to the precise moment at which this offering takes place there was no unanimous opinion among the theologians of that time. For Albert the Consecration of the oblation (*sanctificatio oblationis*) begins with the prayers following the Sanctus and is concluded with the prayers after the Consecration (De Sacrif. Missae 3:6; Borgnet 38:96).

For others, as Lepin notes (p. 178), it embraced the entire section from the Consecration to the Communion. Strikingly enough, Albert held that the sacrifice takes place even when the sacrament is not performed, that is, even when there is no Consecration, as for instance on Good Friday (4 Sent. 13:2). He was not alone in this view; it was expressed also by Bonaventure: there is no "consecration, yet the sacrifice is offered" (4 Sent. 12:2 ad 2; 4 [Quaracchi], p. 299). That is indeed a far cry from identifying the performance of the sacrifice exclusively with the Consecration.

2. St. Thomas Aquinas

Not even in St. Thomas Aquinas do we find an answer that is perfectly clear on first sight. In his teaching on the Eucharist he too focused chiefly on the question of the nature of the sacrament and the Real Presence. Part III, q. 83 of his Summa Theologiae is devoted to an explanation of the Mass; in the celebration of the mystery he distinguishes between offering and Consecration: Mass is "both offered as a sacrifice, and consecrated and received as a sacrament" (*offertur ut sacrificium et consecratur et sumitur ut sacramentum*). Hence, first comes the oblation, then the Consecration of the matter offered, and finally its reception (ST 3a, 83:4).

In another place Thomas distinguishes the sacrifice from the oblation. The holy sacrifice comes about if "something is done" to the object offered up (*aliquid fit*; ST 2a2ae, 85:3 ad 3). Obviously, as Lepin points out (pp. 192–95), he was thinking here of the Consecration. Indeed, Thomas stated of the sacrifice of the Mass that it is accomplished when in the "Supra quae" the priest prays that it will be accepted (ST 3a, 83:4).

On the other hand, Thomas revealed a certain reserve in calling the Mass a sacrifice. For when he thought of sacrifice his mind turned immediately and totally to the sacrifice of the Cross; the suffering of Christ was a true sacrifice (*verum sacrificium*; ST 3a, 74:4), a true immolation (*vera immolatio*), of which the Mass is only a re-presentation (*imago quaedam repraesentativa*; 83:1). But insofar as this sacrament is the re-presentation (*repraesentatur*) of Christ's suffering, in which he has offered himself to God as victim, it "has the nature of a sacrifice" (*rationem sacrificii habet*; 79:7).

Now, what does the *repraesentatio* of Christ's suffering involve? In answering this question St. Thomas did not at first reach beyond the concept and the allegorical interpretation of ceremonies prevailing in his time. Thus he saw the re-presentation of Christ's suffering extended over the entire course of the Mass by means of the priest's different movements and gestures, genuflections and bows, through the breaking of the Host, especially through the prescribed number of signs of the Cross (83:5). But in another context he stressed that the most essential re-presentation takes place in the Consecration; and he is the first to bring out so clearly the idea that the separate consecration of the two species represented the separation of Christ's body and blood in his Passion (80:12 ad 3; 76:2 ad 1; additional references in Gaudel, p. 1058).

As for the celebrant's power at the altar, according to Thomas, the priest consecrates "in the person and through the power of Christ," so that Christ is in a special manner (*quodammodo*) also the celebrant (83:1 ad 3). Even a schismatic priest, who cannot act in the name of the Church, does not lose this power that is his from Christ. Thomas thus gives an affirmative answer to the question that had been answered negatively in preceding centuries, that is, whether a priest separated from the Church can still validly consecrate (82:7).

Thomas spoke also of the efficacy that is inherent in the sacrifice of the Mass. Thus, through the Mass we are enabled to share in the fruits of Christ's suffering (83:1). Those for whom it is offered are benefited by it — not, however, absolutely, but "according to the measure of [their] devotion" (*secundum quantitatem suae devotionis*; 79:5c). It is now agreed that with this last precision Thomas corrected the view he had put forth in his Commentary on the Sentences.[61]

3. Duns Scotus and Gabriel Biel

Duns Scotus (d. 1308) spoke only in passing of the Eucharist as sacrifice. What particularly stands out in his speculation and has been developed by his successors is an unusual emphasis on the Church's sacrifice. While it is Christ who has given the mandate and now gives the sacrifice its efficacy, yet in the Mass he is not the one offering directly (*offerens immediate*); otherwise, says Scotus, every Mass would have the same value as the Passion. In other words it would be an absolute sacrifice. Further, this would call into question the fact that the sacrifice has been offered once for all. The Mass is the sacrifice of the Church (*sacrificium Ecclesiae*) that is being repeated. In it the Church re-presents the suffering of Christ and appeals to it in her prayers (Quodlibetum 20, n. 22).

Accordingly, Christ's presence in the sacrament reserved in the ciborium is not a sacrifice, since the *oblatio* is wanting (n. 21). The offering priest acts in the person of the Church (*in persona Ecclesiae*). By *Ecclesiae* here he does not mean the worshiping community gathered around the priest; Scotus assigned no special active role to this community, but, as he expressly states, he is speaking of the Church as a whole (*Ecclesia generalis*; n. 22). With uncanny logic Scotus concludes from this that a schismatic priest may indeed consecrate, but may not offer the sacrifice validly (4 Sent. 13:2:5).

The distinct role assigned by Scotus to the celebrating priest corresponds also to the distinctions he made regarding the fruits of the Mass. Like prayer in general, the Mass benefits the priest himself in a very special way (*specialissime*) and the Church as a whole in a general way (*generalissime*), but in a special way (*specialiter*) those for whom the Mass is offered and those to whom the priest wishes to apply the fruits; and this efficacy follows from the nature of the action (*ex opere operato*), that is, by virtue of the merits of the Church as a whole (*virtute meriti generalis Ecclesiae*; Quodl. 20, 1:3). For the rest, Scotus hardly mentioned the sacrificial gift, the body and blood of Christ.

While in certain marginal areas the theologians of High Scholasticism introduced one or another distinction, on the pivotal matter of the Eucharist as sacrifice they followed their predecessors on the whole in passing along the familiar teaching of the Church by means of the patristic quotations available from tradition. This holds good for subsequent centuries as well. Several theological treatises of the fourteenth and fifteenth centuries are devoted to questions of rubrics and to casuistic discussions of the Eucharist, but they keep away from the sacrificial aspect of the Mass. Among these later masters the founder of nominalism, William of Ockham, is outstanding.

Others who touch upon this aspect simply repeat what had been said before them.[62] Only Gabriel Biel (d. 1495) handled the subject thoroughly; in his Canonis Missae Expositio he summed up the views of his predecessors without always reconciling them. In Biel, too, the basic theological threads become entangled in a maze of canonistic and casuistic discussions and minute word analyses.[63]

On the essence of the sacrifice in the Mass, Biel follows Duns Scotus. According to Biel the only sacrifice in the New Testament is the sacrifice of the Cross offered by Christ. The Mass is only a memorial, a representative image (*imago repraesentativa*) of this one sacrifice (Lectio 75 F), and hence of limited efficacy from the start. The re-presentation of the sacrifice of the Cross takes place chiefly through the Consecration and Communion, the chalice standing in the foreground. The duality of the species serves on the one hand as a re-presentation of spiritual nourishment (Lect. 52 F) and on the other as a re-presentation of the Passion (53 X). While in the Mass it is the priest who performs the action immediately, ultimately and principally it is the offering Church (26 H).

But since the Mass is the re-presentation of the sacrifice of the Cross and has an efficacy similar to that of the sacrifice of the Cross (85 J–L), the Mass is itself also sacrifice; its value and its efficacy, however, are contingent as being in direct proportion to the disposition of the one who offers, and to the disposition of the Church, which can be no holier than the holiest of her members and is not as such infinite (27). Only once did Biel invoke Augustine's authority: when he stated that in the Mass Christ is the real though invisible High Priest; he thus perpetuated this tradition, but without taking it too seriously.[64] Still, he was thoroughly sound in his approach when he stressed (precisely in Augustine's sense) the interior sacrifice of oneself and the surrender to God's will that the

Christian must bring to the Mass (16 E). In emphasizing the priest's role and the "application of the fruits and merits of the sacrifice" (*specialis, specialissima, generalissima*), he fell back on the thought of Scotus (26 K).

4. THE THEORY OF LIMITED FRUITS AND ITS EFFECTS

The theory that every Mass yields sure but limited fruits became predominant in the later Middle Ages, partly in conjunction with the questionable principle on which it was based, i.e., that the Church's holiness is limited. The consequence was that the multiplication of Masses, considered as a great good in itself, was pushed to the very extreme, with no thought of a celebrating community.

As already in an earlier age, so in the later Middle Ages some did protest against this excessive multiplication of Masses. Francis of Assisi (d. 1226) exhorted his brethren to celebrate Mass only once a day in their houses. When there were several priests in one friary, the others should be content for the love of Christ to attend the Mass of one of their brethren.[65] Likewise Praepositinus of Cremona (d. 1210) maintained that when psalms or Masses are offered for the whole assembly, each individual benefits no less than if they were said particularly for him. He based his argument on a similar expression in the canon *Non mediocriter* of the Decretals of Gratian (De Cons. D. 5 ch. 24; Friedberg 1:1418). And he drew a comparison with the candle that may have been lighted for one single person yet gives light to all.[66]

While again and again during the next period canonists commented on that decretal of Gratian, Iserloh tells us that from the time of Huguccio (d. 1210) they interpreted it in the opposite sense. Theologians of the nominalist school simply followed the teaching of Scotus, and without bothering to argue from basic principles, assumed that the value of the Mass is limited because the Mass must be effective by way of satisfaction (*per modum satisfactionis*). Neither its identification with the sacrifice of the Cross nor the disposition of the participants was taken into consideration. Of course there were exceptions, like the Franciscan Michael Aiguani (d. 1400), who reflected the ancient teaching.

This overemphasis on and isolation of the part played by the Church and the celebrating priest in the Mass have left a few traces even in the ritual of the Mass of the late Middle Ages. In many ways the offertory was now considered and handled as a self-contained part of the Mass. Thus Henry of Hesse the Elder (also known as Henry of Langenstein; d. 1397) divided the principal part of the Mass into the three sections of *Oblation, Canon,* and *Communion,* a division that has since been perpetuated in many books. Since the fourteenth century, as noted by the present author (in MRR 2:97, n.2), the offertory has been called in some missals the "Minor Canon," and it has been very much expanded through added blessings over the bread and wine. The Preface, which comes between the offertory and the Canon, became something of an embarrassment for the liturgists of this time, for as mere prayer it interrupts the progress of the liturgy.[67]

The Mass was accessible to the devotion of the faithful chiefly in its function as a re-presentation of Christ's suffering. The Dutch humanist Johannes Gansfort proposed the view that during the Mass one need do nothing but meditate on the Lord's Passion and death (Franz, pp. 26f.). This tendency to allegorize grows apace, despite Albert the Great's firm protest against it in his treatise *On the Mystery of the Mass (De Mysterio Missae).* At this stage the allegory often had Christ's Passion exclusively re-presented in the ceremonies.

5. CONCEPTION OF THE REAL PRESENCE; MULTIPLICATION OF MASSES

From another angle, the Eucharistic devotion of the late Middle Ages is closely correlated with theological development on two points in particular: first, a concentration on the cult of the Eucharist within and outside the Mass rather than on the celebration of the Eucharist and participation in it; second, the increasing frequency of the celebration of Mass for individual members of the faithful upon the offering of a stipend.

The elevation of the body of Christ at the Consecration was a first manifestation of special veneration of the Eucharist as well as an encouragement to intensify that veneration. After the mid-thirteenth century new liturgical forms made their appearance. The feast of Corpus Christi, created in the thirteenth century, brought in its train the procession of the Most Blessed Sacrament, exposition of the Blessed Sacrament, and the Benediction service; and devotion to the Blessed Sacrament increased.[68] Still, the Mass was no less prized at this time than before. The faithful came to Mass not only on Sundays but even daily, and in large numbers. True, the foreign language created a bit of distance between them and the Mass, but compensation was found (apart from the allegorical interpretation of the ceremonies) in the sheer possibility, newly opened up, of gazing at the sacred Host. As for Communion, the people only rarely made bold to receive it.

So then it was only natural that the teaching on the fruits of the Mass found a lively response in the people and that the frequency of the Mass should have increased substantially. Ultimately, at the end of the Middle Ages, this development led to the rise of numerous "altarists," whose only job was to recite the Office and to say Mass at a specific altar. All this soon brought about certain circumstances that degenerated into open superstition and abuse. Nor should contemporary theology be blamed, except in the sense that it did not resist this tendency energetically enough. Whatever, devotion to the Mass often took a utilitarian and distorted turn. From participation in the Mass, or even from a glimpse of the elevated Sacrament, people hoped for spiritual gain, of course, but also for earthly advantages: thus, on that day one would not become blind, one would not die a sudden death, through every Mass one soul would be freed from purgatory, and so on. Popular writings and sometimes even missals contained long lists of such "graces" or meeds as flowing from attendance at Mass.[69]

The theology of the time neither advocated such excesses nor still less defended them. By and large, despite mutations of emphasis, the heritage of earlier times was faithfully preserved and handed on, as is objectively attested by the article "Missa" by the humanist John Altenstaig in the Vocabularis Theologiae, a theological lexicon that appeared in the year 1517 and sums up the entire tradition.[70]

In contrast to the narrow view of the Mass prevailing at the time is the grand vision of Cardinal Nicholas of Cusa (d. 1464), who compared creation to a temple built by God, in which he has set up an altar, namely, the Word become man, who is at the same time altar, priest, and oblation for the glorification of God. Nicholas also fought most decisively against the abuses mentioned above; but since his efforts remained isolated, the cry for reform — including even the Mass — turned into revolution.[71]

6. ATTACK AND COUNTERATTACK

It was the concept of the Mass as a good work with which one could please God rather than as a free gift of God to men that was the target of Martin Luther's indignation and reforming zeal. He had seen with his own eyes the abuses, the multiplication of Masses, the belief that the Mass was efficacious by merely going through the motions. He had developed his new teaching as early as 1520 in his "Sermon on the New Testament, that is, on the Holy Mass." According to Luther, the words with which Christ instituted the sacrament were his testament, his last will, namely, the promise and assurance that our sins have been forgiven; his body and blood are the seal with which he confirms this testament.

Hence it is an abuse for the priest to pronounce these decisive words softly, and a further abuse to make a good work out of what is a "testament and a sacrament," or to convert the Mass into a sacrifice. Nevertheless, Luther was prepared to grant the notion of sacrifice, if by sacrifice one understood the self-offering of the faithful: the Mass would then be somewhat like the "invisible sacrifice" of Augustine, viz., the people's praise and thanksgiving, which are laid "before Christ our Mediator." But this, Luther adds, requires no priesthood, since we are all priests.[72]

In his later writings Luther drew the logical conclusions from these principles. Thus, because the Mass is merely a testament and not a sacrifice, man can do nothing but accept, and that he does through faith (6:516f.). But since one can have faith only for oneself, the Mass cannot be offered for others, whether living or dead (6:521f.). As a consequence, in a special tract in 1521, he rejected the private Mass as offending particularly against the fact that Christ was offered only once (8:411-76).

In the *Formula missae et communionis* of 1523 and in the *Deutsche Messe (German Mass)* of 1526, Luther went on to propose a reorganization of divine service in accordance with these principles. The most important change was that of the Canon, in which only the words of Consecration are retained. All the rest, in particular any reference to the sacrifice, is dropped. It is not surprising that in many other details Luther adopted the ideas of the late Middle Ages, and that, e.g., he did not grasp the full beauty and depth of the thanksgiving prayer of the Preface, converting it into an admonition to the communicants. True, he assigned to the people a certain active function in praying and singing as compared with the clerical monopoly of liturgy in the Middle Ages; but for the rest, he made passivity a theological principle.[73]

The first Catholic writings in defense of the Mass apppeared as early as 1520, as Iserloh tells us in *Der Kampf um die Messe*. These are polemical works that confront individual statements by Luther with traditional Catholic teaching in order to expose their contradictions or prove them erroneous. The humanists among these controversialists quote several of the Church Fathers to make their point that the Mass is not merely sacrifice but also memorial (*memoriale sacrificium*) as well as sacrifice in mystery.

Yet they in turn advance questionable arguments: for example, Christ, they argue, offered himself not only once on the Cross, but likewise at the eating of the paschal lamb and at the institution of the sacrament. They make the sacrifice of the Mass consist in an oblation of Christ, made present in the Consecration. Johannes Eck defends the theory of the "limited" value of the Mass and the necessity of frequent repetition. His argument in support of this as late as 1542 (in his *Apologia*, 50f.) is that the Mass is in fact only a memorial of the death on the Cross, and hence in considering it as a sacrifice we should not simply identify it with the sacrifice of the Cross.

The basic theological questions, however, are almost never confronted for thorough and clear discussion. Among the isolated exceptions are Kaspar Schatzgeyer, who pointed out that the sacrifice of the Mass is "truly the sacrifice of Christ more than of the Church or of her minister."[74] And Cardinal Cajetan stressed the unity of the sacrifice of the Mass with that of the Cross, since the Cross is made present in the Mass under the aspect of immolation (*immolaticio modo*), and the priest consecrates not in his own name but "in the person of Christ" (Opuscula Omnia, 341).[75]

7. LUTHER AND THE OTHER REFORMERS

These isolated voices, however, were drowned out by the general clamor of the controversy. The defenders contended themselves with "refuting the opponent instead of coming to grips with his meaning and intention and doing justice to them" — to quote Iserloh's assessment in *Der Kampf um die Messe* (p. 57). No notice is taken of the fact that Luther's concept of the Eucharist is based on his theory of justification by faith alone (*sola fide*). Because of this (his basic) principle, the Eucharist too can be for him only a testament, a gift of God, an assurance of his grace, "a visible word," that man accepts in faith; as such it can be only a duplicate of absolution and is really superfluous; at any rate it is not a sacrifice offered to God.[76]

Thus in no way did Luther deviate from his basic position. In the objections of his opponents he saw only evasions and subterfuges with which they attempted to justify the old abuses. Even when the Mass is described as the memorial of Christ's Passion, said Luther, it has really been made a work of man that must be meritorious before God (30.2:611).[77] From 1530 onward Luther's attacks became less hostile.[78] Nonetheless, the concept of the Mass as sacrifice was rejected in the *Confessio Augustana* of 1530 and in the Schmalkaldian articles of 1536–37; and in the presence of the Council called by Pope Paul III, Luther declared that the Mass was a point on which there was no agreement (50:204). Melanchthon's condemnation of the Mass was a little less sharp; he did not exclude a "Eucharistic sacrifice" in the Mass, understanding it of course in a very broad sense.

Despite their disagreement with Luther on other points of their teaching on the Eucharist, Zwingli and Calvin were one with him in rejecting the Mass as sacrifice. Both reformers argued further from their common denial of the Real Presence: thus, since Christ is not present in the sacrament, neither can he be offered as sacrifice. They further support their rejection of the sacrifice by pointing out that, according to a widespread Catholic conception, in such a sacrifice Christ would have to be *slain* every day.

It is precisely these ideas of the Swiss reformers, apart from Luther's influence, that have played so significant a role in the founding of Anglicanism and its teaching on the Eucharist. As a consequence the thirty-first of the forty-two Articles of the year 1553 contains the rejection of "Mass sacrifices," which are called "blasphemous fables and dangerous deceits." So too in the 1552 Book of Common Prayer, every mention of sacrifice is carefully avoided.[79]

VIII. FROM THE COUNCIL OF TRENT TO THE PRESENT

1. THE WORK OF TRENT

Appropriately enough, the Council of Trent initiated its reform action with the very principles where the fundamental division lay, that is, with the sources of faith and with the teaching on justification. After that, however, the character of the controversy and of the defense as well as external conditions determined the direction taken by the proceedings. This meant that with regard to the Eucharist no unified presentation of the whole theme could be prepared, and only the points under strongest attack were reinforced, and in the order of their controversial importance at the time. Thus, in the thirteenth session in 1551, the Council dealt with the sacrament and with questions related to the Real Presence; in 1562, in session 21, Communion was taken up for discussion for the first time; and the Mass, only in session 22.

On the Mass the Council encountered a real difficulty. In contrast with the state of the question on the Real Presence, there had been no comprehensive theological work preparing the ground for a thoroughgoing treatment of the subject, with the possible exception of the writings of Cajetan.[80] There was even less possibility of grasping and expounding the Eucharist as an *action* in the light of its original liturgical form. The most important sources of the primitive liturgy were only just then becoming available in print; Gregory Dix draws our attention to the fact that the Apology of Justin was published only in 1551, the Liturgy of James in 1560, and the Apostolic Constitutions in 1563.[81] Naturally there could have been no question of working with such sources.

Already in the proceedings of 1551–52 the reformers' objections to the Church's teaching and practice of the Mass had been collected and the pivotal issues thoroughly thrashed out at the Council. As a reflection of the medieval emphases, attention had long been directed toward proving that the Mass was a propitiatory sacrifice just like the sacrifice of the Cross, and that it therefore contained within itself an immolation-slaying (*immolatio-mactatio*). Only gradually was it recognized by the Council Fathers that the burden of proof lay on showing the Mass to be a true sacrifice. Accordingly, three elements constituting the sacrifice of the Mass were singled out for scrutiny: consecration, oblation, and re-presentation of Christ's suffering.[82]

In the final Council decree of 1562 these elements were recombined into a broader synthesis. At the same time the points attacked by the reformers were explained more precisely. Thus, as is anticipated in chapter 1, in the Last Supper Christ offered a sacrifice and gave it over to his Church so that by it his sacrifice of the Cross would be forever made present (*repraesentaretur*). This sacrifice is also truly propitiatory (*vere propitiatorium*), since in it the same Christ who offered himself in a bloody manner (*cruente*) on the Cross is now offered in an unbloody manner (*incruente*). In it the sacrificed gift-offering is the same, the same too the sacrificing priest (*nunc offerens sacerdotum ministerio*); only the manner of the re-presentation is different. Hence, as chapter 2 brings out, this sacrifice does not take anything away from the one sacrifice of the Cross, but only makes its fruits accessible; hence too, it can be offered for both the living and the dead. Then some particular points of liturgical practice were defended: the Canon of the Mass, the observance of ceremonies, the permissibility of the private Mass in which only the priest communicates, the use of Latin (chs. 3–9). Finally the decisive points were recapitulated in nine canons (Denz. 1738–59).

2. TRENT AND THE POST-TRIDENTINE THEOLOGIANS

The decree has rightly been called "a masterpiece of synthesis," in Neunheuser's phrase. In reading it one must bear in mind the fact that the emphases were determined by the exigencies of defense and that the formulations had to be phrased in terms of the theology prevailing at the time. The Council deliberately avoided a decision on schools of opinion; it avoided also a speculative approach and the temptation to construct a complete system. A self-contained formulation of the entire teaching on the Eucharist could not yet be produced for the very reason that external conditions had necessitated a treatment of separate sections, i.e., sacrament, Communion, and the Mass. The Council's objective was to achieve something practical and to re-establish the order that had been disrupted. In this same spirit, too, under Pope Pius V in 1570, the Missale Romanum was published in an improved form and as the norm henceforth for the whole Western Church.

Theologians in the subsequent age should have integrated into a comprehensive context what the Council had treated in separate parts for purposes of careful *ad hoc* clarification. This integration, however, was achieved only in part, what with the protracted state of controversy. The casually introduced division of the subject matter into sacrament, Communion, and Mass was perpetuated in almost all the theological tracts and catechisms of the ensuing centuries. The devotion of the faithful was directed far more toward the veneration of the sacrament than toward the co-offering of the sacrifice. In fact, it was at this time that the Communion of the faithful became more and more disjoined from the Mass as a devotional practice in its own right.

During the three subsequent centuries the theological treatment of the subject was based on the freshly verified postulate that the Mass is a sacrifice; and it centered upon the question of *how* the Mass becomes a sacrifice. By far the larger number of theologians were no longer thinking in terms of the Church's sacrifice, an aspect only touched upon by the Council. Even without adverting to the language of the liturgy, in which indeed the "Offerimus" (i.e., we are offering) is characteristic, there was no doubt that the sacrifice offered by the Church was the aspect predominating not only in the writings of the Latin Fathers in particular, but also in medieval thought patterns originating in Saints Augustine and Isidore. But in its Scotist isolation the sacrifice of the Church had become a rock of scandal to Protestant critics. Now, however, the attention was concentrated, in the manner of the Greek Fathers, on the question of the way in which the same sacrifice that Christ had offered on the Cross was present in the Mass. Several explanations were now proposed: the so-called *destruction* theories of sacrifice. A. Michel, who has studied these theories in detail, has arranged them in an order providing the clear general perspective that we shall follow.[83]

3. DESTRUCTION-THEORIES OF SACRIFICE

Common to all these theories is the intent to show that what inheres in the Mass is not a mere memorial (*nuda commemoratio*) of the sacrifice of the Cross, but that in some way this sacrifice becomes *present*. In this they evidently refer to the objection raised by Zwingli after 1523 and later repeated by Calvin and the English reformers: when Christ is offered in the Mass, he must be slain anew, for to sacrifice means to slay.[84]

The striking thing in the reaction of Catholic theology is that it never challenged this understanding of the notion. In his Commentary on Part III of the Summa Theologica of St. Thomas (Disputatio 220.2:15), Gabriel Vásquez (d. 1604) rejected the idea that on the part of the priest a simple oblation (in the manner of Leviticus 23 and 24) could suffice. For no doubt such an oblation without destruction could express in general the recognition of God's dominion over things, but not his dominion over life and death (Disp. 220.3:20-24). How then was the reproach of the reformers to be met? It must be shown that in the Mass something happens through which the Lord's death on the Cross becomes present on the altar.

At an early stage one was satisfied with the answer that in the Mass we have a likeness of the sacrifice of the Cross. This likeness, according to many commentators — *pro* or *contra* — on Thomas Aquinas, is to be found in the fraction (Melchior Cano) or in the Communion (Dominic Soto), or in the separate species without further distinction (Alfonso Salmerón, Gulielmus Estius, and many others).

a) Mystical slaying

Vásquez went a step farther: the Mass is a sacrifice because in it a mystical slaying (*mactatio mystica*) takes place, so that by virtue of the double consecration not only does Christ become present but even his death on the Cross is re-presented. For although Vásquez, like Thomas Aquinas, considered a change to be essential for the sacrifice to take place, still in the same commentary he maintained that in the case of the Mass a re-presentation is sufficient precisely because it is not an absolute sacrifice, but merely a commemorative or relative one (Disp. 220.3; 223.4:37). This position was upheld by many theologians up to the twentieth century.

In a developed form of the same position, Leonard Lessius

(d. 1623) argued that by virtue of the double consecration not only is an image of the sacrifice of the Cross created, but also "by the power of the words" (*vi verborum*) the body and blood are separated from one another (*De perfectionibus moribusque divinis* 12.13:95-97). This idea has been handed down in the expression "virtual slaying" (*mactatio virtualis*) to the present day, chiefly in the Thomistic school. According to others like Z. Pasqualigo (d. 1664) and Bishop Bossuet (d. 1704), it is enough that Christ becomes present with the external appearance of death (*repraesentatio mortis*), since with that we have the external sign required for a sacrifice showing the inner surrender, here the interior surrender of the whole Mystical Body. This explanation was revived by Cardinal Billot (d. 1931).

b) Real "slaying"

Another solution believed to have adequately met the Protestant attack on the sacrificial character of the Mass is that associated especially with Suárez in his commentary on St. Thomas (*De Sacrificio Missae*, Disp. 75), and based on the idea that for an actual sacrifice an actual destruction of the sacrificial victim is necessary.[85] That through the double consecration a mystical slaying (*mactatio mystica*) takes place, he did not dispute. This, however, he pronounced inadequate, since in fact it is not an actual slaying. As against this, an actual "destruction" or at least a "change" is present in another manner, namely, in the substance of the sacrificial gift-offerings of bread and wine, when these are transformed into the body and blood of Christ. For while bread and wine are not really the sacrificial gift-offerings, yet according to Christ's will they are the object with which the sacrifice begins. This theory has been carried forward by Scheeben (d. 1888) among others; he only replaces the notion of destruction with that of the "change" and lays stress on the significance of the sacrifice as an expression of the interior surrender of the Mystical Body.

Cardinal Bellarmine (d. 1621) also considered the "destruction," seen in relation to the species of bread and wine, to be an essential element of the sacrifice; but he found the destruction realized at another point: the Communion. On this principle the priest's Communion belongs to the substance of the sacrifice. Thus by virtue of consecration the sacrificial gift-offerings (Christ's body and blood) are ordained to an actual destruction, and this takes place when they are consumed.

While in these theories the destruction required for sacrifice is found in the species of bread and wine, the theology of Juan de Lugo (d. 1660) posits it of the sacrificial victim, Christ himself. By means of the Consecration, Christ is reduced to a lower state (*statum decliviorem*), to put it in human terms, i.e., that of food (*De Venerabili Eucharistiae Sacramento* 19:65-67). This theory was revived in the nineteenth century by Cardinal Franzelin (d. 1886). From the sixteenth century onward, however, there were theologians who argued that the oblation itself was enough to make the Mass a sacrifice.

4. OTHER THEORIES

In his commentary on 1 Corinthians 11:21-25, Maldonatus (d. 1583) raised no objection to the idea that a sacrifice should take place through the destruction of the victim, but he argued that this is only one of the possible ways it could happen, the essential thing being only the oblation; and the oblation was present already at the institution of the sacrament. This view was later developed chiefly by the theologians of the so-called French school founded by Cardinal de Bérulle. Without denying the significance of the *immolatio mystica*, they laid stress on the interior self-giving practiced by Christ throughout his earthly life and consummated on the Cross, the self-giving he continues in his life in heaven. In the Mass, too, the crucial action consists in this, that by virtue of the words of Consecration, Christ becomes present under the visible species, with this will-to-surrender; and further, that he subsumes the Church into this surrender.

Lepin himself is numbered among such theologians (see pp. 730–58). And Maurice de la Taille's work *Mysterium Fidei* (1921; ³Paris 1931) has contributed much to the growth of this theory. According to him the unique sacrifice of Christ consisted in his death on the Cross and in its liturgical oblation at the Last Supper. The sacrifice of the Mass therefore consists in the Church's renewed offering of this same Victim with the same act of oblation as at the Last Supper, and with Christ renewing it along with his Church.

Since the turn of the twentieth century the increasing opposition to the still influential theories of destruction asserted itself in another direction. This new tack took on radical form in James Bellord (vicar general of Gibraltar), who theorized in two articles [86] that the sacrifice was performed not in the death on the Cross but at the Last Supper, and therefore without the death symbolism. In the Mass it is the Communion that realizes this sacrifice more particularly.

In another, somewhat more guarded way F. S. Renz arrived at a similar conclusion (*Die Geschichte des Messopferbegriffes*). The only real sacrifice, he held, was the death on the Cross; in the Mass this sacrifice is re-presented; and this re-presentation, together with the Real Presence, realizes the idea of the sacrifice. Objectively the sacrifice is performed at the Consecration; subjectively, in the Communion. In its essence, therefore, the Mass is "a meal that has a sacrificial character"; "sacrificial," inasmuch as it sanctifies man (2:500-503).

The theory that the Mass is essentially a meal has appeared several times since then, at times with reference to the New Testament account (e.g., Yves de Montcheuil in *Mélanges théologiques*, pp. 23–48, stresses the idea as one essential aspect); at times in the interest of ecumenical understanding; at times simply in view of the actual liturgical appearance. Along this last line Romano Guardini (d. 1968) has stated; "The basic structure of the Mass is that of the meal; the sacrifice does not appear in it as a figure, but stands behind the whole." [87] Similarly J. Pascher in his book *Eucharistia* (pp. 28–30 of the 2nd, revised edition) looked upon the Institution of Jesus as above all a meal preceded by a thanksgiving prayer like grace before meals.

5. A NEW APPROACH AND ITS SOURCES

The decisive shift toward a radically new attitude is associated with the names of two theologians of the flourishing Benedictine revival. One of them, Abbot Ansgar Vonier (d. 1938), in his classic work *A Key to the Doctrine of the Eucharist*, addressed himself, with repeated reference to Thomas Aquinas, to refuting the view that in the Eucharist the glorified Christ first becomes present and only then is transformed into a sacrificial victim. Rather, he insists, the sacrament as such is itself sacrifice: a sacramental sacrifice. Through transubstantiation Christ's body and blood are brought into the present as they were on Calvary (*Christus passus*). This sacramental "rendering present" alone is adequate in itself to effect the sacrifice (ch. 13).

At almost the same time Dom Odo Casel (d. 1948) began publishing his studies based on the history of religions and unfolding his thesis on mystery cult (*Die Liturgie als Mysterienfeier*). According to this argument, to a certain extent and in certain aspects the Eucharistic celebration is analogous to the ancient mystery cults. From this viewpoint what becomes present in the Mass is not merely Christ but (under the veil of ritual or "in mystery") also his whole work of redemption along with its nucleus, the death on the Cross: and this presence is not only subjective but objective as well. In performing the ritual the Church shares in the act of salvation. Even though not a few critical objections have been raised to particular points of the Casel theory, his postulate of "making present" has been found fruitful, for if in every Mass the death on the Cross is simply made present, then the unity of the sacrifice follows of itself, and new light is thus thrown also on the Church's share.

The change revealed in these publications did not come about by accident; it was prompted by the new awareness of the ancient historical origins made possible through the burgeoning patristic scholarship, the discovery of the old liturgies, the developing study of comparative liturgy, all of which went hand in hand with a practical interest in renewing liturgical life itself. As a consequence, attention was once more focused on the sacrifice of the Church as the assembly of the faithful, the faithful themselves actively offering the sacrifice with the priest, as Pope Pius XII was to insist in his encyclical *Mediator Dei* of 1947. At the same time many liturgists were coming to understand the notion of a thanksgiving prayer once more; too, they were growing more receptive to the deeper significance of the memorial, about which the Fathers had likewise spoken with so much emphasis. And it was but one step from the objective memorial to the idea of making-present.

Moreover, at the same time Protestant criticism ceased to influence the Catholic concept of the Eucharist as it had for several centuries. Of course, in cases where criticism had already reached the pitch of complete denial of Christian revelation, there could be no question of influence. But believing Protestantism, too, had undergone a change, although the concept of the Last Supper in the theology of the reformers was no doubt still very far from Catholic teaching, to judge from the Arnoldshain Theses of 1957, which are the fruit of collaborative work and thus represent some degree of consensus.[88] In various publications the Catholic concept of the sacrifice of the Mass was still accused of violating the uniqueness of the redemptive sacrifice or of overemphasizing the human part in the action.

The same historical insights, nevertheless, engendered significant modifications in the understanding of Jesus' Institution within Protestant communions. Frequently changes filtered even into liturgical texts, with the momentous effect that certain essential elements of a genuine Eucharistic Prayer, of a Preface, of an epiclesis, of an anamnesis, even the *presenting* of the gift-offerings sanctified by the words of the Institution were restored to their services.[89]

6. CONTEMPORARY TRENDS

The Catholic teaching on the Eucharist could now concentrate all the more directly on grasping fully and deepening its speculative understanding of its tradition.[90] The new light thrown on the re-presentation of the one unique sacrificial act also helped to reveal more clearly that in the Mass there is an actual sacrifice and that it is in fact the same one sacrifice as offered by Christ. And if this sacrifice is made present in the church, then it follows that the Church as the body of Christ is associated in this action of its Head, and that when it offers the sacrifice the Church does not act in a vacuum or simply in its own capacity.

At the same time a perspective on the Eucharist has taken hold in which the action, the sacrifice itself, is emphasized, and the Real Presence is seen in relation to this sacrificial action. The more recent studies on the subject, precisely by reason of their fidelity to tradition, round out and complete this new perspective, so that sacrament, Communion, and Mass are not merely juxtaposed, but the "mystery of faith" (*mysterium fidei*) is embraced as a whole. For example, Charles Journet, in his *La Messe présence du sacrifice de la croix*, proceeds from the sacrifice of the Cross and treats the entire teaching on the Eucharist under the concept of the Mass. So too, Michael Schmaus in *Katholische Dogmatik*[91] and L. Scheffczyk in "Die Zuordnung von Sakrament und Opfer in der Eucharistie."

The new orientation in the Church's liturgical practice corresponds to — and indeed has preceded — the new orientation in theology, since the emergence of the liturgical movement (first in Belgium 1909) under the impetus of an ideal intuited rather than seen. This impetus proceeded from the newly awakened realization that undiscovered treasures lie hidden in the liturgy of the Mass, treasures that the present age stands desperately in need of; from the realization, too, that the Church that celebrates the Eucharist must be the actual gathering of God's holy people. From this arose the move to make the Mass intelligible to the people and to invite them to active participation. Pope Pius XII's encyclical *Mediator Dei* was the first official recognition of this tendency.

The same realization led to the Vatican Council II resolution in favor of radical reform of the Mass "to the earlier norm of the holy Fathers" (Constitution on the Liturgy [henceforth CL], § 50). Now, it was not the ritual of the Mass considered in isolation that should be the basis of reform, as was the case of the 1570 reform, nor the ritual's performance by the celebrating priest. Rather, *the Mass celebrated with the people* was henceforth to constitute the norm. This basically accepted principle led to the conclusion that in carrying out the reform in 1967 there was to be a universal shift to the language of the people and also that the reform should penetrate even to the heart of the Mass, the Canon.

Accordingly, in 1968 three new forms of the Eucharistic Prayer (*prex eucharistica*) were added to the old Roman Canon, forms in which the original structure and thematic content of a Eucharistic Prayer find clearer expression. Further, in order to counteract the distracting multiplicity of private Masses celebrated simultaneously in the same church (a fact that all but eclipsed the image of the sacrament of unity and, as mentioned above, was a special scandal to the reformers), the Council proposed the practice of concelebration. As for Eucharistic doctrine, nothing new needed saying in the Council. It was enough to sum up briefly, in the introduction to the chapter on "The Most Sacred Mystery of the Eucharist," the teaching of the Council of Trent.

PART TWO

The Theology of the
Eucharistic Sacrifice

I. THE WORK OF REDEMPTION AS A SALVIFIC SACRIFICE

1. CHRIST CAME TO OFFER A REDEMPTIVE SACRIFICE

The redemptive suffering and death of the God-Man and its culmination, the resurrection, lie at the very heart of the Christian message. The Son of God became man in order that as the new Adam he might lead the new people of God back to him. But it was a sinful humanity that he entered, a humanity that had rebelled against God and thus brought continuing misery upon itself. And so it was his wish to descend to the depths of sinfulness and as the Lamb of God to take away the sins of the world in perfect obedience to his Father's will. Only in this way was he willing to precede mankind into the glory of the Father; and this is why his self-surrender in death may be said to have crowned his life.

Jesus' whole life was oriented toward the redemption of the world from sin through his salvific suffering and death on Calvary. As St. Paul observed (in Hebrews 10:7), it was under this sign that he became man. His incarnation was an emptying (*kenosis*); and, as with his entire life, it pointed toward the Cross (Phil. 2:7-8). For, according to God's dispensation, Christ was to be not merely the preacher of a new doctrine and the model of a new way of life; he was to restore the broken bond of man with God.

The office with which Christ Jesus came into the world was not merely that of teacher and king but, above and beyond these, that of priest. As God-Man, he is essentially the head and representative of humanity before God, the only one competent to make a new beginning. He is priest. By virtue of his total and living surrender to God's will, Christ redirected the obedience of mankind toward God; and thus man was reabsorbed into the love of God. Access to God was once again open for all who accepted Christ in faith.

In recounting this redemptive action of the Lord Jesus, the New Testament does so in the concepts and language of sacrifice.

97

The notion of sacrifice is brought out in the words of Jesus himself when he speaks of his blood "to be poured out in behalf of many for the forgiveness of sins" (Matthew 26:28), and declares that he has come "to give his life in ransom for the many" (Mark 10:45).

In the primitive Church, too, the redemptive suffering of Jesus was invariably designated and described as a sacrifice. For St. Paul, "Christ our Passover has been sacrificed" (1 Cor. 5:7); in the Acts, Christ has bought the Church "at the price of his own blood" (20:28). St. Peter asserts that the ransom paid to free man was not "any diminishable sum of silver or gold, but Christ's blood beyond all price; the blood of a spotless, unblemished lamb" (1 Peter 1:18-19). The blood of the lamb clearly signifies a sacrifice; and in Paul's language even this metaphoric character of Old Testament imagery disappears. It is the stark and simple reality that Paul gets at when he refers to Christ as one who "gave himself for us as an offering to God, a gift of pleasing fragrance" (Eph. 5:2).

On the surface, what happened at the Lord's death on the Cross had really little in common with any of the customary or conventional sacrifices. For the deed of his enemies was a crime, not a sacrifice. He alone was the offerer. It was the free acceptance of anguish and death by a guiltless one-for-others that had been foretold of the Servant of God (Is. 53:2-10). It was precisely what the prophets had demanded as the essence of a sacrifice: the external gift-offering, yes, but dictated by obedience toward God; a gift-offering motivated by the interior sentiment without which, as Jesus had taught, all sacrifices would be worthless: "It is mercy I desire and not sacrifice" (Matthew 12:7). It was a total self-surrender, motivated by the greatest love.

2. A NEW KIND OF "SACRIFICE"

If we wish to understand the death on the Cross as well as the sacrifice of the Mass, it will not do to start from conventional and established cultic forms, whether from the Old Testament or from the history of religions in general. The Old Testament Book of Genesis may indeed allude to sacrifices that have no cultic character in the sense of an established ritual order; but sacrifice in the New Testament sense is clearly dissociated from traditional cultic forms. We have here a new beginning, and hence it is not yet a sacrifice "in the transferred sense." If, in Ephesians 5:2, for instance, the word *sacrifice* has an "ethical ring" (as G. Delling notes in *Der Gottesdienst im Neuen Testament*, p. 22), this is not a deviation from the prevailing concepts of sacrifice but only the accentuation of its essential content; and Delling rightly speaks of a "total transformation of cult-language" in the New Testament (p. 20).

The essential elements of the concept of sacrifice become clear if, with Averbeck (779) and in the spirit of the Letter to the Hebrews, we define sacrifice as "a person's total self-surrender to God, represented in an exterior gift-offering." At the same time it is clear that man has nothing properly his own to give to God; he must first have received it. In the case of the sacrifice of the Cross, nonetheless, there is a genuine giving. The Lord, in his humanity, gives himself totally and unreservedly to God; this self-giving is exteriorly manifested in the surrender of blood and life, just as he had already foretold: "I lay down my life to take it up again. No one takes it from me; I lay it down freely" (John 10:17-18).

Not surprisingly, it is at precisely this point that profound objections are raised by Protestant theologians to the Catholic concept of sacrifice: objections specifically based on the idea of a God who is alone efficacious and all-efficacious, and that of man incapable of anything on his own power. Together with this, they disagree with the Catholic understanding of the human nature of Christ himself. Luther had already declared that what Jesus instituted at the Last Supper was merely a "testament," an assurance to believers that their sins were forgiven, and hence in effect a pure infusion of divine grace that obviated every action of man toward God. Quite in the sense of Luther, Protestant theologians are opposed to construing either the earthly life or the death of Jesus on the Cross as an act of glorifying the Father, since even in the death on the Cross it is God who acts, God who sits in judgment over man and finally grants him grace. In this purview a "sacrifice" of Jesus the man would involve legalism and anthropocentricity.[92] The humanity of Jesus is thus denied a true function at the most critical point.

On the contrary, Catholic theology, following the mind of the Gospels and of the Ecumenical councils of Chalcedon (451) and Constantinople III (680) against Monophysites and Monotheletes, holds firmly that in Christ human nature remained undiminished and capable of genuine activity in its own right; that Christ as man could thus perform his work in behalf of humanity; that thus he is truly the mediator between God and men, not only in a downward direction as the bringer of grace, but also in an upward direction as the perfecter of the new humanity, as is borne out by the titles Sacred Scripture confers on him: *High Priest, King, Head* of his Church.[93]

The sacrificial death on the Cross was Christ's decisive action for the redemption of the world, but it was also the culmination of the glorification of God. Indeed, it was the redemption of the world precisely because it was the glorification of God to the highest conceivable degree.

On the Cross the sacrifice was offered by Christ alone, offered in the greatest abandonment and loneliness; but that was the moment when the "new and everlasting covenant" was established, the covenant by which God planned to draw redeemed humanity unto himself. Hence it was only proper that redeemed humanity of all subsequent ages should not only be taken into this covenant through Baptism but should also have the opportunity to confirm it, to ratify it. The sacrifice should have continuity, not merely to the extent that it is continued in heaven; it should have continuity in his Church upon the earth, in the community of the redeemed, who should in this way grow into this covenant, and in this way, too, become ever more and more authentically the people of God, body and soul.

3. THE LAST SUPPER, AN ACTED PROPHECY

That is why the Lord instituted the mystery of the Eucharist on the eve of his last day on earth. Along with that, he committed to the apostles the charge "Do this in remembrance of me." In this manner he fulfilled visibly what he was destined to fulfill everywhere and through all the centuries: the promise "I — once I am lifted up from earth — will draw all men to myself" (John 12:32).

What was immediately effected in Jesus' action at the Last Supper was, as is universally accepted and established, a *symbolic gesture*, an "acted parable" (in Brilioth's words), or, more precisely, an acted prophecy. As in the case of the anointing in Bethany, which Jesus had interpreted as relating to his burial, so also now he announced through his own action his approaching sacrificial death. He seized upon a traditional table convention and by means of the accompanying words gave it special significance. The bread that he breaks and passes around to be eaten, the wine — blood of the grape — that he hands to his disciples in the chalice, in his own chalice, is his body given up for all, his blood shed for all.

And this takes place within the setting of a meal characterized by the Synoptics as a *paschal* meal at which all thoughts center upon liberation from the condition of slavery, a liberation in time past and a still greater liberation to come. Through this analogy Jesus indicates the redemptive suffering and death he is about to take upon himself. In this sense, too, St. Thomas Aquinas calls the sacrament "an image representing Christ's Passion" (*imago quaedam repraesentativa passionis Christi*; ST 3a, 83:1).

From this one point rationalistic exegetes jump to the conclusion that this is simply the last parable of Jesus and nothing more — which is to say that the meaning of Jesus' action is exhausted by its parable character, as is suggested by the very title of the book by K. G. Goetz, *Das Abendmahl eine Diatheke Jesu oder sein letztes Gleichnis?* As mere parable, however, some other action would have been more appropriate. When the prophet Jeremiah wanted to pronounce destruction upon the idolatrous people, he smashed a jug to bits before the eyes of the elders with the words: "Thus will I smash this people and this city, as one smashes a clay pot so that it cannot be repaired" (Jer. 19:11).

But Jesus does not break a jug, he gives food and drink to his companions at table, in that way indicating at the same time the redemptive significance of his death: it is a work whose fruit they will share in and are even now sharing in; and he charges them to repeat his action.

So then, what we have here is an efficacious, effective, "acted" parable. The type was not altogether unfamiliar to an Israelite. Word and reality went hand in hand in his cognition process. The Hebrew *dabar* itself already signified both. In the prophets one reads of symbolic actions that were still environed by reality. Thus the prophet Eliseus bids the king, who is at war with Aram, to strike the ground with arrows. When the king strikes the ground only three times, the prophet angrily remonstrates, "You should have struck five or six times; you would have defeated Aram completely. Now, you will defeat Aram only three times" (2 Kings 13:18f.). In our case, what we are dealing with is not the action of a prophet but that of a God-Man. And what he plans to accomplish for the redemption of the world and announces through this prophetic *word,* he already anticipates with this word and on it confers a sacramental presence. He performs a sacramental sacrifice and commands that it be performed continually in the future in remembrance of him.

II. THE COMMEMORATION OF THE REDEMPTIVE SERVICE

As associated inseparably with the mandate "Do this in remembrance of me," memory is a key concept for the understanding of Jesus' institution of the Eucharist. *Remembrance,* of course, could be understood as merely subjective commemoration, as merely a mental recalling. Indeed, such a recalling is certainly an integral part of the Eucharist, and most of the prayers and readings associated with the Eucharistic celebration serve the purpose of such recalling. But by no means does simple *recalling* exhaust the significance of the remembrance intended here. For it is the very action itself that Jesus imposes upon his disciples ("do this") to transform into a memorial. What he orders to be done is itself to be a commemoration. What the Lord directs with his mandate is in some sense an objective commemoration, a memorial, a sign projected into the world so that it becomes a palpable, objectivized fact to which even subjective recalling may be conjoined.

1. AN OBJECTIVE MEMORIAL

In every culture there are manifold forms of objective memorializing such as: a monument in various expressions; a portrait; in our case a painting or sculpture of the Crucified. A higher and more telling form of such a memorial may be reproduced through an action, especially a dramatic action. Thus the so-called Passion Play is certainly one means by which an objective memorial of Christ's suffering may be made: objective, of course, only in the sense that there is an external sign or happening outside our consciousness. And many of the feasts we celebrate, secular as well as religious, are such memorial celebrations.

Of special significance for the proper understanding of Jesus' institution of the Eucharist are the feasts in the Old Testament, and in particular the paschal feast, as is brought out by Max Thurian in Part I of *The Eucharistic Memorial*. By means of the Passover the exodus from Egypt was celebrated every year. According to an instruction in the Mishnah (or Talmudic teachings), "In every generation each individual must think of himself as having come out of Egypt," because God has liberated not only the fathers, but "all of us with them" (Hänggi-Pahl 24).

Certain Protestant theologians profess to find in this Old Testament memorial the identical parallel to the memorial intended in Jesus' Institution. Even in the Old Testament, they maintain, God's work for the salvation of his people was not confined merely to an event that happened once in history, i.e., to the exodus from Egypt or to the creation of the covenant. Each time it became "a present reality, a Today" in the cultic feast, especially so in the case of the Pasch.[94]

At the same time, however, we must note carefully that different gradations are to be distinguished in this re-presentation. What we have in the cultic feasts of the old covenant is certainly a re-presentation that goes beyond a merely subjective recalling, even beyond a mere remembrance through some kind of sign or symbol. When at the feast of Tabernacles the exhortations of Deuteronomy were read out and every generation was told: "Remember that you too were once slaves in Egypt, and the LORD, your God, brought you from there" (5:15), far more was indicated than that the feast should awaken the memory of the liberation of their fathers. As Schildenberger observes, "What we have here, in this ever-recurring *today* of Deuteronomy, is therefore an actualization of the covenant of Sinai that continues to survive through the centuries." [95] This is all the more true of the annual paschal feast, for, as he adds, "The paschal memorial is thus a re-presentation of God's salvific work, which is ever continually effected and which therefore is ever present."

We should note, too, that in the case just discussed we were dealing with an action of God that forms a single motif right through the Old Testament and was readily recognized and re-experienced by receptive man in a memorial celebration. In the

New Testament the situation is different, for here the question is of an action of the God-Man circumscribed by space and time: his death on the Cross. If the memorial of the crucifixion was to be not a mere focus for the purely subjective recalling of the past historical event, if it was also to have significance in itself as a commemoration, then this event must in some way be actually contained in and have efficacy in the memorial itself.

That the redemptive act of Christ, the paschal mystery, continues to be effective through all the centuries, especially in the sacraments of the Church, is a basic teaching of Christianity. But while in the other sacraments this continued efficacy takes place under a particular aspect, such as rebirth, or as communication of the Holy Spirit, in the Eucharist the very event of redemption is its content. This, in a not yet closely articulated form, is the traditional teaching of the Fathers, conspicuously the Greek Fathers, who express it in various ways. They stress, as we have seen, that in the Eucharist we have the very same sacrifice as on Golgotha. They use words such as *symbolon, eikon, homoioma* when speaking of the sacrifice on Calvary.

Again, as we have seen, St. Thomas Aquinas designates the Eucharistic celebration as "an image representing Christ's Passion" (ST 3a, 83:1). As the Council of Trent asserts, the Lord intended that through the Eucharist his sacrifice on the Cross should be made present (*repraesentaretur*), and in the same sense the Liturgical Constitution of Vatican II notes that it was the Lord's intention at the Last Supper that his sacrifice on the Cross should continue through the centuries (*perpetuaret*, § 47). What takes place in the celebration of the Eucharist is thus a continuation, a making-present, of the event of redemption. Hence it is an objective memorial: objective not merely in an external sign (however solemn the ceremony surrounding it), but objective in the sense that the very event celebrated thereby becomes present.

2. NATURE OF THE RE-PRESENTATION

The next question is that of how we are to understand this re-presentation. Are we to understand the event celebrated as being present only according to its outcome, in its effect (*virtute*), or also in itself (*actu*)? More particularly to our purpose, is it only the Christ who has suffered (*Christus passus*) that becomes present in the memorial of the Eucharist, or is it Christ in his suffering (*passio*) as well? True, in the passage cited above, Thomas Aquinas quotes the well-known Sunday prayer: "Whenever the commemoration of this sacrifice is celebrated, the work of our redemption is enacted" (*opus nostrae redemptionis exercetur*); but in his exposition he never goes beyond a presence of *Christus passus*.

Theological discussion in the present century has tended more and more to assert also the presence of the *passio*, and thus to accept the actual presence of the very event of redemption. But the ways in which an explanation of this objective memorial is sought take different directions.[96]

The question here is how the sacred event, the historical fact of the death and resurrection of Jesus (which like every other historical event belongs to the past), can become present to us in the celebration of the Eucharist. Certain Protestant authors (e.g., W. T. Hahn, G. Bornkamm) have advocated the Kierkegaardian-based view that men in the worshiping community must become contemporaneous with the past sacred event. This theory, however, conflicts with the fact that the Eucharistic celebration is performed in the Christian era. And hence we must take another approach, and explain how the relation between a past event and our time may be understood.

Odo Casel's "mystery" theory yields this precision: The historical fact itself becomes present to us not in its historical appearance of that time, but *in mysterio*. Johannes Betz accepts this explanation, but with one modification: that the historical fact contains not an *absolute* (as Casel presumes it) but a *relative* presence, namely, the presence implied in the symbol, in the ritual established by the Church; since otherwise the Church would seem to be merely receptive, merely passive.[97]

According to still others it is not the historical event that must now become immediately present, but rather its continuation in eternity, since the transfigured Redeemer continues forever the same self-surrender he made on the Cross. The re-presentation would be achieved not so much horizontally, not as something traversing the centuries, but vertically, flowing directly from the continued self-surrender of Christ in heaven. But it must be noted that the sentiment of surrender would not yet constitute by itself the sacrifice that should become present.

Another solution, as tentatively suggested by Gottlieb Söhngen, proposes that the sacred event becomes present not in itself but in the effect its celebration produces in the participants, in that they are made the image and likeness of the suffering and risen Lord.[98] Finally, it has been suggested that it is not the sacrificial act itself that must become present in its historicity; rather, it should suffice that the supra-temporal content of the historical act — the attitude, namely, of total self-surrender to God for the sake of men, which informed the entire life of Jesus (and this is more than a mere sentiment) — becomes present anew in the Church's celebration.

With such qualifications the thesis of the presence in mystery should become a valuable means to deeper understanding of the sacrifice of the Mass in its unity with the sacrifice of the Cross. First, however, it might be useful to consider the question from yet another angle.

3. THE VARIOUS PRESENCES OF CHRIST

In this final purview, the presence of Christ's death on the Cross in the Eucharist is only a special instance of his presence in his Church. While during the past few centuries theologians thought of his presence almost exclusively under the species of bread and wine, our age has once again become much more aware of the manifold aspects of Christ's presence. This was, of course, already expressed in our Lord's words: "I am with you always, until the end of the world!" (Matthew 28:20). Both the encyclical *Mediator Dei* and the Vatican II's Constitution on the Liturgy (§ 7) have again drawn our attention to this aspect. Thus, besides the Lord's presence according to substance, as we have it in the sacramental species, we should also distinguish a presence according to act, an *actual presence* (Journet, *La Messe* [pp. 82–86], uses the designation *présence opérative* in the same sense). The purpose of both modes, however, is the continuing presence of the Lord in the hearts of the faithful about which St. Paul speaks, so that Christ may "dwell in your hearts through faith" (Eph. 3:17); and which may be called also (as Neunheuser says in *Opfer Christi*) a presence through the Holy Spirit, a spiritual presence.

We have in the Mass not merely the substantial presence of Jesus Christ by which he becomes present *on* the altar as our gift-offering, but also his actual presence by which he is present *at* the altar acting through his instrument, the ordained priest. This actual presence of our Lord, however, is not restricted to the Eucharist:

we have it in all the sacraments. It is this presence that is meant when in conventional theological parlance Christ is referred to as the primary minister (*minister principalis*) of the sacraments. He is the priest in the proper sense, the High Priest.

In the Mass of the Mozarabic Missale Mixtum (PL 85:550), this concept finds full expression in the prayer the celebrant recites immediately before the words of consecration: "Be present, be present, O Jesus, thou good High Priest, in our midst, as thou wast in the midst of thy disciples, and sanctify this oblation." [99] This presence may also be found, as Vatican II finds it, "in his Word when the holy Scriptures are read in the church" (CL § 7). Moreover, at the distribution of Communion St. John Chrysostom sees in the hand that presents the consecrated Host the outstretched hand of the Lord himself.

The presence found in the performance of the Eucharistic action evidently goes even deeper, for in it is contained a memorial of the redemptive sacrifice itself sacramentally re-presented; hence the Mass is a sacramental sacrifice. That is why some authors speak of a *commemorative* actual presence. Now, in relation to this *commemorative* presence, what we have been discussing until now is, in Betz's terminology, the *principal* actual presence. It is an actual presence that brings before us the remembrance of a fact. [100] When the words of consecration are spoken over bread and wine, Christ becomes present not in any vague, indefinite manner, but precisely as the one who took suffering upon himself, conquered it, and entered into the glory of the Father. He becomes present as Christ who has suffered and risen from the dead (*Christus passus et resuscitatus*). The redemptive act of that moment of history is not to be separated from him. [101]

Every human being we encounter is in some way branded by his own life experience; his personal history leaves its mark or stamp upon his "character." Something similar, but on a higher level, obtains in our case in that of the God-Man and his work for the salvation of the world. His death on the Cross was simply the climax of the essential role of savior that he accepted when he became man. In assuming human nature and in thus actuating it to a personal being in the manner of a quasi-formal cause, the Logos has become the head of the human race and its High Priest with the task of redeeming this human race. His life is informed by the spirit of surrender to the Father for humanity. The climax of this redemptive life was the sacrificial death on the Cross. As an external fact this death was an event happening at a particular point in history; but in its substance, as the redemptive self-surrender of the God-Man, it shared the supra-temporal character of the Logos, could be anticipated at the Last Supper, continues in eternity in a transfigured state, and therefore can be realized also in time and within the framework of the Church.[102]

In the foregoing explanation there has been no necessity to point to a continuous sacrifice in eternity, one in which the historical sacrifice of Christ lives on and becomes present in the Mass. Such a sacrifice there certainly would not be if merely the continuing sentiment of sacrifice, the God-Man's interior attitude of self-giving is meant. For without the symbolic expression in an external sign, the sentiment of sacrifice would not yet constitute sacrifice. Other theologians on the contrary point out (rightly) that Christ in his elevation to the right hand of the Father has ascended to the presence of God together with his entire salvific work on earth, and remains forever present there, so that we may truly speak not only of a continuing intercession but also of a continuing oblation.[103] Understood thus, the relation to the sacrifice in heaven actually comes to the same thing as has been explained above.

4. THE COMMEMORATIVE ACT AND ITS CONTENT

All these considerations, however, are simply attempts to explain in depth the fact, borne out by tradition, that we must hold fast to: *in the commemorative act of the Church the redemptive act of Christ becomes present.* Further, that just as the substantial reality of the one body of Christ becomes present in several places, so, too, through the commemorative actual presence, the one event of the death on the Cross becomes present at several points of time.

This new-old perspective on the problem, restored to currency chiefly by Odo Casel, has provoked the interest of non-Catholic theologians and to a large extent won their approval.[104] To the extent to which we grant the sacrificial character of the Lord's death on the Cross, the sacrificial character of the Eucharist should also be granted, since in this way it becomes clear that the Eucharist yields not a new sacrifice but only a new presence of the one sacrifice. This logical sequence has in fact been so recognized. Of course, among Protestant theologians there are some who now draw the opposite conclusion and resist this idea of presence because it would necessarily lead to the recognition of the sacrifice.[105]

We may now enquire further into the precise content of this presence. It is clearly brought out first of all by the very sign used to designate it. The essential elements of the sign have been set down by Christ himself: bread and wine and the words spoken over them by his representative, the priest. Even with these words the sign is not a naturalistic re-presentation of what is meant; nor is the ritual accompanying the words a portrayal or even a dramatic performance of the redemptive event. It is a symbol: certain elements of the object are emphasized to bring out the significance of the whole.

But if symbol on a natural level is suited to re-present in some way the intended object (this concept is one of the fundamental principles of Plato's philosophy), a sacramental symbol is all the more suited to make the redemptive event present. What was thus minimally necessary and sufficient as a sign, the Church has with reverence and devotion enriched out of the treasury of revelation confided to her — with what result may be seen in the varied liturgies of the Church; for they concentrate above all on the *eucharistesas* of our Lord and the mandate "Do this in remembrance of me," and fashion it into the Eucharistic Prayer in order to bring out still more sharply what is signified while making the people fully aware of it.

As we have already seen, what is signified is primarily the redemptive self-surrender of Christ: *his sacrificial death on the Cross*. In the plan of redemption, however, the Calvary event is not complete in itself, but reaches its full dimensions only with Christ's resurrection and his ascension to the Father. And so it is that the Church's retrospective commemoration of the redemptive act embraces all these aspects as constituting one single whole. The glorification was the necessary complement to the sacrificial death of the God-Man; and yet it was at the same time the acceptance of the sacrifice. That is why almost all the liturgies contain in their anamnesis, after the words of consecration, clear reference to the resurrection and ascension together with the death of Christ, as the object of the memorial. In fine, what is signified extends to Christ's whole paschal mystery (*mysterium paschale*): the entire process of the redemption and renewal of the world, as hymned in several passages in the New Testament, especially in 1 Timothy

3:16; Philippians 2:5-11; Colossians 1:12-20, texts to which a cultic character is justly attributed.

On the other hand, the Incarnation, the starting point of the redemptive action, was adverted to only occasionally in the liturgies. The Greek Fathers asserted with some emphasis that the Incarnation, too, was involved in the object of anamnesis, and described Christ's coming at the consecration in terms of his coming at the Incarnation (cf. Betz 1.1:260-300). Most anaphoras of the Eastern Churches also include Christ's second coming, which, of course, must be celebrated not in commemoration of the past but only in expectant anticipation of the future.

In the anamnesis no specific verbal mention is made of one aspect of the redemptive work identified with the Church, the founding of the Church. Redemption is the redemption of humanity; it means the gathering of a new people of God in the Church. This aspect does not need to be expressed in words: it finds its expression in the very celebration. The Mass is nothing if not the presence of the redemptive work formalized in the Church.

Besides, of course, this identification finds due expression in every elaborated parallel text of the liturgical anamnesis, i.e., in the thanksgiving prayer, as for example in the third Eucharistic Prayer of the new Roman Missal, where the theme of the Preface is carried forward thus: "From age to age you gather a people to yourself, so that from east to west a perfect offering may be made to the glory of your name." The sacrifice that becomes present in the Mass is given into the hands of the Church so that the Church may offer it. It is the sacrifice of the Church as well as Christ's.

III. THE SACRIFICE OF CHRIST AND OF THE CHURCH

1. PROTESTANTS AND THE SACRIFICE OF THE CHURCH

If the sacrifice of our redemption becomes present in the Eucharist, then it is self-evident that the Mass is the sacrifice of Christ. This teaching has today found acceptance even among Protestant theologians. And yet the same theologians seem to find insurmountable difficulties with the "Offerimus" (we offer) of the Catholic liturgy, which at the same time brings out its nature as a sacrifice of the Church.[106]

The Church, they argue, can only receive; it can receive, possibly, with prayer and thanksgiving. But perish the least suggestion that the Church, on its part, should offer the sacrifice of the Cross made present among us![107] Thus, in his foreword to M. Seemann's work *Heilsgeschehen und Gottesdienst*, Peter Brunner holds firmly to his view that the action of the God-Man should not be combined with an action of the creature (pp. xiv–xv), for that would mean a new sacrifice and would call into question the "once and for all" (*ephapax*) theology of the Letter to the Hebrews. That is why even the new Protestant liturgies carefully avoid every expression that could be understood to suggest an offertory action on the part of the community.

The Lord's mandate "Do this as a remembrance of me" does indeed imply that the Church must do something; and she must do it in commemoration. It is what St. John Chrysostom paraphrases in the words, "We perform the commemoration of his death." The Church must present the sign with which Christ anticipated his self-surrender of the following day, so that in this sign that self-surrender of time past may now be made present anew in the Church's midst. And if the Church is to do what Christ has done, it must present the sign "in thanksgiving," for Christ performed that action in an ambience of thanksgiving (*eucharistesas*).

111

Thus the Church must follow him even in this: fulfilling its commission out of a sense of gratitude, in faith, hope, and love, addressing itself to God.

Accordingly, all the Catholic liturgies of both West and East pronounce the Institution account while praying before God — as in the old familiar Roman Canon: Jesus raised his eyes to God, "to you, his almighty Father." In each version the account is set in a framework of prayer. Indeed, it caused a serious breach in Christian tradition when Luther enjoined that the words of Consecration be recited as proclamation in the Gospel tone. This is why he also desired the celebrant to stand behind the altar and address the words to the people.[108] The question whether the prayers surrounding the words of Consecration should determine the way those words are projected was raised again during the preparation of the German Lutheran liturgy in 1955, and the way was left open for an answer in the affirmative.[109]

What the Church must do, in the Lutheran purview, is bring about a memorial or recalling, with the face turned toward God. The Church re-presents Christ's sacrifice before God and thus offers it to him — with the intention, of course, that it should be indeed pleasing to him. That, however, is nothing but an offering, an *oblatio*. The logical implications are seen even by those strict Lutherans who on this ground reject a prayer framework around the Institution account. In that type of thinking it is immaterial whether the word *offerre*, which has come down to us through a long tradition is used, or if one deviates from the line of tradition and substitutes *praesentare* in its place (as is, in fact, done at Taizé: "We present to thee . . . the signs of the eternal sacrifice of Christ" [110]).

2. THE CATHOLIC TRADITION

In Catholic theology, however, the Mass is definitely a sacrifice under a two fold aspect: it is the sacrifice of Christ re-presented or made present anew; and as re-presentation it is also itself an offering, an *oblatio*, a sacrifice.

What is correctly connoted by this offering, however, is not an independent, autonomous action of the Church, an action proceeding purely from human power. It is an action proceeding from divine power and divine grace: "from the many gifts you have given us" (*de tuis donis ac datis*). It is performed totally with the power communicated to the Church by Jesus Christ. And in performing that memorial the Church acts as the community of those who through Baptism have become members of Christ's body and in whose hearts he already dwells through faith; it is they who have gathered together in his name. The Church performs the memorial through his commission and in his behalf, by the authority conveyed to it through his mandate, and as sharer in his priesthood.

This was how the Fathers looked at it. This was also why they called Christ *High Priest* not only in relation to the death on the Cross and to his office as universal mediator in heaven, by virtue of which office our praise and adoration are offered to God "through him," but also and explicitly in relation to the sacrifice offered by the Church. Thus we hear Pope St. Clement of Rome calling Christ "the High Priest of our gift-offerings," while the presbyters exercise their office "in the place of Christ" (*vice Christi*), according to St. Cyprian's Letter (63:14). Although in later times the words *mediatorship* and *priesthood* were used cautiously of Christ in view of Arian misinterpretation, expressions of this type are not wanting even during that period.

Bishop Braulio of Saragossa (d. 651) speaks of the sacrifice as being "offered by the true High Priest, Christ Jesus" every day upon our altars (*a vero pontifice offertur Christo Jesu*; Ep. 42). Isidore of Seville designates the Church offering the sacrifice of Christians as the "body of Christ" (Quaestiones in Vetus Testamentum; PL 83:394 D).[111] More precisely, Thomas Aquinas described the priest as one who "bears Christ's image, in whose person and by whose power" (*gerit imaginem Christi, in cujus persona et virtute*) he pronounces the words of Consecration; and so even here priest and victim are "in a measure [*quodammodo*] one and the same" (ST 3a, 83:1 ad 3). And the Council of Trent sums up the tradition with the following formulation:

> For it is one and the same victim: he who now makes the offering through the ministry of priests (*idem nunc offerens sacerdotum ministerio*) and he who then offered himself on the Cross; the only difference is in the manner of the offering.[112]

So it is that in the sacrifice of the Mass, Christ and the Church are at work together. As for the physical appearance, every time the sacrificial act is performed anew, we have the person of the celebrating priest delegated by the Church. As the Church's mouthpiece authorized by Christ, the celebrant pronounces the blessed words set down by Christ himself over the gift-offering of bread and wine, determined again by Christ himself. Christ acts in him in a sacramental manner. From this point of view, there are as many acts of Christ as there are Masses offered.[113]

The Mass is Christ's continuing act of sacrifice taking place sacramentally at many different points of space and time; its value is determined by that one act. Hence, what we have said above does not imply that the multiplication of Masses and of the sacramental acts means a multiplication of the value. This point will be discussed below in greater detail. On the other hand, neither should we think of a new physical act of sacrifice on the part of Christ every time; the efficacious continuation of the one lasting act of sacrifice is enough.[114] Otherwise the Mass would be a new, an absolute sacrifice when in fact it is a purely relative one that by its very essence is only a new presence or re-presentation, a new revelation of the one saving sacrifice of the Cross in the Church.

Nevertheless, the Church does have a genuinely active role to play in the sacrifice of the Mass: that of performing the sacrament continually at a definite point of space and time, performing it as the spatio-temporal expression of Christ's attitude of self-giving, in order that the faithful assembled at various times and places may unite themselves with his self-giving, and that the invisible sacrifice of their faith and commitment may find expression in this visible sacrifice. Or, still more precisely, that Christ may draw the faithful unto himself and include them in his one unique sacrifice, so that in this manner his promise may be realized ever more surely: "I — once I am lifted up from the earth — will draw all men to myself" (John 12:32).

3. A Sacramental Sacrifice

It is this one and same sacrifice that took place on Calvary in one form and takes place now in another form in the Mass repeated so often. The Council of Trent has expressed the distinction between the two forms of appearance by contrasting the *bloody* with the *unbloody* sacrifice. In order to bring out the difference in the manner of offering the sacrifice, the Council has appropriated a terminology inherited by the Greek liturgies from olden times and familiar to Latin theologians by the end of the Middle Ages, just as an earlier age had expressed the same distinction with the terms *real* and *mystical.*

The word *unbloody* undoubtedly alludes also to the difference in the manner of offering the sacrifice; but this is primarily a negative criterion, for it describes how the sacrifice of the Mass is *not* offered. For a positive idea we should have to turn to the content. Thus, on Calvary Christ offered the sacrifice alone; in the Mass he offers it with and through his Church. Christ is not satisfied to draw the Church unto himself by means of Baptism.

Of course, even Baptism brings about an actual presence of Christ and of his redemptive work, but the manner in which this is achieved is not that of a sacrifice. In Baptism the recipient of the sacrament plays a predominantly passive and receptive role (though in the case of an adult the recipient is also expected to *do* something). In the liturgy of the Mass the Church is called upon to play an active part, to join in offering the very sacrifice to which it owes its origin, to ratify on its part the covenant to which it has been committed.

Only through this active participation of the Church does the sacrifice of the new covenant reach its destined fulfillment. At first it was offered *for* everyone. Now it must be offered also *by* everyone, by all who enter into this covenant. Only in this way can Christ's world-redeeming action attain its goal. It is here that mankind is integrated in Christ's death as well as in his resurrection. In this sense what happens in the Mass is a "process of integration" — to use the terminology of Michael Schmaus, who bases his exposition of the Mass on this fundamental idea and calls his own theory "the theory of integration" as opposed to the former "theories of destruction." [115]

The Mass is the sacramental presence of the one sacrifice of Christ, and now, as a sacramental sacrifice, it is entrusted to the Church's hands. Hence it is the Church's business to develop and adapt the form of this sacrifice further, to give it suitable structure, to the extent that Jesus himself has made provision for such development and adaptation. Concretely, what the Church has in the past understood as being her job in this development of form and structure has crystallized in several key concepts, the most important of them emerging at the very dawn of Christianity. These key concepts have exercised a many-sided influence on the contours of the Mass at different times and in different places. We can best identify these concepts under their Greek names: anamnesis, epiclesis, eucharistia, prosphora.

a) anamnesis

The whole Mass is before all else an anamnesis. As J. Betz notes, "The anamnesis is not a part but the basic principle of the Mass."[116] The relation between the Church's action and Christ's work finds its clearest expression in the concept of anamnesis, which is like a cord uniting Jesus' sacrifice of the past to the Church's present sacrifice (Betz, p. 113). The very word implies that the mind turns back to the past action — Christ's world-redeeming work — to bring it down to the present moment and into the midst of the celebrating community. This comes about through the *memorial*, which is more than mere subjective recalling. Thus in the anamnesis the emphasis is on the object of the memorial more than on the Church's commemorative act. As we have already seen, the concept of anamnesis is prominent in the writings of the Greek Fathers of the fourth century and after, and lives on still in all the liturgies. Moreover, it gives its name to the prayer in which it finds immediate expression, that is, the prayer beginning with *Unde et memores* directly after the Consecration in the Roman Canon.

b) epiclesis

The Mass as a whole, or at any rate its Canon, was considered an epiclesis (invocation), as brought out by Odo Casel.[117] In this sense St. Irenaeus speaks to the heretics of bread that *receives* (Adv. Haer. 4:18:5) and is no longer ordinary bread. Among the Church's institutions not found in Sacred Scripture St. Basil mentions the words of invocation (*ta tes epikleseas remata*) pronounced at the offering of the Eucharistic bread (in his book on the Holy Spirit, De Spiritu Sancto 66; PG 32:188). Apparently what he means is the entire Eucharistic Prayer. The notion of epiclesis implies that the re-presentation of Christ's sacrifice takes place through the sacred word "proclaimed" over the gift-offerings prepared upon the altar. This sacred word can be understood as the "word coming from him [Christ]" of which Justin spoke (in his Apology, 66), whether in the narrower or broader sense; or even as the word of petition, as prayer for the power from above by which the material gift-offering becomes Christ's body and blood. In the Eastern rites since the fourth century the word epiclesis has been applied in the narrower sense of a special prayer. The prayer for the power to transform, which must come from God, found in this epiclesis a special sanction, for through it the power of God —

or often more specifically the Holy Spirit — is called down upon the gift.

c) eucharistia

Commemorative re-presentation and prayerful acceptance of Christ's sacrifice are closely associated with the idea of eucharistia or thanksgiving. From very early times the Mass was most often called: eucharistia. The concept of eucharistia differs from that of anamnesis only in that it recalls the manifestation of God's generosity expressly in the form of prayer directed toward God himself. The two notions as handled by the Church Fathers are very closely related, as Betz indicates in *Die Eucharistie* (1.1:158-60).

As a term designating the "awe-ful mysteries," eucharistia is explained by St. John Chrysostom in his Homily on Matthew 25 in these words: "The best way of preserving a benefit is the remembrance of this benefit and the continued expression of gratitude" (PG 57:331). Literally it denoted the attitude of the one who has experienced a blessing (*charis*), or, better still, one richly endowed with *charis*, who therefore is *eucharistos*, and moreover meditates on it, acknowledges it, and gives expression to it in word or action. Even etymologically *to thank* is in the final analysis nothing but *to think about* benefits received. The great *charis* for which the Church had to give thanks was Christ himself, the mystery of faith that so transported Paul (as in 2 Corinthians 8:9 and Titus 2:11).

Just as the anamnesis sometimes encompasses a larger field that embraces the whole period from the Incarnation to the Parousia, so too eucharistia (thanksgiving) tended to widen its scope beyond the fact of the crucifixion considered in isolation, and so was not limited to this one point. Just as Christ's *eucharistesas* seems to have embraced God's gracious interventions for both his old and his new people, so too the Church's Eucharist could embrace the whole dimension of salvation history from creation to the very consummation of the world.

Thus the example of Jesus' thanksgiving worked together with a Christian insight into the reasonableness of this thanksgiving to structure the Mass essentially as "eucharistia" quite early in its history. In the "Gratias agamus" (let us give thanks), which to this day precedes almost all versions of the Eucharistic Prayer of the East and the West, eucharistia has become, so to say, the general heading over the entire prayer that follows, and over the sacramental action contained within it. And the gift-offering inspired by this thanksgiving prayer has been known as the Eucharist from Justin Martyr to our own day. Moreover, as we have seen above, in the time of the apologists, the Eucharistic celebration was known also by the most general expression "Prayer." But this term was used particularly in communicating with nonbelievers, more to characterize its content than as a simple label for the Eucharist.

d) prosphora

The God-ward impulse, man's countermovement to the descent of divine grace, is his response to the concept of eucharistia. The eucharistia is the corollary and echo of *evangelion*. And this countermovement is not confined to the words of the prayer but must be actualized in gift-offerings. This is the point of the concept of offering (*prosphora, oblatio*). Interestingly enough, the idea makes its appearance early in the development of the Mass, as Betz shows in "Die Prosphora."

While one may doubt whether the Didache's *thysia* (a more powerful concept than prosphora) does not rather mean Christ's sacrifice as re-presented in the Mass, there can be no doubt that the *prosphorai* of which Pope St. Clement of Rome speaks refer to the Church's action. St. Irenaeus lays special emphasis on the gift-offerings "which earth has given" (new Order of Mass), to be transformed into Christ's body and blood and offered to God. *Oblatio, sacrificium*, and their Greek equivalents now become the accepted names for the Mass. From the time of Hippolytus of Rome the "Offerimus" appears at the climax of the Eucharistic Prayer just as regularly as the "Gratias agamus" does at its beginning. Indeed in Hippolytus the two concepts — to give thanks and to offer (*gratias agere* and *offerre*) — prove to be all but synonymous, if we follow H. Elfers in *Die Kirchenordnung Hippolyts von Rom* (pp. 209f., 230–32).

From thanksgiving it is really but a small step to offering. Indeed, from the very concept of *eucharistein* it is not yet certain whether the thanksgiving should be expressed in words or in a gift-offering. When the Church re-presents Christ's sacrifice of the Cross, it does so in the act of giving thanks and as co-offerer. Into the Church's hands Christ entrusts the sacrifice that he has offered in its stead — a sacrifice the Church alone can apply as he wishes.

Into the Church's hands he commits it so that the Church may now offer it with him by enacting the sacramental sign he has determined.

This is precisely what is meant when in the liturgies the "Offerimus" follows close on the heels of the "Memores." This very fact that the Church must act or place the sacramental sign determined by Christ clearly implies that the Mass is the sacrifice of Christ *and* of the Church. As representing the sacrifice of the Cross it is, in the words of Baumgartner, "the cultic expression constitutive of the gift the Church must offer to God — of itself, of Christ, of the world."[118]

If we accept the distinction of the older authors that *oblation* means a simple offering, and *sacrifice* an offering involving a destruction or transformation, then we can say that the sacrifice of the Cross is what becomes present anew and constitutes the actual content of the celebration. While the re-presentation itself, effected by the Church's action, is as such only an oblation, the two offerings meet and merge into one single act.[119] The significance of the Church's oblation lies solely in this, that in faith, hope, and love it enters into the self-surrender that found its consummation in the sacrifice of the Cross. Thus Betz could say in "Die Prosphora" (p. 115) that in the sacrifice of the Mass Christians must "convert Christ's self-surrender into their own act and their sacramental act into Christ's self-surrender." So again, the whole Mass is a real sacrifice.

The essential sacramental consummation of the oblation is reached when the sign determined by Christ himself is placed, that is, in the consecration of bread and wine. But the Church, since it must at the same time express its own self-surrender, is bound to broaden the scope of this expression. This is precisely what happens in the prayers of offering, which, like the memorial, belong to the classic structure of every liturgy. Most of these prayers go beyond the simple "Offerimus" directly following the "Memores," a fact that is particularly noteworthy in view of the special accent on the "Offerimus" in the traditional Roman Canon.

4. OTHER EXPRESSIONS OF THE CHURCH'S SELF-SURRENDER

Moreover, in the offering rituals, as much as in the prayers they accompany, the Church finds wide scope for the expression of her self-surrender. These rituals, despite being reduced to the minimum in the new order of Mass, still assert themselves in the four Eucharistic Prayers of the reformed Liturgy of the Eucharist: in the extending of hands over the sacrificial gifts during the epiclesis before the Consecration, originally (in the 1968 text) also in the deep bow at the prayer for the acceptance of the gift-offering after the Consecration. In the traditional form of the Roman Canon, too, there were gestures of pointing with the hand (which were stylized into signs of the cross) to accompany the corresponding prayers. Finally, even the elevation of the species at the Consecration derives from an Offertory ritual: specifically the ritual observed by Jesus himself at the Last Supper when he raised the cup to the height of a span above the table in a gesture of offering as prescribed by Jewish ritual for the thanksgiving ceremony after the meal, as we have described above.

The Church's offering finds clearest expression in the importance given the preparation of the material gift-offerings and in the way the liturgy utilizes the underlying symbolism of this act. This is the genesis of the ceremonial found in the Eastern as well as in the Gallican liturgies in which the gift-offerings are brought up and placed on the altar; it is also the genesis of the Offertory in the Roman liturgy.

While the Offertory should not be isolated to the extreme proposed in the Scotist approach, the tendency today is to swing to the opposite extreme, as might be discerned in R. A. Kiefer's article "The Noise in Our Assemblies" (otherwise a valid and urgently serious plea for more emphasis on the people's acclamations).[120] Some liturgists favor abolishing the Offertory entirely and avoiding every sign of an "offering" of material gifts; the most they would grudgingly allow is the offering pronounced after the Consecration. But we should not forget that Christ himself chose these creaturely gifts, gifts with a definite significance. No doubt he singled out bread and wine principally because, as bodily nourishment, they were suited to become bearers of spiritual nourishment.

But there is more to it than that. In taking bread and wine Christ chose precisely those gifts in which human life as well as human work — indeed, the entire earthly cosmos — is assimilated into the divine mystery. This multi-dimensional symbolism should find a place in the Mass liturgy and be included in the rite of offering. It would be unnatural not to exploit the symbolism contained in the very nature of the act; and it would be utter folly to exclude it altogether. At any rate, no great theologian from Irenaeus all the way to Suárez has expressed any fear that the essential act of sacrifice would be eclipsed or obscured if allowed to begin with earthly gift-offerings.

What we have in the liturgy of the Mass is what the Church does by way of enhancing the sacramental sign and giving it form and structure. The sacramental sign we are concerned with here is contained essentially in what happens at the Consecration of bread and wine. Throughout the Middle Ages theologians were at pains to discover at various points or in various rituals the anamnesis implied in the Consecration. In all the fully developed liturgies the thanksgiving implied in the same rituals is articulated even before the Consecration in a more or less profusely expanded Preface.

Hence also, it is at least permissible to let the oblation begin even before it is actually made, and not confine the activity to the practical task of preparing the gifts that have somehow to be readied. But in that case it should be clearly understood that the Offertory is not simply the Church's sacrifice isolated and independent of Christ's sacrifice, nor even an anticipation of the sacramental event, but actually a kind of overture to the sacred action. As such, the well-structured Offertory, with at least an intimation of the sacrifice about to take place, is a valuable occasion for all participants to realize what the Mass as the Church's sacrifice should be: an expression of the God-ward orientation of our whole life with all its joys and sorrows, its hopes and longings; an acknowledgement that all this is mingled and united with the sacrifice that Christ, our High Priest, has offered and continues to offer with us.

IV. THE OFFERING CHURCH

For a long time liturgical theologians found it necessary to concentrate on a defense of the sacrificial character of the Mass by emphasizing that in it Christ himself acts. Since the need for this emphasis has now become less urgent, the ground has been cleared for a closer look at the Church's action.

The Church offers. This fact should now be brought into sharper focus. Left very much in the background during the past centuries, even if never actually disputed, still its reappearance has been looked upon with suspicion on the part of some liturgists who have feared that it might appear to attribute the power of consecration to the ordinary faithful. Thus A. Michel refuses to include the Church in his definition of the Mass.[121] According to his theory, it is enough if the definition mentions Christ, the head of the Church and the actual celebrant, offering the sacrifice through the instrumentality of the visible priest. And yet, as we have seen, that offering role was the ancient Church's authentic tradition, as emphatically attested by St. Augustine and transmitted uninterruptedly right through the early Middle Ages, as R. Schulte has shown in *Die Messe als Opfer der Kirche*.

More recent theology has helped to rehabilitate the ancient tradition. One has only to mention works like those of Maurice de la Taille (1921) and of Maurice Lepin (1926), the historical study of Schulte (1959), or the collections on the sacrifice of the Church compiled by R. Erni in 1954 and Burkhard Neunheuser in 1960. In *Katholische Dogmatik 4*, Michael Schmaus sums up his meditations on the subject in compressed statements such as, "The Mass is Christ's and the Church's sacrifice" (4.1:382). The documents of Vatican II bear in this same direction. Thus, according to the Constitution on the Liturgy, the Church "comes together to celebrate the paschal mystery" (§ 6); her liturgical celebration is "an action of Christ the priest and of his Body the Church" (§ 7).

1. THE WHOLE CHURCH OFFERS

But now the question arises: what really is meant here by *Church*? That the Mass is the Church's sacrifice in the sense that ecclesiastical authorities have the duty to watch over it, regulate its rubrics, and the like, was never called into question even during past centuries; in fact, it was asserted with special emphasis. This duty of the Church has been underlined in the encyclical *Mediator Dei*, and Vatican II adverts to it as well (§ 22). Significantly, however, the Council here does not use the general term *Church* but the more precise expressions "authority of the Church" or "Mother Church" (§§ 14, 21). Moreover, it has always been considered self-evident that in the celebrating and consecrating priest the Church itself acts. What we are concerned with in the present chapter is the Church as the community of the faithful, as the people of God; and the question is: Can we say of the Church understood in this sense that it offers the sacrifice? [122]

The historical documents indicate that this concept was universally accepted as self-evident and was transmitted without reflection up to the Middle Ages. The clarity with which St. Isidore of Seville makes the point is particularly striking. In his language the subject of the Eucharistic offering is "the Church" or "the Christians" or "the faithful" or simply "we." Once Christ has been mystically anointed as High Priest, writes Isidore in his work on the ecclesiastical offices, "the whole Church" has also been anointed and consecrated, because the Church is incorporated into him (De Eccl. Off. 2.26:2; PL 83–825).

As for the generality of the faithful (*tota fidelium unitate*) who are brought together spiritually in the unity of one faith though not physically in one place, Walafrid Strabo states that they offer the sacrifice (De Exordiis et Incrementis ch. 17). Equally clear and emphatic is his contemporary Florus of Lyons' well-known assertion appearing in his Commentary on the action of the Mass and often repeated even to our day: "What the priests in their special ministry do, all do through their faith and devotion" (*Quod enim adimpletur proprie ministerio sacerdotum, hoc generaliter agitur fide et devotione cunctorum*; De Actione Missae; PL 119:47).[123]

Hence one could without misgiving say of the faithful who participated in the Mass during those centuries that they *celebrated* the Mass, as, for instance, it was in fact said of Alcuin (who was only a deacon) in his Vita (ch. 26).[124] Finally, the whole accent on the people's offering at the very climax of the Canon ("We, your people and your ministers" — the new rendering of *nos servi tui sed et plebs tua sancta*) expresses this idea in such unmistakable terms that one wonders how the rich significance of this liturgical language could ever have fallen into oblivion as the centuries passed by.

St. Thomas Aquinas speaks emphatically of the power conferred upon every Christian "pertaining to the worship of God" through "a certain spiritual character" he receives in Baptism and Confirmation (ST 3a, 63, 1). But after Thomas this concept was lost sight of, and in the thirteenth century a new viewpoint gained ground. With Thomas one could indeed speak of the priestly role of all the faithful; but in speaking so, one was not so much concerned for the distinction between the priesthood of the baptized lay person and that of the ordained priest. The priest's proper role was never questioned; rather, one thought of Christ as the fountainhead of every priestly power. From this viewpoint the Church on earth was already the beginning of the Church in heaven. In fact, the two were rarely conceived of as distinct from one another. As Congar maintains (pp. 254–60), it is simply the one integral Church, the one filled with the Holy Spirit, the holy Church.

2. HISTORICAL SHIFTS

But then historical developments precipitated a change of perspective, a shift of emphasis. Theologians increasingly viewed the Church's action in the Mass as well as all the sacraments under the aspect of the power or authorization required for validity, whereas in former times the Church had been seen above all as the Bride of Christ and the Body of Christ the High Priest, and, as such, called to offer with him the one and everlasting sacrifice.

The full flowering of Scholastic theology coincided with the emergence of new heresies attacking the Church's hierarchical order. The struggle became particularly strenuous after the sixteenth century. The upshot was that the former ecclesiology withdrew into the background and the Church's action was now seen not under the aspect of grace and the Holy Spirit common to all the faithful but under the aspect of the *powers* inherent in the Church, the powers, namely, that are conferred upon chosen members of the Church by Christ himself. Since (it was reasoned) the priest alone can consecrate, the participation and action of the faithful became insignificant under this new orientation. Other factors had also been at work in the same direction for a long time; the result was a continuing devaluation of the role of the laity until nothing more than their devout presence at Mass was required.

Happily, Vatican II has restored the old order, not only reviving at the theoretical level the total concept of the Church in its integrity and richness, but also calling for "that full, conscious, and active participation" of the faithful in the liturgy "which is demanded by the very nature of the liturgy" and to which the Christian people have the right and the duty "by reason of their baptism" (CL § 14). We are reawakened to the consciousness that the entire Eucharistic celebration in the assembly of the faithful is the most convincing proof of the living Church; that precisely in this celebration is the Church's essence visibly realized.[125] And we can achieve this awareness without having to go all the way with the Russian theologians (Afanasieff among others) who equate the Church with the Eucharist, asserting that where the Eucharist is, there is also the Church, and vice versa.[126]

3. THE GATHERED ASSEMBLY IS THE ACTIVE SUBJECT

So now that we once more recognize in the community of the faithful the Church offering the sacrifice, it remains for us to explain how, within this community, the liturgical assembly in the concrete relates to the whole Church. Doubtless it is to the whole Church that the Eucharist has been entrusted; but is the whole Church as such also the subject that acts? The whole Church is certainly more than the totality of the faithful; it is the mystical unit held together through Christ's Spirit. This is why it is called *Mother* and *Bride*, why also characteristics of a human being are attributed to it.

And yet the Church should not be conceived as a person standing between Christ and the faithful.[127] Nor for that reason can the whole Church offer the sacrifice; this can be done only by the individual local Church. Even assuming that the mandate to celebrate the Eucharist derives from the Church's authority, such a mandate does not alter anything in the nature of the Mass itself, nor, according to Rahner-Häussling (p. 36f.), does it increase its value.

No, the whole Church can offer the sacrifice only insofar as it is present in the concrete community gathered around the altar, in the faithful acting together here and now. This is exactly what Vatican II declares in the Dogmatic Constitution on the Church (*Lumen Gentium*): "This Church of Christ is truly present in all legitimate local congregations of the faithful . . ." (§ 26). The document points out also that these are called *churches* in New Testament writings and makes special mention of the community gathered around the altar to celebrate the Eucharist, the symbol of the Mystical Body's unity. The Constitution on the Liturgy likewise envisions the most perfect manifestation of the Church in a Eucharistic celebration in which priests and "a full complement of God's holy people" surround the bishop in vital participation of the sacred action (§ 41).

Further, several key phrases appearing in the liturgy may be traced to the local community gathered around the altar. The *Church* with which the liturgy in the (old) Roman Canon is concerned is principally the faithful present, as is unmistakably the sense of the word *circumstantes* applied to them, and of the phrase "oblation of your whole family" (*oblatio cunctae familiae tuae*). The "Oremus" (Let us pray) and the "Gratias agamus" (Let us give thanks) are invitations to the faithful to pray; and the prayers that follow allude to the faithful in expressions like *ecclesia tua* and *populus tuus*. It is only of actual participants that the priest can say in the Postcommunion, "With sacred gifts you have loaded your people" (*Satiasti familiam tuam muneribus sacris*). So, too, nothing but actual persons can be meant by "my sacrifice and yours" (*meum ac vestrum sacrificium*) in the "Orate, fratres," or by "your servants as also your holy people" (*servi tui sed et plebs tua sancta*) in whose name the decisive "Offerimus" is pronounced. Even the General Instruction of the new Order of Mass of 1969 expressly states that the priest should recite the prayers of the Mass "in the name of the entire assembly" (§ 10; see also § 13).

Hence it is not necessary to conclude that the priest functions in the name of the Church (*nomine Ecclesiae*) only in so far as he is authorized (*deputatus*) to do so by the whole Church (i.e., by papal authority), and that by reason of this authorization he represents the whole Church. The priest functions as the representative of the community assembled here and now, in which the whole Church is truly present (*vere adest*). As such he recites the prayers and as such he also exercises his consecrating power received from Christ.[128] The idea that the Church *consecrates* is not unknown in the older tradition, as we gather from Florus of Lyons' *De actione Missae*: "The Church consecrates the mystery of the sacred Body and Blood of the Lord with these words received from tradition" (*Ecclesia ex traditione in his verbis consecrans mysterium sacri corporis*; PL 119:53).[129]

The bond with the whole Church is naturally and necessarily present in every legitimately constituted community gathered round the altar. In the sphere of ritual, too, a bond is created by the fact that the ritual itself is what Church authority has laid down or approved, as well as by the fact of prayers for Pope and for bishop offered among the Intercessions at every Mass.

4. Conclusion

In the total picture of the liturgy of the Mass there is no doubt that the Church's sacrifice is accorded far more powerful expression than Christ's sacrifice. After what has been said so far, however, this should not surprise us or cause any anxiety such as that betrayed by Journet in his *La Messe* (p. 130). The whole point of the Church's sacrifice is simply to offer the sacrifice that Christ has placed in its hands. The Church's action is wholly oriented toward the sacrifice which Christ offers and in which he includes his Church. Thus the Church's sacrifice remains entirely and absolutely subordinated to Christ's sacrifice and is realized only through the initiative from Christ himself, who has authorized and empowered the Church to offer the sacrifice, and himself works in the Church through his Spirit.

All this throws new light upon the role of the individual Christian participating in the Mass. What the Church does as the community of the faithful and what the local community assembled around the altar does, individual Christians do as well: *they offer the sacrifice.* Pope Pius XII has asserted this fact in clear terms in *Mediator Dei.* The faithful offer the sacrifice "not only by the hands of the priest, but also, to a certain extent, in union with him" (§ 92). It is the act par excellence with which the faithful exercise their own sharing in Christ's priesthood in which they participate by virtue of Baptism; thus it is primarily in the Church's divine service, in the Mass, that they fulfill the duty assigned to them in 1 Peter 2:5 to offer "spiritual sacrifices acceptable to God through Jesus Christ."

V. THE SACRAMENTAL ACTION AND ITS REQUISITES

Now that we have explored the broader questions, we come to the central point: the conditions that must be fulfilled for the realization of the sacrament of Christ's sacrifice. These conditions have to do with the *subject*, the *matter*, and the *consecrating word*.

1. THE SUBJECT OF THE EUCHARISTIC ACTION

a) The ordained priest

The subject of the Eucharistic action is the Church. Within the Church it is the priest's function to perform the sacramental sacrifice. With his ordination through the laying on of the bishop's hands, the priest has received from Christ the power to pronounce the sacred words over bread and wine effectively. The denial of this power by the Waldensians was the occasion for a definition of the doctrine in the Fourth Lateran Council (Denz. 794). A similar need arose when the reformers of the sixteenth century again denied it; and this time the same teaching was confirmed by the Council of Trent, in Session 22, canon 2 (Denz. 1752). Vatican II's Dogmatic Constitution on the Church (*Lumen Gentium*, § 10) has summed up in a few words the relation of the ministerial or hierarchical priesthood to the common priesthood of the faithful:

> Acting in the person of Christ, [the ministerial priest] brings about the Eucharistic sacrifice and offers it to God in the name of all the people [*nomine totius populi Deo offert*]. For their part, the faithful join in the offering [*oblationem*] of the Eucharist by virtue of their royal priesthood.

Note the precision of the language: the ordained priest *brings about* the *sacrifice* and *offers* it; whereas the faithful join in the offering of the oblation. The terms *in persona* (of *Christ*) and *nomine* (of the people) are practically synonymous. The "In"

128

before *nomine* came into use among canonists of the fifteenth century under the influence of Humanism.[130]

The above doctrine corresponds to the teaching of Sacred Scripture. Certainly it would be a mistake to cite Old Testament law, as some theologians have done, in order to show that it is exclusively the priest's function to offer sacrifice. For the Eucharist, like the sacrifice of the Cross, is a sacrifice of a unique type and as such it brought the Old Testament priesthood to an end. And yet even the New Testament has special office-bearers for the sacred ministry. It is true, the more ancient sources, which had still to maintain the distinction, do not give these officials the designation *hiereis* applied to the Old Testament priest or the pagan priest.

New names were coined for the new thing (e.g., the word *priest* derived from *presbyter*). The mandate was given to the Apostles, who in turn handed it down to their successors. For what Christ has ordained unto his memorial is to be performed "until he comes" (1 Cor. 11:26). All are invited to receive Christ's body and blood (John 6:53-58). For the Institution of the sacrament, however, only the closed circle of the Apostles were present. To them alone was given the mandate, "Do this."

The tradition in the infant Church is unanimous on this matter wherever we can find expression of it. Pope St. Clement I, as we have seen, in his Letter to the Corinthians writes of office-bearers whose duty it is to offer gifts (ch. 44:4). According to Justin Martyr it is only the *proestos* who recites the Thanksgiving. Hippolytus of Rome brings out the same idea still more clearly. Tertullian (De Virg. Vel. 9:2) speaks of the "priestly office" (*sacerdotale officium*) to which no member of the order of virgins should lay claim despite her other privileges, and of the "holy minister" (*sanctus minister*) who performs the sacred action (De Exh. Cast. 10). For Cyprian the priest really functions in Christ's place (*vice Christi vere fungitur*; see Letter 63:14). And in Letter 76:3 he bewails the hard lot of bishops and priests who have been condemned to the mines and find it impossible to offer the divine sacrifice.

Nor does the tradition of the Eastern Churches deviate from this consensus. The only point remaining somewhat obscure is found in the observation in the Didache (10:7) that prophets should be allowed "to give thanks as much as they wish"; but it probably means that they are counted among the office-bearers.

The special power of bishops and priests may be called into question only if one questions also the more fundamental fact that in his Church Christ instituted bearers of certain powers that were to be the means of communicating the graces of his redemption to all future times.

The priest's action is most fully significant at the moment when, standing at the head of a more or less "full complement of God's holy people," he exercises his priestly office. One is not a priest for oneself alone. This is why all Christian liturgies are so structured that the priest begins the Eucharistic Prayer only after he has invited the people present to participate in it. Similarly, the liturgies are unanimous in requiring the people to say the ratifying *Amen* at the end. As St. Augustine put it in Sermon 272, "To say *Amen* means to give one's signature" (PL 38:1247).

b) The priest is always able to consecrate

The priest does not receive his power from the people, however, but from Christ himself. It is stamped upon him with an "indelible mark" and, as with Baptism, cannot be lost or eradicated. Hence, it can be validly exercised even outside the Church and against the Church's will, though it can be meaningfully exercised only in the service of the Church and within the community of its faithful.

For a long time certain theologians hoped to evade this conclusion, which follows necessarily from the premise that the priestly office is inherited from Christ. Most often the question was not stated in clearcut terms between valid and invalid action. Accordingly, several Fathers of the Church tended to deny the validity of the Eucharist celebrated outside the Church.[131] Thus Leo the Great could declare, in his letter to Patriarch Anatolius of Constantinople, that where there was a schism, "there is no valid priesthood or authentic sacrifice (*nec rata sunt sacerdotia, nec vera sacrificia*; Ep. 80:2; PL 54:914 B). This text was popular among medieval canonists, as we gather from Gratian's Decretals (II.1.1.c.68; Friedberg 382). Several medieval theologians — among them Peter Lombard in his Sentences — held that the Consecration pronounced by a schismatic priest was invalid (4.13:1). Others who dared not go that far, denied to the schismatic priest only the power of offering but not the power of consecrating. Among these was Duns Scotus, whose teaching on the Church's sacrifice leads to this conclusion, as we noted above.[132]

The problem was finally solved by St. Thomas Aquinas (ST 3a, 82.7). In doing so he cited the authority of St. Augustine, who had emphatically asserted (in Contra Epistulam Parmeniani; Book 2, ch. 13, no. 28) that in those who stand outside the Church the sacrament of Orders, like Baptism, remains unaffected (*integra*). For, as Thomas observes, it is one thing to possess and exercise it improperly, and another thing to possess and exercise it rightly (*recte*). Even the priest who is separated from the Church's unity "can indeed consecrate" in the person of Christ (*in persona Christi*) and truly change the bread and wine into Christ's body and blood. But it is no longer a *spiritual sacrifice*. The sacrament becomes present, but the prayers he recites in the person of the Church (*in persona Ecclesiae*) lack efficacy because they do not have the necessary ecclesial sanction.

The principle underlying Thomas' solution was later articulated by the Council of Trent in the formula: As on the Cross, so also in the Mass, it is Christ who offers, making use of the priest now as his instrument (*idem nunc offerens sacerdotum ministerio*; Sess. 22, ch. 2). The priest pronounces the words of Consecration not in his own name but as Christ's herald, in the name of the one and only High Priest who has taken him into his service. If sometimes this occasions among Protestants even today the attribution of some "magical remnant" to the Catholic teaching on the sacrifice of the Mass,[133] we might argue that such a reproach would touch every incidence of belief in the efficacy of a sacrament; further, it is hardly relevant to speak of magic when the issue involved is not of independent powers but of the continued efficaciousness of Christ as High Priest.[134]

2. THE MATTER FOR THE EUCHARISTIC ACTION

The *matter* required for the sacramental sacrifice is bread and wine. In the Church, bread (*artos*) has always connoted wheaten bread, which had in any case been prescribed for the paschal meal. And since the Passover was associated with the Feast of the Unleavened Bread, it was unleavened wheaten bread that was used at the Last Supper. But down the centuries the Church has placed no great importance on the distinction between leavened and unleavened bread in the Eucharist: both were in use.

In the West, Rabanus Maurus (d. 856) becomes the first reliable witness for the practice, common since then, of using only unleavened bread (*panem infermentatum*; De Institutione Cleri-

corum 1:31; PL 107:318 D). The thin white wafer, as he observed, seemed best suited to the reverential handling due the sacred
species. In Eastern theology of the time of the Great Schism, the
unleavened host was considered an offense against faith, since in
the East the leaven (*fermentum*) was believed to symbolize Christ's
soul; to be without leaven (*azyma*) would mean to be without
life (*apsycha*).[135] Later on, however, this criticism subsided considerably.

So much for bread as one component of the matter. As for the
other, wine, it is to be obtained from grapes (*vinum de vite*); but
detailed regulations regarding its quality and color have never
been laid down. Within certain circles in the early Church there
was a tendency to use water instead of wine; but, as we have seen,
St. Cyprian put this down with a firm hand. That such a tendency
could appear is understandable, since in the four Institution accounts only the chalice (*poterion*) is specified, not the content.
Still, the full text (i.e., the account in Luke 22:18) makes it clear
that the "fruit of the vine" is meant. Moreover, the Last Supper
was indeed a paschal meal, a feast-day dinner; and for the paschal
meal, wine — specifically red wine — was expressly prescribed, as
J. Jeremias demonstrated in *The Eucharistic Words of Jesus* (p.
53).

3. THE CONSECRATING WORD

a) Repeating what Jesus said

As for the *consecrating word*, which is the sacramental form,
the mandate "Do this" meant that those receiving this mandate had
to do what Jesus had done. In the Church's tradition this has always been understood to mean that the priest, who functions in
the place of Christ, should pronounce over bread and wine precisely the words Jesus had pronounced, and that this should be
followed by the eating and drinking, that is, by the Communion.

For a long period the question hardly came up as to the precise scope and wording of the formula to be pronounced in fulfilling this mandate. According to the oldest and the most universal
tradition it was in the form of a thanksgiving prayer corresponding
to Jesus' *eucharistesas — eulogesas*, and within it the Institution
narrative in the traditional words of Jesus. It is these words that
Justin Martyr seems to allude to when, in his Apology 66, he says

that the change into Christ's body and blood takes place "through the words of the prayer [derived] from him." [136]

Liturgical tradition in both the West and the East is unanimous and invariable in this respect, with just one exception in the East. Although in the East Syrian liturgy the two later anaphoras, that of Theodore and that of Nestorius, contain the Institution narrative, in the oldest written documents of the Anaphora of Addai and Mari the narrative is missing; so also in the fragments of a sixth-century anaphora, which, however, contains a short paraphrase of the Institution narrative (Hänggi-Pahl 374–80; 401f.). Of the several attempts to explain this absence of the Institution narrative, the most tenable is the supposition that the narrative was dropped only at the time when the status of the epiclesis began to be exaggerated among the Nestorians, as A. Raes has proposed.[137]

In any event, St. Ambrose's testimony in his commentary on the sacraments leaves no doubt that the mandate, "Do this in memory of me," embraces the Institution narrative (De sacramentis 4.4.14, 21–22). Ambrose also uses the term *consecratio*; thus, through the Consecration the bread becomes Christ's flesh. To the question he poses, How does the Consecration come about? With what words and prayers? (*quibus verbis est et quibus sermonibus?*), he answers: "Those of the Lord Jesus" (*Domini Jesu*). Indeed, he maintains, the power of Jesus' words is comparable to that of the words with which God created the world. Then he quotes the Institution narrative.

The Church's magisterium has defined the point in the Decretum pro Armenis in these words: "The form of this sacrament is the words of the Savior with which he effected this sacrament" (*forma hujus sacramenti sunt verba Salvatoris quibus hos confecit sacramentum*).[138] This, however, merely stipulates the conditions for valid performance; the words, "This is my body," "This is my blood" are the minimum required and are sufficient for the sacrament to be actualized. All ancient Christian liturgies, however, have held that these words should be embedded in a thanksgiving prayer, just as Jesus himself spoke them in the context of a thanksgiving prayer. The restriction of the outlook to a merely legalistic concern for the minimum requisite has sometimes led to an undervaluation of the thanksgiving prayer and, in the splinter Churches of the reformers, partly to its loss.

b) The blessing or epiclesis

This thanksgiving prayer has to be understood at the same time as a benediction, especially if the *eulogesas* of the Institution narrative in Mark/Matthew is taken into account. But this benediction, as a calling down of heaven's blessing, was suggestive of what later came to be known as the epiclesis. Benediction is always a prayer for God's blessing, and in a larger sense this prayer is the epiclesis. The blessing for which one prays to God may relate to the gift-offerings of bread and wine, which are to be transformed by God's power to a higher order of gift-offering (Consecration-epiclesis).

But it may relate to the participants as well, so that by virtue of their participation they "may be filled with every heavenly blessing and grace" (Communion-epiclesis). The epiclesis contained in the Eucharistic Prayer of Hippolytus already belongs to this latter kind, and various pointers show this to be the more primitive and basic form of epiclesis. And so the blessing may be a prayer that the divine power or the divine Word or the Logos or the Spirit (best understood as the person of the Holy Spirit himself) might come upon us. All these expressions appear in the history of the Mass.

At the point when the Trinity controversy centered upon the person of the Holy Spirit (whose divinity the Arians denied), both camps — the opponents as well as the defenders — spontaneously preferred the epiclesis that prays for the descent of the Holy Spirit in the Mass. This epiclesis appeared around the year 380 in the Apostolic Constitutions, and evidently not long after that it was also incorporated into the Anaphora of James, which is the basic form of all anaphora texts in the West Syrian and Byzantine liturgies.

Remarkably, the prayer for the transformation of the gift-offerings by the power of the Holy Spirit comes only after the words of the Institution narrative, but this is explained by the text of the Apostolic Constitutions itself, for the Eucharistic Prayer it contains is found to be merely an expansion of Hippolytus' Eucharistic Prayer; and at that very point in the Hippolytan version, that is, after the Institution narrative, comes the prayer that the Holy Spirit be sent down "upon the gift of your Church," so that all may become one and "be filled with the Holy Spirit." At bottom, then, what we have here is a Communion-epiclesis, though not without some suggestion of an effect upon the gifts themselves.

c) *The place and meaning of the Consecration-epiclesis*

This prayer for the descent of the Holy Spirit upon the gifts evolved further into the prayer for the central and all-important transformation of the gifts; and it took root in the spot where it had been planted: *after* the words of Institution, albeit in its new form it would have been more appropriate and meaningful *before* them. In fact, in the Egyptian liturgy it preceded the Institution narrative, as is seen especially in Serapion's anaphora, where in the manner of earlier times the prayer calls down God's power to fulfill this sacerdotal gift-offering. In the anaphora of the West Syrian Byzantine type the prayer between the Sanctus and the Institution narrative was devoted largely to recalling the history of salvation, and as such was not a suitable context for the insertion of a Consecration-epiclesis. Hence this was joined to the Communion-epiclesis, so that even though the epiclesis comes after the Institution narrative it prays that the Holy Spirit may come down and "change" these gifts into Christ's body and blood. The term denoting *change* varies with different liturgies: *apophene* in the Apostolic Constitutions; *hagiasai kai anadei* in the Liturgy of Basil; *poieson metabalon* in that of John Chrysostom; *poiese* in James' *anaphora*. All these expressions, however, are understood as identical in the sense of transubstantiation. It was all the easier for this identification to come about, as not one of the proto-liturgists ever demanded precisions as to the moment the transformation took place; it was simply assigned to the Eucharistic Prayer as a whole.

Together with this unchallenged insertion of the epiclesis after the words of Consecration there is the fact that in the East, even in the early Middle Ages, the Institution narrative was accompanied by rituals that can be understood to mean only that at this precise point through Christ's words his body and blood become present. That is clear in the Byzantine Liturgy of St. John Chrysostom as it has come down from the ninth century in the Barberini manuscript (Brightman 328). While the preceding section of the anaphora is recited in a low voice, Christ's words are recited or sung aloud (*ekphonos*), and the people answer with a ratifying *Amen*.

Even earlier, in the eighth century, the Syrian Liturgy of James attests that the Institution narrative and the ratifying *Amen*, said twice (after both the words over the bread and the words over the chalice), had gained in prominence as focal point and climax. While the fragments published by O. Heiming date from the eighth century, the practice was evidently in effect in the Syrian Liturgy of James as far back as *c.* 700, as the texts edited by A. Rücker show.[139] In the ninth century this practice, by then deep-rooted, was protested by Moses bar Kepha since he (rightly) saw in it the implication that the Consecration took place at this very point. For meanwhile the view that the Consecration of bread and wine took place only at the epiclesis had somehow worked its way into Eastern theology.

d) A new interpretation of the Consecration-epiclesis

St. John Damascene (d. 749), who appeared at the beginning of this new emphasis, found that between the Institution narrative and the epiclesis in Basil's Anaphora, the gift-offerings were called *antitypa* of Christ's body and blood. In the context of the iconoclastic controversy raging at the time, he interpreted the word not in its old sense in which *antitypon*, like *typos, symbolon, eikon,* and *homoioma*, was used to designate the reality itself (as Betz explains in *Die Eucharistie* 1.1:217-39), but only in the sense of *image.* From this, as he logically concluded, Basil could have applied the word to the gifts "not after the Consecration but before the Consecration, and therefore the Consecration took place only at the epiclesis"; he develops this position in his doctrinal compendium entitled: De Fide Orthodoxa (4:13; PG 94:1152-53).

From then on this theory was almost universally accepted in the Eastern Churches. Yet it was understood to mean only one thing: the epiclesis was necessary if the words of Jesus were to become efficacious. It was only after the fourteenth century that the significance of the Institution account began to be depreciated to no more than a mere "narrative" and the significance of the epiclesis was increasingly underscored as *the* point of doctrinal difference with the Latins, as S. Salaville has shown.[140] As against the West's emphasis on the words of the Institution narrative which the minister pronounces *in persona Christi* by virtue of the power conferred upon him, C. Kern, in presenting current Orthodox thinking, lays stress on the epiclesis pronounced *in persona Ecclesiae.*

Ancient traditional rituals, which seemed to ascribe an immediate efficacy to Jesus' words, were given a new meaning to suit the shift of emphasis from Institution account to epiclesis. This is particularly the case with a rubric in the Byzantine Liturgy of St. John Chrysostom that prescribes that at the words "This is . . .", the deacon point with his Orarion to the gift-offerings. A note in the Euchologion of 1839 insists that this gesture is meant to point not to the gift-offerings on the altar but to those at the Last Supper, just as Jesus' words are pronounced only as a historical narrative (*diegematikos*; Brightman 386).

That the use of a Consecration-epeclesis even after the words of the Institution narrative is not contrary to Catholic faith is shown by the fact that the Eastern Churches in communion with Rome have used this very Consecration-epiclesis. A prayer for the operation of the Holy Spirit even after the actual moment of transubstantiation is no more extraordinary than, for instance, the centuries-old practice, at ordination in the Roman liturgy, of ritually conferring priestly power upon each individual priest only after the sacramental act. In fact, numerous forms of the "Post-pridie" prayer in the Gallican and Mozarabic liturgies contain epicleses petitioning for sanctification (*sanctificare, benedicere*), even sometimes for transformation (*transformatio, transmutatio*), of the gift-offerings, as may be discovered in Lietzmann's survey of the epiclesis texts of the Gallican and Mozarabic rites (pp. 93–113).

Moreover, even in the earliest forms of the epiclesis following the Institution narrative, i.e., in those of the Syrians (Theodore of Mopsuestia and Narsai of Nisibis), a distinction was already made between the effect of the words of the Institution narrative and that of the epiclesis. While by means of the narrative Christ's body and blood were believed to become present as in his death, the prayer for the Holy Spirit's descent (along with the commingling) was believed to effect their revivification through the operation of the Spirit, as in Christ's resurrection; and only in this manner was the gift-offering supposed to become the food of immortality.[141] This distinction, however, corresponds to a mode of thought in terms of symbols and images rather than of strict logical categories, and was hardly meant as a precise theological definition of the reality.

The temporary acrimony of the discussion over the epiclesis may also be accounted for by the West's exclusive preoccupation with the essence and conditions for validity, questions that the East was far from willing to enter into, since it was satisfied with the ritual it had inherited from ancient tradition. Further, the East's theological approach was different: it viewed all supernatural graces and effects within a Trinitarian framework and traced their concrete efficacy to the Holy Spirit's operation. This Eastern viewpoint has meanwhile come to be increasingly understood and appreciated in the West. Thus, for example, all three Eucharistic Prayers introduced in the Roman Mass in 1968 include a regular Holy Spirit epiclesis.

VI. COMMUNION AS SACRIFICIAL MEAL

The Eucharist is constituted of bread and wine. Bread and wine are meant to be eaten and drunk. At the Last Supper Jesus himself gave the gift-offerings to his disciples with the express invitation, "Take and eat," "Take and drink." Communion therefore is of the very essence of the Eucharistic celebration. There is a tendency among some to posit Communion as only an integral but not an essential part of the sacrifice, since a sacrifice without a sacrificial meal is conceivable, as is borne out by the history of religions. Even in the Old Testament, sacrifices not associated with a sacrificial meal were performed (as in Leviticus 3 and 6). But no conclusion can be drawn regarding Christ's Institution by comparing it with other sacrifices. It is atypical, unique. In the Eucharist, partaking of the gift-offerings is a constitutive element. The performance of what Christ has instituted would not be complete without Communion. The priest's Communion, at least, belongs to the essential nature of the Eucharist.

1. THE MASS IS MORE THAN A MEAL

In the New Testament Institution accounts, Jesus' action of presenting the species as food and drink is given so much prominence that upon superficial consideration one could be tempted to read into the action nothing more than a meal and thus to reduce the Institution to a mere meal ritual. The reformers of the sixteenth century in fact did succumb to the temptation. And the same temptation seems to hold an attraction for Catholics keen on ecumenical dialogue: as witness, for instance, the tendency not only to take over from the Reformed churches the expression *supper* or *banquet* as a possible synecdoche (a part for the whole) but, further, to adopt the concept itself as adequately describing the whole reality.

The Council of Trent expressly rejected the view that the offering in the Mass is nothing other than "Christ . . . given us to eat" (*Christum ad manducandum dari*; Sess. 22, can. 1). Nor is it enough to say that *under* the visible process, under the species of the banquet-meal, something that can be called sacrifice becomes mysteriously present. The sacrifice itself is a visible process; it is itself the essential sign. In the Mass Christ offers the sacrifice in a visible manner through the ministry of the priest. If the visible sign itself did not have the sacrificial character in the Mass, then every other sacrament would with equal right have to be called sacrifice; for in all the sacraments it is the sacrifice of the Cross that is effectively at work.[142]

But what impression does an onlooker get of the Mass if not that of a banquet or meal? True, what appears to the external eye seems to exhibit all the elements of a banquet-meal: a table is covered, bread and wine are placed on it, and these are passed around as food and drink. But it would be equally true to say that, as we have shown above, through the centuries and even today, the elements of an *offering* are just as visible, even to the external eye, in the appearance of the Mass. Furthermore, everyone must agree that in the sacramental sacrifice, too, the sacramental sign is of two kinds: what one sees and what one hears. And what one hears is the factor that determines the meaning of what one sees. If today (as Schillebeeckx indicates[143]) the "word" has acquired so much importance even in the Eucharist, this very fact should help us realize that the entire Eucharistic Prayer expresses a Godward movement, an offering.

The Eucharistic celebration was dissociated from the context of a regular meal more than nineteen centuries ago and has remained so ever since; and we ought not to encumber it again with a meal or make *banquet* the basic form of the Eucharistic celebration. Moreover, in this connection, as J. H. Crehan rightly points out,[144] Hippolytus of Rome applied the expression *the Lord's Supper* to the Agape and not to the Eucharist. As was noted above, before the sixteenth century the Mass was never called *meal* or *supper* or *banquet* in any liturgy.

2. THE MASS AS A MEAL

Even though the meal is not the basic form of the Mass as a whole, it is still an indispensable and essential part of it. Communion is the sacrificial banquet. No Mass can be celebrated without Communion. In the Church's tradition this teaching finds clear expression in the rule prescribing that when the celebrating priest is forced to terminate his Mass before Communion, it must be consummated by another priest. Communion is the climax and consummation of the Eucharistic celebration, not only by reason of Christ's mandate but also because the whole point of the sacrament is to involve the individual man in the gift of salvation granted all men through Christ. God's great condescension to man, manifested in this world first through the Incarnation, reaches the extreme limit possible this side of eternity in Eucharistic Communion. For the recipient it is a pledge of eternal life, of participation in the life of the God-Man as in Christ's death and resurrection; of the "resurrection on the Last Day" that is promised to him (John 6:54). The reception of Christ's sacramental body constitutes as well as confirms anew the recipient's incorporation into his Mystical Body.

The Eucharistic celebration achieves its fullest form when the community assembled for the celebration takes part in the sacramental Communion, just as it has taken part in the offering and announced this participation through its ratifying responses. The people's Communion is the fulfillment of Christ's desire to draw his own unto himself and to take them with him to his Father. At the same time it also means on their part a final *Yes* and a sacramental self-abandonment in his sacrificial self-surrender. This is why Vatican Council II heartily endorsed "that closer form of participation in the Mass whereby the faithful, after the priest's communion, receive the Lord's body under elements consecrated at that very sacrifice" (CL § 55).

Still, a participation in the Mass without Communion is not empty and meaningless. Through their reverential presence and their *Amen* the people exercise faith and say *Yes* to the priest's offering as an expression of their own self-surrender to God, even if for some reason or other they do not receive Communion. Theirs is a genuine and fruitful participation even when it is not fully realized on the sacramental level.

Even when the people communicate under only one species, their full participation in the Mass is assured, since such a Communion adequately and actively involves the participants as sacramentally sharing the sacramental sacrifice. Of course, since an absolutely complete sign would naturally require both the offering of the two species and Communion under both, at least the priest must communicate under both species. Communion under one species is an abridgment, but an abridgment that may be referred to the mode of expression used by Jesus himself (John 6:57-58). At any rate it is permissible in a situation where there is proportionate reason for it, viz., the practical difficulties entailed in distributing the chalice among a large number of participants. And all the more so if people are sensitive about the possible danger of irreverence toward the sacred blood, as was the case in times past.

The search for ways and means to avoid or minimize the danger of irreverence started early, but it was during the thirteenth century that a definitive solution was hit upon. This was the age when veneration of the sacrament received special impetus. At the time, it was made easier to forego the chalice by the doctrine of "concomitance," which has in the meanwhile been clarified by recognition that whoever receives Christ's body receives the whole Christ. It was the heretical denial of this fact that spurred the Council of Trent to defend the doctrine and its practice (Sess. 21, cans. 1–3); it was the reason also why exceptions to this rule were thereafter granted only very rarely and temporarily. For the rest, the question of the laity's partaking of the chalice is not a theological one, but merely liturgico-pastoral. Vatican II has made provision for a wider participation in the chalice as far as it is practicable, and has re-emphasized the full sacramental sign in that way.

VII. THE MEANING AND VALUE OF THE MASS

Historically Christ's work for the renewal of the world took place in a small country and within a short span of years. In the Eucharist this same work becomes present to men of every land and age in its central and decisive events, namely, Christ's suffering, death, and resurrection. This is not the only way his redemptive work becomes present, nor is the presence of the same kind in every instance. For Christ becomes present also when his word is preached. He becomes present in all the sacraments. What we have discussed above is his actual presence. When the sinner is absolved through rebirth in the sacraments of Baptism and of Penance, it is chiefly Christ's redemptive power to overcome sin that becomes present. The Eucharistic celebration, on the contrary, is the gathering of those who have already been redeemed and sanctified in the sacrament. Christ includes them here in the great and final glorification of God that he alone could accomplish.

1. A CELEBRATION OF THE ASSEMBLED COMMUNITY

If we wish to understand the real meaning of the Mass we should not start with the case of a private Mass celebrated by a priest alone for the intention of some particular person. We should start from the Church's official celebration. As in the second century (and probably even in the first), so also today, this official celebration takes the form of the assembly of the faithful "on the day named for the sun."

This celebration of the assembled community is the very foundation of the essential structure of the Mass. It is a celebration that presupposes a congregation prepared for sacramental participation in Communion, and thus is structured as a thanksgiving prayer; in fact, its principal section begins with the call: "Let us give thanks to the Lord our God." So then the Church's official

Eucharist is the weekly commemoration of the redemption on Sunday, the day on which the redemptive action was consummated; it is a celebration through which the community of the redeemed becomes aware of its dignity and of its hope; and ordinarily it is the community gathered around its officially appointed pastor. Hence the principle, valid even today, that the parish pastor must not accept a private intention for his Mass on Sunday (and on feast days of the same grade as Sunday). He should say Mass for his community — or, more correctly, with his community.

It is the importance given to a secondary good that led to misunderstandings regarding the Mass. One such misunderstanding is abetted by the fact that the above-mentioned Sunday obligation has come to be called the duty of *application* in connection with the way of treating private Masses (CIC can. 306). Thus already Duns Scotus spoke of this *applicatio* prescribed by Church law, according to which a pastor should celebrate Mass "in particular for his parishioners" (*specialiter pro suis parochianis*; Quodlibetum 20:16). According to the original and real purpose, however, the whole point is not that the pastor performs something but that the actual *Ecclesia* celebrates the Eucharist with its legitimate pastor.

The real meaning of the Mass unfolds in the community's Sunday Eucharist: thanksgiving and worship. Thanksgiving for grace received, and worship in the highest sense of an outburst of the whole man in faith, hope, and love to glorify the divine Majesty. Only secondarily is it also an act of humble supplication; for thanksgiving and worship that rises from sinning, contingent mortals is at the same time petition, petition for God's further grace and mercy toward us, as St. Thomas Aquinas explains.[145]

2. TRENT AND THE MASS AS EXPIATORY

In discussing the purpose of the Mass, "four ends" are usually mentioned: *adoration, thanksgiving, petition, expiation*. And since the Council of Trent they are frequently enumerated one after another, thus giving the impression that they are of equal weight. The Council itself was not responsible for this enumeration, but in fielding the questions that came up, the Council Fathers did declare that the Mass was also an expiatory sacrifice. Indeed, they condemned those who held that the Mass was "merely an offering of praise and thanksgiving . . . and not propitiatory" and that it was "not to be offered for the living and the dead" (can. 3).

Pointing out the identity of the Mass with the sacrifice of the Cross, the Fathers strongly defended the expiatory character of the Mass and declared that with this sacrifice before his eyes, God grants us the grace of penitence as well as forgives "wrongdoings and sins, even grave ones" (*crimina et peccata etiam ingentia*; ch. 2). At the same time, in another passage, the Council asserts with sufficient clarity that such forgiveness is brought about not immediately through the sacrifice of the Mass but mediately through the sacrament of Penance.

We should be doing an injustice to the Council if we took its declarations out of their context and age. The Council felt no need to examine or develop points not being disputed, e.g., that the Mass is above all worship and thanksgiving. It only defended and settled the point that was disputed. The Protestant reformers had before their eyes the undoubtedly distorted views underlying certain practices prevailing at that time, such as the innumerable votive Masses for the living and the dead and the superstitious faith in their efficacy. But the reformers were not content with fighting the distortion and superstition; they went on to attack the very foundation without pausing to ask whether the foundation was actually responsible for the abuses.

Thus the Protestants denied that the Mass had any value whatever as petition and expiation. They went so far as to deny even the sacrificial character of the Eucharist. At any rate in the Formula Concordiae of 1577, a document considered to be basic to orthodox Lutheran doctrine, the sacrifice of the Mass "offered for the sins of the living and the dead" (*quod pro peccatis vivorum et mortuorum offertur*) is thrown overboard.[146] Even Protestant theologians such as are not averse to rapprochement declare that the Catholic doctrine of the Mass as expiatory sacrifice is the greatest single stumbling block. It is considered variously the Catholic Church's "radical error" (*per* Ortenburger[147]) or the doctrinal difference that "divides Churches" (*per* the prominent liturgist Peter Brunner[148]). The Catholic teaching is challenged as claiming to add something to the sacrifice of the Cross, which alone was the all-embracing and all-sufficient expiation for the sins of the world.[149]

Is this reproach really justified? The Mass is an expiatory sacrifice only to that extent to which the one and all-embracing expiatory sacrifice of the Cross is made present in it. In Warnach's words, only Christ's sacrifice "is expiatory and salvific in the proper sense, whereas the Church's sacrifice of gift-offering and of prayer, the Eucharist, provides the container or the form."[150]

This sacrifice becomes present, as we have already seen, principally as the Church's sacrifice of thanksgiving and of worship (the Church here denoting, of course, those who are redeemed and sanctified through that sacrifice). But because the Church is a pilgrim Church and, as St. Paul puts it in his Letter to the Hebrews (5:2), "is beset by weakness" because it is a "sinful Church" and is oppressed by manifold hardships, its sacrifice of praise and thanksgiving necessarily becomes also a petition for God's gracious mercy.

3. HISTORICAL SHIFT OF OUTLOOK

This faith-conviction found a place in the structure of the Mass prayers already in the early centuries. A typical example occurs in the account of the Fifth Mystagogical Catechesis of Jerusalem:

> Then over this sacrifice of reconciliation we pray for the peace of the Church and for the welfare of the world . . . and for all who have fallen asleep before us, convinced that it will be of the greatest benefit to the souls for whom we offer petitions, while the holy and awesome sacrifice lies before us (5, 8, 9).

These "petitions" are the Intercessions associated with the offering in all the liturgies.

The votive Mass, to which we referred briefly above, made its appearance in the West around the sixth century, and by the end of the Middle Ages its popularity had grown to unprecedented proportions. Fundamentally, however, this brought about nothing more than a new emphasis that contributed to a change in subjective appreciation and to a questionable outlook. In the traditional teaching itself nothing was changed; the sacrifice remained the Eucharist introduced by the "Gratias agamus." But now its offering was no longer solely associated with mere prayer and worship; the offering itself was made as petition for some special intention.

Thus, the Eucharist was no longer seen primarily and exclusively in relation to the gathering of God's people, who, united with one another and in Christ, go before God in a spirit of worship and adoration. Rather, it tended to be appreciated in relation to a particular case of human need and to a small circle of the oppressed. In a growing number of instances, this relation became restricted to the celebrating priest and the Mass server who represented those who had requested the Mass. The Mass is offered for *someone*, for the living or for the dead.

This appreciation of the Mass became so prevalent that it found its way into the ordination formula incorporated in the Pontificale Romano-Germanicum (*c.* 950), when the ordaining bishop, presenting the chalice and the paten to the newly ordained priest, says, *Accipe potestatem offerre sacrificium Deo, Missamque celebrare tam pro vivis quam pro defunctis, in nomine Domini* ("Receive the power to offer sacrifice to God, and to celebrate Mass, for both the living and the dead, in the name of the Lord").[151] As is well known, it was this formula in particular that later roused Luther's indignation. For the record, in the 1968 revised ritual for priestly ordination it was modified to *Accipe oblationem plebis sanctae Deo offerendam* ("Receive the oblation from holy people that is to be offered to God"; § 26).

To offer *for* someone can mean to offer *in his name*, as his representative; such, in any case, was the implication when in the Mozarabic liturgy even the dead were referred to as "offerers" (*offerentes*). But as a rule it simply means that the offering is made for the benefit of someone, who is frequently mentioned by name. As Berger points out, however, at the root of this practice there was always the feeling that the person named was somehow present (see pp. 163–240). Often, too, the special intention embodying one's petition was worded *for* health, *for* liberation from enemies, *for* peace.

Finally, the hope implied in mentioning an intention or a personal name was that God might be gracious and merciful to the person involved, a sinner like all of us. Every sacrifice of petition thus becomes at the same time propitiatory sacrifice. Yet even as propitiatory sacrifice the Mass does not state a right or declare payment of a debt; rather it is no more than a humble supplication, a prayerful reference to the unique sacrifice once offered for our redemption and made present anew before us, a petition rooted in the conviction that the new presence of the redemptive sacrifice cannot remain inefficacious, that it brings us closer to God, that it opens and disposes our hearts to God's mercy.

4. The "Efficacy" of the Mass as Propitiatory Sacrifice

Even though this solution may not always have been clearly articulated, theologians have long since known and upheld it; and St. Thomas Aquinas cites the intercessory prayers in the Canon of the Mass as proof for it (ST 3a, 79:7c). The solution is satisfactory also because it does justice to the Tridentine Council's description of the Mass as "a sacrifice of propitiation" (*sacrificium propitiatorium*). True, some popularizers attributed to the Mass an infallible efficacy "by reason of the work done" (*ex opere operato*), similar to what they held concerning the sacraments. In orthodox studies (as, e.g., Journet's *La Messe*, p. 165) *ex opere operato* meant only that the celebration is valid whenever the conditions are fulfilled, even should the celebrant be an unworthy priest. But more often the expression may have been used with regard to the effects: as in the sacraments, so too by "hearing" Mass and by virtue of the consummated sacrifice, participants were expected to share in the fruits of redemption, obtaining forgiveness of sins and an increase of grace.

Suárez, in his Commentary on the Eucharist (Disp. 79:1), and still more De la Taille, in his *Mysterium fidei*,[152] underline the essential distinction between sacrament and sacrifice. Thus, in the sacrament one receives, whereas in the sacrifice one offers. In the case of sacrifice the concept of "work done" (*opus operatum*) is inapplicable in the usual sense, because sacrifice is homage rendered to God.

To produce an effect in the offerer is not of its very essence. Only to the extent to which it is pleasing to God can it operate as a moral cause, as the object of divine pleasure, to dispose God toward the offerers and to incline him to have mercy on them. To that extent it is, in De la Taille's language, "pragmatic impetration, or impetration by way of action" (*pragmatica impetratio*). It is only in this sense of petition expressed and vivified in and through the sacrifice that we can say that the Mass operates *ex opere operato*: to the extent, namely, to which in the Mass "over and above any prayer or ours, the impetration of our High Priest, now ratified and heard by God . . . goes up to heaven" (in De la Taille's words, p. 321).

In this passage De la Taille rejects also the distinction Suárez makes (79:2.6-7) between supplication (*impetratio*) and prayer that derives its efficacy only from its association with the sacrifice. The impetration, according to Suarez, is infallible in the sense defined above, namely, that it comes about necessarily, while with regard to the prayer this infallible necessity does not exist. At any rate, if looked upon as propitiatory sacrifice, the Mass remains only a petition. A. Michel, who adopts De la Taille's thesis, calls the Mass a "prayer action" (*prière en acte*); and McCormack draws the practical conclusions from this view of the Mass, in his article "The Act of Christ in the Mass." [153]

No new act of God's will to grant grace and mercy is posited by the sacrifice of the Mass, according to this view; nothing is added to the propitiatory power inherent in the sacrifice of the Cross. It is the same will of God posited once at Christ's sacrifice on the Cross that now (in the words of Rahner-Häussling, p. 64) "approaches man in his concrete situation so that man makes this gracious will his own in and through its visible manifestation." In this way the fruit of Christ's sacrifice is *applied* to men of different times. Even when occasionally the Church texts speak of God being propitiated through the sacrifice of the Mass, either the expression is used in the above sense of application or "the Mass is being envisaged as the liturgical representation of the sacrifice of the Cross and the latter included in its concept, so that the *placari* can be affirmed of the Mass thought of in that way" (*ibid.*, n. 5).

5. The Fruits of the Mass

Since the late Middle Ages the belief that the sacrifice of the Mass necessarily and always brings spiritual gain to the participants has issued in a teaching on the *fruits* of the Mass that had beginnings in Duns Scotus' theology. Scotus distinguished three ways in which the Mass becomes fruitful to the participants: for the celebrant "most especially" (*specialissime*); for the whole Church "in a very broad way" (*generalissime*); and "in particular" (*specialiter*) for those to whom it is applied (Quodlibetum 20:3-4). Characteristically, however, Scotus selected his examples of these types from the intercessory prayer, which makes clear that every prayer benefits first of all the one who prays; so, too, that the prayer of a member always benefits the whole Church as well; and above all, that it benefits him for whom one prays. It is equally clear that the power and efficacy of such prayer, as of every human endeavor, are limited.

Scotus could apply his distinction and its conclusions directly to the Mass, for he considered the Mass only as an action of the Church, and hence an action of limited and finite value, since the criterion for the value of the sacrifice is not the gift but the giver. While not much attention was paid to this questionable premise in the subsequent period, the teaching on the finiteness of the fruit, especially of the "special fruits" (*fructus specialis*) accruing to the person for whom the Mass is said, had come to stay; and this was one of the factors behind the growing conviction that it was reasonable and necessary to have Masses celebrated again and again. Another factor, one that is fundamentally valid, was precisely the impetratory nature of the sacrifice offered as petition. Thus, since the petition is directed toward a limited object, for a particular intention, repetition of the petition is a sign of its urgency.

What was less clearly seen was that the value and the efficacious power of the Mass considered in themselves are the same as the value and efficacious power of the sacrifice of the Cross represented in the Mass; that consequently these are unlimited in themselves and are limited only through human capacity to receive, through the receiver's disposition. This is the participants' "faith and devotion" (*fides et devotio*) to which the Roman Canon of the Mass made reference. For in every Mass Christ's sacrifice becomes present anew with its entire redemptive power and grace, as the work that has established perfect peace between heaven and earth and has restored total rapport between man and God. And in becoming present it sends up petition for one person or another, for one intention or another. But our capacity as contingent beings is limited.

Hence there is little point in forcing distinctions between *fruits* of varying value or in arranging the different grades of efficacy in neat categories. For the ultimate success of a prayer does not depend on the one who prays but on the free will of the One who grants, and that One does not need a computer. Finally, regarding those for whom the Mass is offered, as in fact regarding all those who participate in its actual offering: *the fruit they receive depends on their attitude and disposition*; this is true whether one has in mind the celebrant, or others who are bodily present, or still others who have the Mass celebrated for their intentions by offering a stipend (see Rahner-Häussling, pp 77–87).

Since the participant's disposition is a decisive factor, one might imagine an extreme case in which a Mass becomes altogether fruitless or worthless. If, for instance, the required dispositions were to be totally absent, if an unworthy priest were to offer the sacrifice in an unworthy manner, and if none of the other participants had even the minimum of that *fides et devotio*, such a Mass would indeed be a new time-and-space re-presentation of Christ's sacrifice, but without actual value and without efficacy; it would only be an insult to God. Neither could it be efficacious as the Church's sacrifice for the benefit of the whole Church, since, first, the Church cannot will such an offering, and second, there can be no question of efficacy in favor of the whole Church unless particular members of Christ's Mystical Body concretely receive such an efficacy.[154]

6. THE STIPEND

A special means of contributing to the sacrifice is the stipend. However, since all gifts of grace are by nature gratis, the stipend does not entitle one to the *fruits* of the Mass; the giver merely binds the priest to say the Mass for his intentions, that is, to pray for him when he enters into God's presence with his sacrifice. This practice was not unknown to the ancient Church. Thus Epiphanius (d.403), in his tract "Against Heresies," reports the case of a newly baptized person who gave the baptizing bishop a certain number of gold pieces with the request "Offer for me" (*prosphere hyper emou*; Adv. haer. 30:6; PG 41:413). The one offering the stipend thereby becomes the *offerens* in a very special sense.[155]

For some centuries the Church has been careful to lay down detailed regulations governing Mass stipends in order to avoid the abuses to which this practice can lend itself; these directions are given in the Code of Canon Law (can. 824–44). The orthodoxy of the practice itself, however, as well as of the teaching on *application* has been upheld by Pope Pius VI in a decree directed against the Synod of Pistoia (Denz. 2630).[156]

7. PROPER UNDERSTANDING OF THE MASS AS PROPITIATORY

Down to this present century Catholic faith in the Mass as propitiatory sacrifice has constantly been a red flag to the Protestant reformers, who have repeatedly accused the Church of trying to add something to Christ's all-sufficient sacrifice offered on the Cross. As a result of the discussions and clarifications of the past few decades, however, many well-disposed Protestant critics have modified their reproach and some have dropped it altogether. The most significant factor in bringing about this reconciliation has been a more profound understanding of the Mass as "the Church's sacrament of the sacrifice Christ offered on the Cross," to quote Michael Schmaus. Significantly, this statement appears almost word for word in the definition of the Eucharist by the present-day Swiss Protestant theologian J. J. von Allmen in *The Lord's Supper*: ". . . the Eucharist is a sacrament of the sacrifice of Christ and a channel of the Church's sacrifice. . . ."[157]

Clearly, when the Mass is understood in this way nothing new is added to the content of Christ's sacrifice; there is only an unfolding of this same sacrifice, but now within the dimensions of the Church. None of the documents containing the Church's teaching and theological commentary on the Eucharist ever speaks of the Mass as adding something to or complementing Christ's sacrifice. Neither does the Church claim to "have free disposal" of Christ or of his sacrifice when it offers this sacrifice for a human intention. The "free disposal" the Church enjoys in the case of the Mass is no more or no less than in the case of any prayer-petition we might offer.

Hence it has rightly been asserted even among Protestants that to admit the propitiatory character of the Eucharistic sacrifice is no more difficult than to admit its thanksgiving character; for even in the case of thanksgiving the decisive factor is God's acceptance, as E. Fincke argues.[158] Of course, the difficulty of reconciliation becomes greater when, fundamentally, the objection concerns any offertory-action of the Church in union with the re-presentation of the redemptive sacrifice or any prayer formula in which the Institution narrative is involved; for in such supposition we can do absolutely nothing more than to have faith. But this position, too, has now been abandoned in certain newer Agendas. Moreover, the principle directly concerns not so much the special case of the Church's sacrifice and propitiatory sacrifice, but rather the basic relation of the Christian to God, and the whole doctrine of justification.[159]

Vatican Council II was not handicapped by the heated atmosphere of controversy in which the Council of Trent had to defend the Church's essential inheritance and work for the renewal of Christian life. The question now was not to defend the Mass or to settle disputed points as in the sixteenth century. The Second Vatican Council's reform of the liturgy and of the Mass was directed simply toward realizing their essential nature more perfectly and unfolding their richness more effectively; and it has already succeeded in clearing away a number of misunderstandings. Most importantly, the contours have been molded in clearer relief, and the right points have been re-emphasized. This is most striking in the enriched texts of the Preface and in the three new forms of the Eucharistic Prayer.

In this connection it is most interesting to read the assessment of the Protestant theologian K. H. Bieritz.[160] As he rightly concludes, for "a theology derived from the Reformers" and their Christology, the contrast offered by the Catholic liturgy still exists, and has "become even clearer and sharper."

PART THREE

The Liturgical Form

I. HOW THE SCHEMA ORIGINATED

In the historical survey given in the previous chapters, we set out in some detail what we know of the structure and form of the Mass from the first years of the Christian era down through the centuries. We were interested to discover in what way the early Church understood the nature of the Eucharist; and of necessity the answer was based principally on what appeared to the eye. Now to sum up our findings.

1. BASIC STRUCTURE FROM APOSTOLIC TIMES

The New Testament accounts of the Institution reflect the manner in which the Eucharist was celebrated in Apostolic times, for they apparently omit everything not relevant to the fulfillment of the mandate "Do this in remembrance of me." In the first Christian community the Eucharist was performed in conjunction with a meal: the person presiding took bread, broke it, gave thanks, and, after pronouncing Jesus' words of Institution over it, distributed it. Then he took the chalice, gave thanks, pronounced the words handed down, and passed it around the table.

By the time of St. Paul it seems to have been only a memory that the bread ceremonial ever took place before the meal and that with the chalice "after the meal." By then the two actions were continuous; and from this arose, at least as early as the first century, the simplified sequence in which the one presiding takes the bread and the chalice, pronounces the thanksgiving prayer, the *eucharistia*, breaks bread, and distributes the consecrated gifts.

The basic structural outlines of the Eucharistic celebration were thus laid down as they were to remain for all times. The meal from which the Eucharistic celebration had been separated could be left out altogether. In fact, it had to be dropped, if only by reason of the practical difficulties involved in serving growing communi-

155

ties. Thus the emphasis, now no longer placed on the breaking of bread (since the meal proper that began with the breaking of bread no longer existed), was transferred to the prayer over the bread and wine, which could not have been a mere grace before meat. The character of the gathering was no longer determined by the fellowship of a meal in common but by that of prayer in common: *a simultaneous appeal to God.*

The Eucharistic gathering had become a prayer meeting where there was only the one table at which the "president" (as Justin Martyr called him) pronounced the thanksgiving prayer, the *eucharistia,* over the gifts of bread and wine. This carried such weight that the apologists of the second century spoke as though the Eucharist were solely a matter of prayer, and Tertullian sometimes described it simply as "prayer" (*oratio*). Bread and wine, however, were included in this act of prayer, and accordingly we find references to an "offering," even to a "sacrifice"; and the rite ended with a partaking of the sacred offerings in Communion. The basic form was the *eucharistia.* The offering was first prepared (the later Offertory), and after that the breaking of bread (fraction) and Communion took place.

An important addition was the Scripture-reading service. As early as the time of Justin, that is, the mid-second century, this service was the approved thing for the first part of the Sunday Eucharistic celebration. Thus a Synagogue custom that was second nature to the Jewish Christians was universally added as a prelude to the Eucharistic service. As Justin witnesses, another Synagogue custom also adhered to was that of following the reading with a prayer for general intentions.

For centuries to come, however, this service of readings was not looked upon as necessarily connected with the Eucharistic celebration. In some localities it might be separated from the Eucharistic celebration, as it was still in the twelfth century in the monastery of St. Sabbas, where the community was divided according to national origins for the readings, and then the Eucharist was celebrated together. The readings could even be omitted altogether if an equivalent preparation was provided for in some other way, as the present author has explained (in MRR 1:261f.). Finally, the emphasis was not exclusively on the readings in themselves, but on the fact that the community gathered in God's presence and in God's name heard his words before glorifying him in the Eucharist.

2. UNIFORMITY AND FREEDOM

Within these guidelines, established not by prescription but by custom and an interest in uniformity, there existed considerable freedom of movement and apparently great variation from church to church. We hear nothing of written or mandatory texts. The Eucharistic Prayer of Hippolytus of Rome was a private work and as such was an exception too; he hastens to note in connection with his manuscript that it is "definitely not necessary" for the bishop to adhere to the words suggested "as though he had to learn them by heart." There is no thought whatsoever of reading them; everyone is to say the prayers in his own way (Botte 28f.). In later editions of the text, however, the word "not" in the phrase "definitely not necessary" was deleted. In both the Syrian and Egyptian Churches this text from a Roman author writing in Greek was in great use. In the Church of Ethiopia the formula of Hippolytus with extensive amendments is today still the basic schema for Mass. At the same time the very fact of such widespread usage is a witness to the extensive freedom that Christians in those early times evidently enjoyed as their natural right.

The same impression of uniformity in essentials and freedom in details emerges from Eusebius' account of an event we have adverted to above. As we read in his History of the Church (5:24), when about the year 154 Bishop Polycarp of Smyrna called on Pope Anicetus, the Pope invited him to celebrate the Eucharist in church. Apparently he felt no anxiety that the bishop from Asia would celebrate the Eucharist in his own way and disrupt the order of the place. Ironically enough, the one who was worried was the leading delegate of the Quartodecimans, a sect with several differing traditions on the important point of liturgical order.

To a considerable degree this variety may be associated also with the Eucharistic Prayer. The version of Hippolytus, in all its clarity and compactness, might have been typical of Rome and Alexandria, but it certainly does not adequately represent the whole tradition. Among other things, it contains no reference whatever to the preparatory function of Old Testament history in the economy of salvation. Parallel with the tradition of Hippolytus there must have been at least a Jewish-Christian tradition incorporating the *eulogia* of the Jewish grace at table and mentioning the election of Israel. The prayers of the Didache, even though they themselves did not form part of the sacramental Eucharist, might yet help us to get an inkling of this, expressing New Testament ideas as they do in archiac terms. (Betz assumes that these prayers were originally Eucharistic but, as they came down to us, were appropriated for use in the Agape.[161])

The East-Syrian Anaphora of Addai and Mari seems likewise to have assimilated a Jewish-Christian tradition, or at any rate a Semitic one. Its triple Sanctus seems to be part of what was assimilated from Judaism into the Eucharistic Prayer in early Christian times. In it the world of angels and the worship of the divine Majesty stand out prominently. Following the investigations of E. C. Ratcliff, several attempts have been made to reconstruct the original form of this Eucharistic Prayer.[162]

Within the Hellenistic world, too, several different types must have existed. Joy in nature and cosmic hymning of praise were favorite themes of Stoic-Platonic philosophers during the early Christian centuries. This mood and attitude could not but exert a powerful influence on Christians and find its way even into their prayer, in particular into the thanksgiving prayer. At any rate, Justin Martyr reports in his Apologia that Christians "worship God and sing songs of praise for creation and for all the means of prosperity, for the condition of peoples, and for the change of seasons" (ch. 13).[163] Even the description of the Godhead as the incomprehensible, infinite, uncreated Being whose nature can be expressed and understood only in negative terms is characteristic of this philosophy. In the Euchologion of Serapion this same language is found.

As has been repeatedly pointed out, the Eucharistic Prayer in the eighth book of the Apostolic Constitutions (Hänggi-Pahl 82–95) is impossibly long and for that reason could not have been used in actual service. Evidently this in itself is a sufficiently clear indication that what we have here is a collection of the texts available at that time, a synthesis of the principal types that had been handed down. In fact, in a basic outline originating in Antioch we may distinguish clearly a cosmological section with a detailed description of nature, an anthropological-religious section recalling the history of salvation from the fall of the first man to God's election and guidance of his people in the old covenant, and (after the Sanctus) a Christological section containing the Institution narrative and fragments of the text of Hippolytus.

3. COMMON TRADITION AND GROWTH OF REGULATION

All this manifests the desire to cultivate a common tradition. And of this disposition we have clear proof in the fact that through centuries of free text composition, certain recognizable traits (that could have been inherited only from the first community of Apostolic times) were everywhere faithfully handed down. Among these are the invitation to prayer and the greeting accompanying it, the doxological conclusion with a reference to God's eternity at its end, and finally remnants of the original language: *Amen, Alleluia, Hosanna.*

Constantine's Edict of Toleration promulgated in 313 A.D. occasioned an influx of great masses of people into the Church. Stricter regulation of the liturgy now became a necessity, not from one administrative center but principally at the hands of each patriarchate on its own initiative. And this is the origin of the many separate, different liturgies. Among them the East Syrian liturgy, which acquired prominence in eastern regions (Mesopotamia, Syria), and later was strongly influenced by the Greek liturgy, spread as far as India, where it is known as the Syro-Malabar rite. In Greek-speaking territory, with Antioch as center, the evolving West Syrian liturgy (the Liturgy of James) among the Jacobites and the Maronites was the parent stock from which the Byzantine liturgy soon branched out, to predominate later throughout the whole East.

Closely related to the Byzantine is the Armenian liturgy. The Egyptian liturgy originated in Alexandria, its center, and branched out later into the Coptic and the Ethiopian liturgies. The Latin West saw the rise of the Roman liturgy (with which that of North Africa is closely related) and those of the Gallic type with branches growing independently of each other: the old Spanish, the Gallican, and the Milanese liturgies. Some authors allude also to a Celtic liturgy, but this can hardly be called an independent branch.

In order to follow the further evolution of the liturgical form and structure of the Mass, we must now examine the several constitutive elements, especially in the context of their historical development in the principal liturgies, with special attention to that of the Roman rite. Such a review should help us to understand the product of that evolution — the Mass in its present liturgical setting — and to appreciate the reforms introduced by Vatican Council II.

In the two-part division of the Mass adopted by Vatican II, the captions *Liturgy of the Word* and *Liturgy of the Eucharist* (CL § 56) can hardly be considered adequate, particularly the first; and the Council text itself added a qualifying "in a certain sense" (*quodammodo*). For in all the traditional liturgies the proclamation of the Word of God is preceded by a "foreword" that cannot be considered an element of the Scripture-reading service and so has been named: Introductory Rites. The introductory rites and the Scripture-reading service together would then constitute the "Fore-Mass," an expression that many present-day writers on liturgy condemn because they fear it implies a derogation of the Scriptural Word.

The term itself, however, expresses no such derogation; it simply denotes the preparatory function that even the Word has in relation to the sacrament. Thus Schillebeeckx assures us that "under a certain aspect the term 'Fore-Mass' should not be considered unfortunate." In the final analysis, the Word too is an integral part of the Eucharistic celebration; and even then it is but a component of a greater thing, the sacrament itself. As Schillebeeckx observes, "The proclamation is a foreword to the decisive Word of the Eucharist." [164]

II. THE INTRODUCTORY RITES

As compared with other ecclesial acts that are related to individual persons (Baptism, for example), the Eucharist is essentially a community celebration. Accordingly, in all the liturgies the Mass prayers are designed with the presence of several persons in view and are meant to constitute at least in part a dialogue. The Eucharistic celebration is the very actualization and manifestation of the Church as community. Normally the Eucharist presupposes the gathering of the faithful in a church, although the mere act of congregating would in itself suffice, for according to Justin's report,

"On the day named for the sun all those who dwell in the city and in the countryside come together."

Over and above this basic presupposition, a developing liturgy had to give thought to imposing a meaningful form and order on the very act of gathering. For it is not a mere secular meeting but a gathering unto God, a gathering called by God himself. Just as he calls the Church, which is essentially a "called community" (*ecclesia*), so too in his behalf the Church leadership calls the Sunday gathering in each place: this is the *synaxis*, the *collecta*, the assembly.

1. Entrance Ritual, Opening Prayers, and Incensing

Accordingly it seemed but proper that when the people had withdrawn from the noise and bustle of the world and passed through the atrium to reach the holy place where the community was going to celebrate the Eucharist, they should await its beginning in silence. It was in this spirit that at the beginning of Christianity in Egypt, the Canones Basilii laid down the instruction (in ch. 95) that psalms should be read while the faithful arrived.[165] A parallel in our own time is the practice in some communities of praying the rosary together before the beginning of a liturgical action.

The wish to give the meeting a more definite starting action led very early in the history of the Roman liturgy to an opening section principally in the form of an entrance ritual, the Introit. The priest passed into the midst of the community already assembled and recited the first prayer. On solemn occasions this became the entrance of the clergy to the acompaniment of the choir: the Introit in the stricter sense.

The Kyrie litany, which spread everywhere after the early sixth century, formed a kind of transition to and preparation for the priest's first prayer, the Collect. Except for the element of Prayers at the Foot of the Altar and of the Gloria, which as a regular element came at a later stage of development, the same ritual was followed when, on the occasion of a procession, a halt was made to visit a church, or when the bishop or a prelate on an official visitation was solemnly received by the community. The *Pontificale Romanum* in use even today contains such directives in its "Ordo ad Recipiendum Processionaliter Praelatum."

The idea that in the gathering of the community one must enter into God's presence in an attitude of prayer was developed still further in Eastern liturgies. In the Byzantine liturgy the readings are preceded by an "opening" (*enarxis*) consisting of a series of prayers somewhat like our Little Hours. At its center are three psalms (with antiphons), the first two of which are concluded by a short litany recited by the deacon and a prayer said by the priest. On Sundays the third psalm is usually replaced by the chanting of the eight Beatitudes. This Little Hour format has been retained and is clearly recognizable also at the beginning of the East Syrian liturgy (Hanssens 34–37). If the Enarxis of the Byzantine liturgy forms a sort of vestibule before the sanctuary, this vestibule itself is preceded by at least two more "entrance halls." The liturgy opens with a lengthy ritual for the preparation of the offerings (*proskomide*) that have to be carried up to the altar afterward, and this is followed by a ritual of incensing.

The incensing ritual in a variety of forms is common to all Eastern liturgies. The altar, the sanctuary, the nave, the congregation, the clergy are incensed in turn, to the accompaniment of appropriate prayers. In the Byzantine and Maronite liturgies the accompanying prayer is Psalm 50, the "Miserere." From this we may gather the function of incensing for these liturgies: the blessed smoke is intended to signify and awaken sentiments of purification and sanctification. The exact parallel to this in the West is the custom, familiar since the eighth/ninth centuries, of beginning the Sunday Eucharistic service with the sprinkling of holy water on the people to the accompaniment of the initial verse of the same Psalm 50 and the verse "Asperges me."

In pre-Christian times incense and incensing had primarily an apotropaic significance, i.e., it was supposed to have the power to keep demons away. Whatever vestige of superstition survived in the popular mind at the time incensing was introduced into the liturgy, the significance the Church conferred on it is conveyed unmistakably in the words of the accompanying prayer for God's grace to purify us.

In the Coptic Mass great importance is attached to the incensing, and it is repeated in several places. Even the power of instant forgiveness of sins in the manner of a sacrament has been attributed to it (Hanssens 86–91). At the beginning of Mass the incensing is preceded by a solemn penitential prayer in which the priest, with explicit reference to the power given the Apostles to forgive sins (John 20:22-23), prays that the forgiveness of sins may come down upon himself and upon the entire people "from the mouth of the Most Holy Trinity" and "from the mouth" of the Holy Church and of the Twelve Apostles and of all the Saints (Brightman 148f.).

2. DEVELOPMENT OF PENITENTIAL RITES IN THE MASS

Since early times a similar prayer, though with less emphasis on the incensing, has dominated the formal act of penance (*Sedro poenitentiae*) at the beginning of the West Syrian Mass (Hanssens 45f.; Brightman 115f). Moreover, during the preparation for Communion, the Syrian liturgies contain distinctly recognizable forms of a penitential act with the clear expectation of sacramental efficacy.[166]

A penitential rite of one form or another occurring at the beginning of Mass, and usually associated symbolically with the incensing, would thus seem to be a commonly prevailing practice in most (not all) Eastern liturgies. Though the form varies, the idea itself evidently belongs to a very old tradition. Even as early as in the Didache, a confession of sins is prescribed before the Sunday celebration of the Eucharist (14:1).

It is not surprising that the same principle became operative in the West as well and that the entrance ritual of the Roman liturgy was expanded to include a penitential rite, though it never attained the dimensions accorded it in the East. In the West, too, the opening of Mass was not the only place for the expression of penitence, as the present author has demonstrated.[167] The general petition of the Church in the Expositio of the Old Gallican Mass is thought to have a penitential character, for priests and deacons had to prostrate themselves and call down God's forgiveness "for the sins of the people."

It was only after the Roman liturgy spread into Gallo-Frankish territory that the elements of a penitential act emerged at three points: at the beginning of Mass, after the Gospel, and before the Communion. We are not including here the above-mentioned Asperges ritual, which was never considered part of Mass and which has remained in use only on Sundays in parish churches. From the very first, a penitential act occurred at the beginning of

Mass, in the prayers at the foot of the altar; but it was always the priest's private prayer, never extended to include the people.

Since the tenth century, however, a public act of penance modeled on the reconciliation of sinners on Holy Thursday was inserted directly after the readings. Even today the Caeremoniale Episcoporum depicts it as a solemn act (2:39 and also 2:8.50): the Confiteor is first chanted and then the bishop imparts the solemn absolution. In a simplified form and adapted to the role of the priest in his community, the same ritual, that is, confession of sins after the Gospel, followed by the priest's "Misereatur" and "Indulgentiam," became the common practice toward the end of the Middle Ages. St. Charles Borromeo, for one, attached great importance to it. In some European dioceses down to our own day the Sunday sermon was concluded with this penitential ritual, even when it was preached outside the Mass.

The third point at which such a penitential rite was performed was during the preparation for Communion. Before the 1960 reform of rubrics, the Confiteor and two formulas of absolution had to be recited if the faithful wished to receive Communion at Mass.

While in the last two cases the penitential rite pertains to the people, the Confiteor of the missal of Pope St. Pius V, that is, the Confiteor recited at the foot of the altar, was the function of the priest with his assistants prior to the present time. A penitential prayer said by the priest at this point occurs for the first time in the eighth century in the Ordo Romanus 17 (Andrieu OR 3:179). In the style of the Apologies, the priest confessed his unworthiness in a wordy improvisation. After the eleventh century it was usually replaced by the Confiteor in dialogue form, as was already customary for a long time in reciting the Office. First the priest makes the act of confession to his assistants, and they in turn make the same act of confession to the priest, the response each time being the "Misereatur." In conclusion, the priest recites the "Indulgentiam," the formula with which sacramental absolution also was given before the ascendancy of Scholastic theology. Evidently the intention was at least not to rule out a sacramental interpretation of the act. For this reason the priest sometimes added a penance to the "Indulgentiam," as for example an Our Father.

The Confiteor, which constituted the nucleus of the prayers at the foot of the altar, was soon expanded to include names of saints. Psalm 42 was then prefixed to it, for, with its antiphon,

"I will go to the altar of God" (Introibo ad altare Dei), this psalm was originally meant to be recited along the way to the altar. And it was concluded with the prayer, "Remove from us" (Aufer a nobis).

3. 1969 ORDER OF MASS: ENTRANCE RITUAL AND GREETING

It is against this historical background that we must consider the opening of Mass as detailed in the 1969 Order of Mass (Ordo Missae). Here too provision is made for an opening action under the heading: "Introductory Rites." This opening ritual extends through the Opening Prayer, the priest's first official prayer, which climaxes it and gives it thematic unity. The gathering is now officially constituted as the community that is led by the priest of the Church into God's presence. To some extent the confession of sins stands at the beginning as a negative pole to this confident entrance before God's majesty. For the Church standing before God is a Church made up of sinful men. If the Opening Prayer (the Collect) constitutes the community, congregational singing prepares for and supports this active fellowship.

The chanting starts with the Entrance Antiphon and Psalm, the Introit sung while the priest and his assistants approach the altar. This chant had its origin in the Stational Mass and in the great basilicas of Rome. Since the Secretarium, where the clergy vested for Mass, was as a rule situated close to the entrance of the church (at the end opposite to the apse), on festive occasions the procession of the clergy to the altar was a solemn affair calling for choral accompaniment. The chanting at this point, as also at the Offertory and the Communion, was the responsibility of a group of trained singers, the so-called *schola cantorum*. The text was taken from the Book of Psalms, and the verses were chanted alternately by two sections of the choir.

The Entrance hymn had also another function that has retained its relevance through the centuries and even today. It was meant, especially on feast days, as a kind of overture, to give the pitch and suggest the mood and theme of the occasion — a prelude to create the right atmosphere. The General Instruction of the new Order of Mass (§26) considers it desirable that the people take part in this singing, for such congregational effort is all the more significant as it brings a diversified crowd into the unity of an ecclesial community; and voices united in singing are a telling symbol of a closely knit group.

In order to give sufficient play to this effective symbol, the new regulation approved not only the singing of the psalmody as found in the traditional Graduale Romanum or in the newly compiled Graduale Simplex, but in its stead even "another song appropriate for this part of the Mass, for the day, or for the season," provided its text has been approved by the bishops' conference. This opens a wide range of options, whether from the already existing treasury of Church hymns or from compositions contemporary in word and melody.

When the priest arrives at the altar he salutes it with a kiss, after a custom that has come down from ancient times; in current ritual the altar is kissed not several times, as was done before the recent reform, but only when the priest approaches the altar and again when leaving it at the end of Mass. When the hymn is finished, the priest opens the celebration by greeting the people, as in any gathering. Thus Augustine, e.g., began the celebration of the Eucharist with a salutation, as we read in *The City of God* (22:8, "I greeted the people": *Salutavi populum*).

But with that the parallel with a secular gathering ceases. Since we come together before God and in his name, the greeting must be specifically religious, one conveying a desire for God's blessing, rather along the line of what we find in the Letters of the Apostles or of what was traditionally used in the liturgies. Indeed, the religious character of the Introductory Rites is dramatized also by the sign of the Cross at the very beginning and by the Trinitarian formula associated with the sign since olden times: "In the name of the Father . . ." (Ordo Rom. II; Andrieu OR 2:418, 446).

For this greeting the Order of Mass offers a choice of three formulas: first, the expression with which Paul concludes the Second Letter to the Corinthians (13:13), wishing the faithful "the grace of the Lord Jesus Christ," but so as to direct the eye to God our Father as the source of all grace and to the Holy Spirit as the active principle of its unfolding. In some liturgies this salutation initiates the dialogue before the Eucharistic Prayer.

The second form provided by the Order of Mass, the one with which St. Paul began most of his letters, has the structure of a Roman oration: "The grace and peace of God our Father and the Lord Jesus Christ be with you." The third choice is a form in com-

mon use: "The Lord be with you." This formula, whose wording
too is biblical (see Ruth 2:4), aptly expresses the Lord's presence
in the community gathered together in his name (Matthew 18:20;
28:20).

This is the appropriate moment for the priest, in accordance
with the General Instruction of the Order of Mass (§11), briefly
to "introduce the Mass of the day." On certain occasions a similar
introduction is also permitted before the Readings and the Preface.
The new liturgy has thus assimilated an element that Gallican-type
liturgies (at a different point, to be sure, as after the Readings)
expressed in a formula that was invariable in structure but in content varying with the feast; for example, the Eucharistic section as
a rule began with an address to the people describing the mystery
of the feast and inviting the faithful to respond with appropriate
prayer.

4. PENITENTIAL RITE AND KYRIE

After the priest's greeting and preliminary remarks, the first
major element occurs in the form of the Penitential Rite. What was
formerly a private act on the part of the celebrant in the Prayers
at the Foot of the Altar is now publicly performed by the whole
community. The priest invites the people to admit their sinfulness
before God, in words that in themselves clearly describe the penitential act. This is not, of course, the sacrament of Penance but
simply a confession that we are sinners even while we hope we are
in God's good graces.

This humble confession, which the Lord expects of "his own"
(see Luke 18:13), makes us less unworthy to approach the sacred
mysteries. It is for this reason that, of the two traditional responses
to the confession of sins — the "Misereatur" and "Indulgentiam" —
the priest now pronounces only the first, since according to an old
tradition even a lay person could recite this form as a petition for
God's mercy upon the penitent, whereas the second one had served
for centuries as the formula of sacramental absolution. Similar
reasoning supports the practice of reciting the Confiteor only once,
even though it is still addressed to the congregation ("to you, my
brothers and sisters").

The shorter, simpler version of the Confiteor now prescribed
is closer to the oldest Confiteor formulas. The invocation of saints'
names, often senselessly multiplied during medieval times and then

itemized in parallel lists in the two sections of the Confiteor, has now been reduced to the minimum. Moreover, the oldest formulas phrased this invocation of saints only in general terms and attached it only to the first part of the formula: "and all the saints" (*et omnibus sanctis*); the intention was to bring out the public character of the confession. What developed later on as the second part either did not exist originally or was addressed only to the Church on earth and to her minister, the priest, as a petition for prayer: "pray for me" (*orare pro me*).

The Order of Mass does not restrict the penitential act to this Confiteor formula, but provides alternatives for invoking God's mercy. One of these utilizes the "Kyrie eleison" because of the plea for mercy it contains, and expands it each time as an address to Christ, with an appeal to his coming as Redeemer; the actual wording is left to the celebrating priest.

The Kyrie itself has not been dropped. The Greek wording preserved in its Latin context points to its origin. As early as the fourth century, *Kyrie eleison* was the Greek Christians' response to every petition in the litany recited by the deacon. The Synod of Vaison in 529 bears witness that already the "blessed custom" of the "kyrie eleison" ("the sweet and very salutary custom": *dulcis ac nimium salutaris consuetudo*) had spread everywhere in the West, even to Italy and to Rome (can. 3; Mansi 8:727). There is substantial evidence that such a litany was already in use under Pope Gelasius (492–96). Thus, in the litany handed down as the "Prayer of Gelasius" (*Deprecatio Gelasii*, PL 101:560f.), every petition is followed by the invocation *Kyrie eleison*.[168] At the time of Pope St. Gregory the Great (590–604) there existed side by side with the full liturgical form, the custom of repeating merely the invocations *Kyrie eleison* and *Christe eleison* alternately.

Even as a simple invocation in which all human needs and intentions could be covered, the Kyrie eleison contained a built-in temptation to accumulation or repetition in some "mystical" number. In fact, the Byzantine breviary has a twelvefold and even a fortyfold "Kyrie eleison." No specific number of invocations was prescribed in the older Roman liturgy. According to the first Roman Ordo (end of the seventh century), the litanizing carried on until the Pope gave a signal to stop (Andrieu OR 2:84). A century later the number was fixed at nine, in the sequence in which it was known until the most recent liturgical reform (*Kyrie eleison*, three times; *Christe eleison*, three times; *Kyrie eleison*, three times).

While the Kyrie eleison was not intended originally in a Trinitarian sense — nor does the context warrant it — after the ninth century this interpretation became predominant at the hands of liturgists and spiritual writers carried away on a wave of devotion that was cresting at the time. From the very beginning, however, *Kyrie* meant Christ, and from St. Paul's time it was a popular name for Christ. He was being invoked at the beginning of his celebration; he was, so to speak, called into the midst of the community that had assembled in his name.

The 1969 Order of Mass provides for the priest's threefold invocation and its repetition each time by the people; this is a simplification compared to the former ritual of three-times-three invocations. On the other hand, there is nothing in the General Instruction (§ 30) to prevent increasing the number of invocations or even expanding the texts. The possibility of expanding them into a confession ritual has already been mentioned above. During the late Middle Ages it became common practice to augment the Kyrie invocation by way of "troping." Kyrie tropes comprise almost half the contents of volume 47 of the collection *Analecta Hymnica.* [169]

5. GLORIA

While the Kyrie, particularly when said as a genuine prayer, is more invocation than hymn, the Gloria was conceived from the very start as a hymn or song of praise modeled on the canticles and psalms of the Bible and following no fixed metric rules. It is, moreover, a priceless heritage from the earliest period of Christian hymnody. The Greek version appears as early as about the year 380 in the Apostolic Constitutions; and the New Testament Codex Alexandrinus (fifth century) contains it almost exactly as in its present wording.

In the early Middle Ages the Gloria was used somewhat in the manner in which we use the Te Deum today, as a solemn hymn for feast days. In Rome, however, quite early in liturgical history and certainly before the sixth century, the Gloria found its way into the Mass for Sundays and feast days, though at first only when the Pope celebrated it. Only in Frankish territory did it become a regular element of the Mass. At first it was thought of as a congregational hymn and hence was set to simple melodies; but soon it was providing the text for more elaborate, virtuoso compositions and also was augmented by means of tropes.

As in other early Christian hymns, a biblical phrase introduces the Gloria. The popular liturgical understanding, "Glory *be* to God in the highest, and on earth peace to men of good will," is not quite faithful to the Scriptural intent, for God's glory at the mystery of Christ's birth is to be understood in the indicative, as a statement of fact (*is*), rather than in the optative, as a wish (*be*); and the "good will" is not the good will of men, but of God, i.e., God's merciful grace. So then in the biblical text it would be "Peace to men who have found grace with God." In any event, the hymn accords perfectly with the liturgical context: we have indeed come together in order to glorify God anew.

The Gloria is composed of two strophes, one praising God and one invoking Christ. Its structure is the same as that of the Te Deum; in fact, it portrays the basic structure of the Christian message of salvation: "Eternal life is this: to know you, the only true God, and him whom you have sent, Jesus Christ" (John 17:3). If the Gloria is sometimes viewed as an ode to the Trinity, this is admissable only insofar as the Triune God is meant in the first strophe. As a matter of fact, in a large sector of tradition, e.g., in the Antiphonary of Bangor (*c.* 690), even this first strophe ends with the expanded phrase, "God, almighty Father, Lord, the only-begotten Son, Holy Spirit of God" (*Deus Pater omnipotens, Domine Fili unigenite, Sancte Spiritus Dei*). The act of glorifying God is performed in the simplest form, i.e., through a series of expressions of praise. More than that mere mortals cannot do. Perhaps the most striking thing about it is the idea that we "thank" God for his great glory. After all, the fact that God has revealed his glory to us in nature and in history is the most important basis not only for our adoration but also for our gratitude.

In the second strophe the invocations to Christ begin with a twofold series of expressions eulogizing him in his divinity and in his humanity. The designation "Lamb of God" has particularly rich overtones. Following closely is a short litany in which John the Baptist's reference to his redemptive function (John 1:29) as well as the Apocalypse motif of the Lamb's victory are woven in. The succeeding expressions of praise have an authentic early-Christian coloring, with their abundant allusions to the abhorrence of paganism, with its many gods and heroes.

The attribute "holy" (*hagios*), moreover, was often predicated of divine beings; and *kyrios* or Lord was a term applied by several cults to their special cult heroes. In particular, ancient emperor worship gave the name "Lord" (*kyrios, dominus*) to the emperor. As opposed to this, the hymn glorifies Christ as the only Lord, in the spirit of 1 Corinthians 8:6 and Philippians 2:11. In the final verse of the second strophe the Holy Spirit is mentioned along with the Father, thus concluding the hymn fittingly on a Trinitarian note. There is good reason to call the hymn the Great Doxology.

6. COLLECT

The climax of the prayer movement in the Introductory Rites is the Opening Prayer, or, more descriptively as in the (Latin) Ordo Missae, the *Collecta*, i.e., gathering, summing up. While the expression first became current in the Gallic liturgies as a summing up (probably via the *Institutes* of John Cassian; see 2:7, "to gather up the prayers" — *precem colligere*), it appears also in other positions at the end of a division: as a conclusion to the petitions, for example, or at the end of the Offertory or Communion.[170] In the new Order of Mass the Opening Prayer gains in prestige by reason of the fact that once again, as originally, only one such prayer is offered, and there is no second or third round of requests or commemorations. How inseparable the *Collecta* is from its context and how thoroughly it is integrated with the Introductory Rites is also brought home to us in another little touch: the salutation *Dominus vobiscum* no longer immediately precedes it; for the people are addressed at the very beginning of the whole unit. The Prayer is now preceded only by the simplest and shortest form of invitation: "Let us pray."

In other liturgies this invitation is usually more wordy, often sketching the substance of the Prayer or elaborating on the day's motif. This happens too in the Roman liturgy on certain occasions, as for example at the Solemn Prayers of Good Friday. On occasions, too, the Roman liturgy retains also the ancient tradition of inserting the "Flectamus genua" (Let us kneel) in the invitation to prayer; before the priest utters the prayer he asks the congregation to kneel down and pray silently for a moment.

According to a regulation considered important enough to be passed in the Council of Nicea in 325 (can. 20), this gesture of kneeling was to be dropped on Sundays and during the Easter season, when the community prayed standing out of respect for the risen Lord. But the pause for silent prayer announced by the words *Flectamus genua* was by no means discouraged. In the new liturgy the pause comes back into its own, and in the General Instruction (§32) its significance at this point is described: "The priest invites the people to pray, and together they spend some moments [*parumper*] in silence so they may realize that they are in God's presence and may make their petitions."

The very function of summing up prevents the content of the Opening Prayer from being more than general in nature. The important thing here is that the community appears before God by virtue of the very fact that the priest, acting as its mouthpiece, humbly and reverently directs the petition toward God. Ever since set texts have been composed for this prayer and compiled in liturgical books, regulations concerning form and content have necessarily and naturally evolved. Thus, e.g., on every occasion, even saints' and martyrs' feasts, the prayer is to be addressed to God himself.

Again, it must involve *praying* in the full, classic sense of the word: raising the heart and mind to God. Only exceptionally may it be addressed even to Christ, and then only in the few instances retained in the renewed liturgy as having originated in a later tradition; for normally Christ must be invoked only as Mediator at the end of the prayer. Unlike in the Greek liturgies, which so often seek to capture God's inscrutable essence with many oblique descriptions, the approach in the Roman tradition is brief and restrained: "God almighty; Eternal God." The very reticence on God's greatness and majesty is eloquent. Only on feasts and special occasions is the so-called relative predication ("God who . . . ," *Deus qui* . . .) added to the address in the Latin version. After the name of God has thus been invoked, the mystery commemorated on the day or the special basis for our confidence is mentioned in an attitude of praise and worship.

7. Genre and Character of the Collect

As for the literary genre, the Opening Prayer is cast in the style of dignified address. In the whole history of liturgy, that record of man's endeavor to devote to God's glory the best that human art can achieve in materials, tone and word, there is hardly an instance of an Opening Prayer in poetic form. So too, the delivery never goes beyond a plainchant recitative (or: *récitatif*) even though its vernacular is stylized as in the Latin collects. We can and should praise God in song, but when we place ourselves directly and immediately in the presence of his divine majesty, all prolixity of human language collapses.

On the other hand, it would be futile even to attempt to invent a sacral style. While its language does not have to be the flat idiom of everyday life, neither should it be altogether removed from the ordinary experience of men; it should be like the language of formal discourse on a solemn occasion. In any event one refinement of stylization has been preserved from older tradition: the priest recites the Prayer with hands extended (*manibus extensis*) in a gesture of supplication.

The Opening Prayer is a petition in character. It could be an act of adoration and thanksgiving as well, but then thanksgiving is the theme of the whole Mass celebration. In the wording of the petition, which must be as general as the content, the Latin formula betrays a weakness for antithesis: human struggle and divine help, ephemeral deeds and eternal verities, earthly misery and eternal blessedness. One might say that the necessity to formulate a fresh prayer in each case resulted in a number of compositions that are richer in word than in content.

While the Prayer is a petition, the moment comes for praise as well, and this especially in the concluding words, in the implication that our humble prayer has its place in the economy of salvation that God has planned for us. Our prayer ascends to God "through Jesus Christ," a modality that at the same time reflects the basis of our confidence: *Christ is of us as well as of God*. The ancient Latin formula clearly brings out Christ's relation to both parties: he is "our Lord," we are his people; and he is "your Son."

Christ is the bridge between men and God. But he is in "your glory" as the first of our race. He lives (Hebrews 11:25; Apoc. 1:18), he reigns (Apoc. 5; 17:14), "in the unity of the Holy Spirit." This last phrase says in fact more than that the Son reigns "with" the Holy Spirit. The reference is to the unity of which the Holy Spirit is the foundation (see Eph. 4:5). In this context we may understand the unity between the Father and the Son, while at the same time adverting to the further dimension of unity with the Church Triumphant in which Christ lives and reigns. Without being explicitly stated, the mystery of the Trinity is clearly implied.

The expression "through Christ," characteristic of the Latin collect, is an ancient Christian heritage with its source in the New Testament writings (Rom. 4:8; 16:27; 2 Cor. 1:20; Hebrews 13:15; 1 Peter 2:5; Jude 25). In the early Christian era it was common to all liturgical prayer until, as a result of the convulsions in the fourth century, most of the Eastern rites discarded it, except for a small vestige in a few fugitive prayers. "Through Christ" affirms that we no longer stand directly before God in all our human weakness and helplessness; Christ is with us as our Mediator, our Advocate, our High Priest. It is through him that we now enter God's presence.

Hence, in older wordings of the liturgical prayer, petitions and praise are frequently offered "through our High Priest Jesus Christ." Moreover, in the minds of the early Christians the "through" of mediation was not merely or necessarily associated with the advocate through whom one's petitions were conveyed to someone in power. When we relay a letter to a distant friend, we say of the messenger, "Through the kindness of — —." In this sense, when the Christian community prays, it speaks to God our Father through him who has gone before us.

III. THE LITURGY OF THE WORD

In all the liturgies the first part of the Church's Eucharistic celebration consists of readings from Sacred Scripture. The light of the Word must precede the mystery of faith and illumine the way to it. But it must not be just any random reading but one that will be an instrument whereby the Church can fulfill an essential part of her mission, which is to preach the Gospel without ceasing. This is why in all traditional liturgies the readings always culminate in a passage from one of the four Gospels.

1. CHOICE OF READINGS AND CHANTS

As for the antecedents to the Gospel, each liturgy has its own procedure. The Syrian liturgies have adhered to the Synagogue custom of choosing one passage from the Law and one from the prophets, and adding one New Testament reading not from the Gospels. The liturgy of the Jacobites has in most cases as many as three selections from the Old Testament and three more from the New. A pattern of one Old Testament reading before two of the New was familiar in still other liturgies, such as the Byzantine originally, or Gallic types in the West; only during the Easter season was a single passage from the New Testament read.

The principle that before the celebration of the Eucharist — the Easter Sacrament — only the New Testament should be read, took root at a very early time in Egypt only. The Roman liturgy then followed this usage for the Sundays after Pentecost; thus the Gospel was always preceded by an "Epistle," a reading from the Letters. In some places, however, by way of exception, even non-biblical passages were read, for example (as in Milan) on a martyr's feast day the account (*passio*) of his suffering and death.

Since as a rule the faithful came together for the Eucharist only on Sundays and feast days, the selection for the reading had to be limited to the most important books of Sacred Scripture. There probably never was a *lectio continua* in the strict sense of the term.[171] The Syrian method of choosing the readings seems to have come closest to this ideal, as Baumstark suggests.[172] Moreover, the traditional pericope catalogues and lectionaries do show in several cases longer sequences of passages taken from single books, but never a lengthy, complete sequence without abridgment. Thus in the Byzantine liturgy the readings for the first successive seventeen Sundays after Pentecost are taken from Matthew and for the next sixteen Sundays from Luke; but these readings are passages selected beforehand. In the Roman liturgy the old formula announcing the Gospel reading, "Continuation of the holy Gospel" (*Sequentia sancti evangelii*), is reminiscent of one or another form of schedule of pericopes that must have been followed once upon a time.

At a very early time certain books of Sacred Scripture were set apart for the rotating seasons in the Church calendar. In Antioch the pre-Easter readings were taken from the Books of Moses; elsewhere the Book of Job was read during Holy Week, and the Book

of Jonas during Eastertime. The Acts of the Apostles was ear-
marked for the Easter season.[173]

Since the reading cannot, of course, be abruptly inserted in
the liturgy without a proper contextual framework, it is preceded
by an appropriate preparatory formula and followed by another to
complete it. In addition there is the homily to explain its meaning,
and further, by a liturgical instinct or common custom, the hymn
to follow should echo the spirit of the reading, which is then
rounded off with prayer. In the Byzantine liturgy this hymn usually
comes first, in the so-called *prokeimenon* ("that which is set
forth"). The non-Greek Eastern liturgies insert a preparatory
prayer. Sometimes even before the first reading a liturgical salutation greets the faithful and asks them to be attentive to what is
coming.

In the Roman liturgy, according to an ancient practice, the
reading in the Mass as well as in the Office is usually rounded off
with a psalm sung as a response. A cantor specially trained for the
purpose steps forth with his *cantatorium* or book of chants (the
Church's oldest hymnbook) and intones the psalm; in response
the people sing a refrain from the psalm. For chanting the psalm
the cantor was permitted to go as far as the ambo (the reader's
pulpit), but as time went on, he could go only *up to* the highest
step, since this top step was reserved for the Gospel reading. He
was to remain standing on a lower step (*gradus*), whence the chant
came to be known as the *Gradual*. As a rule the refrain was taken
from the psalm chanted by the cantor, but this was replaced by
the Alleluia with regard to the psalm or verse immediately preceding
the Gospel. This Alleluia before the Gospel has its origin in an ancient tradition, for it recurs in one form or another in every liturgy
except the Ethiopian.[174]

2. THE GOSPEL

From very early times the Gospel reading was given a place
of honor. Distinction was shown first of all in the "packaging" of
the book. Manuscripts of the Gospels illuminated with costly silver
and gold lettering on purple foil and bound in ivory covers were
used on feast days. While the other readings might be entrusted to
a lector, the Gospel had to be read by no less than a deacon in
Orders. Although liturgical regulation required that a distinction
be made between the office of celebrant and the ministry of the

reader or lector, yet on major feasts, in the Byzantine liturgy, among others, the celebrating priest or even the bishop was known to have read the Gospel.

In the Roman liturgy the lector was led to the ambo in a small-scale procession, with acolytes bearing candles and incense, and torches and bowls of fire (MRR 1:68, n. 7); all this was by way of conferring on the book of the Gospels the reverence reserved by ancient court ceremonial for the ruler when he made a public appearance. St. Jerome must have had this usage in mind when he wrote (Contra Vigilantium, ch. 7) that even in broad daylight candles were lighted when the Gospel was read. Its parallel in the Eastern liturgies is the Little Entry, in which the book of the Gospels is solemnly borne to the altar before the first reading.

The old Expositio of the sixth century Gallican Mass interprets the procession with the Gospel book as the triumph of Christ, who now ascends his throne to proclaim the "gifts of life" (*dona vitae*; p. 14f. in Quasten edition). The acclamation "Glory to you, O Lord" (*Gloria tibi, Domini*), which occurs for the first time in this Expositio, expresses the conviction of Christ's presence in the Gospel, as does also the later and still widespread "Praise to you, O Christ" (*Laus tibi, Christe*).

While during the other readings the faithful remained seated, as early as in the fourth century the custom of listening to the Gospel in a standing position was in force in the Eastern rites. With the ninth century the sign of the Cross, made by everyone present, came into use in the West. Before long this gave way to the threefold sign of the Cross, signifying that our mind is open to receive Christ's word, that we confess it with our lips, and above all that we intend to take it to heart.

Obviously the readings are meant to be understood by the faithful. For over a thousand years, apart from the mission sermon and the instruction of catechumens, the Church knew of no other way of instructing the faithful than through the Sunday Mass, and above all, through the readings incorporated in its very structure. So then, if this catechetical function was to be fully realized, the Church could not stop with a careful selection of readings.

On occasion the Gallic liturgy even introduced a harmony of the Gospels, so that on feast days a Gospel reading might consist of several passages culled from different sources on the principle of centonization (a kind of anthologizing; MRR 1:404). The

ambo, or lector's pulpit, was introduced with a view to making it
easier for the people to follow the reader.

3. THE LANGUAGE GAP

As during the course of the Middle Ages the gap widened almost everywhere between the spoken language and the written
language of the sacred books and of the lessons read to the people,
the Church was faced with a serious dilemna: Which was to have
priority, understanding of the readings, or preservation of the texts
in the language hallowed by centuries of usage? The Roman (and
the East Syrian) liturgy chose the second alternative, while most
of the Eastern rites switched to the vernacular at least for the
readings — if they did not go all the way with Patriarch Balsamon
(d. after 1195), who advocated the adoption of the mother tongue
for the whole liturgy. Thus in the Coptic and West Syrian liturgies,
the lessons are read in Arabic, while the rest of the liturgical texts
remain in their respective vernaculars.

While the Roman liturgy kept to Latin, the consequent loss
of touch with the living languages was compensated for to some
extent by the sermon, which received new impetus, particularly in
the Romance countries, with the emergence of the mendicant orders
of St. Dominic and St. Francis. Moreover, the people, lettered and
unlettered, were well instructed by means of the sculpture, painting,
tapestry, poetry, stained glass, illuminating, troping, miracle plays,
and the minor arts to which they were exposed in their places of
worship, and which were all thoroughly impregnated with the
Scripture story.

The Sunday Epistle and Gospel were read in the mother
tongue before the sermon, but the other texts of the Mass formulary
became for the people little more than a symbol, an action of the
celebrant alone, and after the thirteenth century he had to read
them even when they were being chanted by subdeacon and deacon
at high Mass. If the Latin texts had by now become to a goodly
degree unintelligible to the people, the setting of these texts to
formally sophisticated compositions, which were a far cry from
those plain recitative chants of early times, operated to reduce the
distance separating the people from the language of the liturgy.

Another compensation was found in the further enrichment of
the ceremonial surrounding the Gospel reading. The Gospel,
honored ever more highly, was read from the right side ("right"

in relation to the bishop's chair or cathedra) or the "Gospel side" as opposed to the left or "Epistle side." The Gospel alone could be proclaimed from the exalted height of the ambo; accordingly, the reading stand was transformed into the "eagle stand," so that the book rested on the outstretched wings of an eagle (symbol of St. John).

This same mentality was behind the erection of two ambos in larger churches from the tenth century on. Before long, however, people began to realize that the ambo had lost its meaning. So away went the ambo, and in its place came the preacher's pulpit towering high in the nave of the church. After that it was but logical that the priest did not stand facing the people for the liturgical readings. Even at high Mass the subdeacon had to read the Epistle facing the altar.

4. THE LITURGICAL REFORM

One of the first steps of Vatican II's liturgical reform was to correct this whole situation; this it did with the Instruction of September 26, 1964, §§49–52. With the restoration of the vernacular liturgy, the ambo has reappeared also, or at any rate a special place for the readings. The whole complex of the Liturgy of the Word underwent a transformation.

According to the mind of the Council, richer food should be offered to the faithful at "the table of God's Word" (CL §51). A decree of August 5, 1969, provided for an adequate selection of readings from one of the three Synoptic Gospels for Sundays outside the two liturgical seasons, the whole cycle covering three years; John's Gospel was to be read during certain liturgical seasons. Further, in addition to the reading usually borrowed from the Acts and the Letters of the Apostles, provision is now made for a third reading for Sundays and feast days, this time from the Old Testament. The pericopes for this third reading must always be selected for their relation to the Gospel of the day and should throw light on salvation history from promise to fulfillment. It is left to each national conference of bishops to decide on the feasibility of this third reading.

The spirit that prompted the use of the mother tongue is also behind the renewed practice of giving to the people the responses hitherto reserved for the Mass server, especially those after the readings: the "Praise to you, Lord Jesus Christ" (*Laus tibi, Christe*) as well as the "Thanks be to God" (*Deo gratias*) in use among Christians for various occasions as early as the fourth century.

The Responsorial Psalm between the readings, too, has felt the hand of reform. This response should always follow the first (Old Testament) reading and relate to it. The Alleluia verse has its place between the Epistle (First — or Second, as the case may be — Reading) and the Gospel, and is dropped during Lent. Since these two chants have more than a merely decorative function, nor are they merely a musical flourish to an action but are in themselves components in the Mass structure, it is not permitted to substitute other hymns chosen at random from popular hymn books.

5. HOMILY

The last unit in the Liturgy of the Word is the homily. The Word proclaimed in the readings had been written in a cultural milieu of the distant past and in an idiom with which we are no longer in touch. The task of the homily is to clothe it in today's idiom and unfold its relevance to the men and women of today. The homily has also a mystagogical function: that of introducing the congregation to the celebration of the sacred mysteries, and as such serving as the link connecting God's Word as proclaimed in the readings with the Eucharistic celebration. Therefore the homily is not an arbitrary interruption of the liturgy, but is rather an integral and organic part of a fully developed act of worship.

For this reason the homily figures in the oldest description of the Mass we have — in Justin Martyr — and flourished particularly during the time of the great Fathers of the Church. Curiously enough, however, there is no mention of it in the documents of the Eastern liturgies or in the older Ordines Romani that provide a description of the Mass; the Coptic Mass is an exception (Brightman 158). In the West the Expositio of the Gallican Mass (15–16) adverts to the "homilies of the saints" (*homiliae sanctorum*) that should be given to the people "in a more accessible style" (*apertiore sermone*). The Synod of Vaison in 529 laid down the ruling that ordinarily the priest should preach, but that when this was not possible the deacon might read a homily (Can. 3). To some extent the Middle Ages carried on the homiletic tradition, but the textual explanation of the liturgy was often replaced by an exposition of the Creed, the Lord's Prayer, or the Ten Commandments. While the revival of preaching in the late Middle Ages had its inspiration almost entirely outside the Mass, still the description of the Mass in the Pius V Missal mentions the sermon after the Gospel as being feasible (Ritus servandus 6:6).

The Constitution on the Sacred Liturgy rehabilitates the homily as "part of the liturgy itself" (CL §52). On Sundays and feast days it may be omitted only "for a serious reason." Its substance should be not merely an exegesis of the text, but an explanation of the mysteries of faith related to the readings and liturgy of the day, especially during the two liturgical seasons. And at all times the homily should apply these mysteries to "the norms of Christian life."

The Instruction of September 26, 1964, interprets this prescription in a somewhat wider sense, permitting even a series of sermons by way of exception, provided they are connected in some way with the course of the liturgical year (§ 55). While it is self-evident that the homily during Mass is not the only form of preaching, it is the most usual form in which the faithful are offered the spiritual nourishment of God's Word; in a goodly measure it is their "daily bread."

6. Creed

That the people should respond with a "Profession of Faith" to the proclamation of God's Word is too obvious to require comment. Soon after the Credo was introduced into the Mass by Patriarch Timotheus (d. 517), it gained wide currency throughout the Eastern Churches. In these liturgies, however, it occurs not at the end of the readings but at the beginning of the Eucharistic Prayer as a kind of preliminary step. Clearly such an arrangement was prompted by the deep and vivid realization that the Credo, as indeed the Eucharistic Prayer itself, contains the substance of the entire history of salvation, if only in the form of a confession of faith.

In the West the Credo appeared for the first time (and complete with the *Filioque*) at the Spanish national Synod of 589. After that it turned up in Ireland (the Stowe Missal) and, by way of Alcuin, in England (York). About the year 800 (and probably again with Alcuin's intervention), it came into use at the palace chapel in Aachen, and from there it spread throughout the whole Carolingian kingdom. When in 1014 Emperor Henry II came to Rome for his coronation, he was surprised to find that the Credo was missing from the Mass, and thereupon had it introduced through the offices of Pope Benedict VII.[175]

The Eastern text of the Credo reflects its Eastern origin, and it was composed with as little view to inclusion in the Mass as was the Apostles' Creed of Roman origin (Symbolum Apostolicum). In a still simpler form it was the baptismal creed of Jerusalem that Cyril of Jerusalem expounded to his catechumens about the year 350 (Catecheses 7–18). Around 374 it appeared in Epiphanius of Salamis (Ancoratus, ch. 118). It was here that the clauses on Christ as the Son of God and on the Holy Spirit were added to counteract the Arian heresy; and with that the text of the creed crystallized substantially into its present form. It is called the Nicaeno-Constantinopolitanum or simply Nicaenum (Nicene) Creed because it contains the articles of faith defined in the two councils of 325 and 381. It was, however, solemnly ratified only at the Council of Chalcedon (451), whence also it was disseminated throughout the East; as could be expected, the several Churches developed their own variations corresponding to their different liturgical traditions (Brightman 574).

The Byzantine liturgy and the Roman liturgy kept to the singular form of the original baptismal creed: *Credo* (I believe). Each individual person must confess his faith, just as in Baptism. Nevertheless, certain Eastern rites introduced the plural form *Credimus* (copied for some inexplicable reason in the American Order of Mass). In the basic text of Jerusalem as well as in the Roman version, the credal affirmations are worded primarily in biblical terms, e.g., the teaching on God, on Christ and his work, on the Church's spiritual riches. In fact, in the Eastern creed a biblical quotation from Paul's Letter to the Ephesians (4:5f.) determines the basic framework: One God, one Lord (in the text of Jerusalem, also: one Spirit), one Church, one Baptism.

By virtue of its anti-heretical formulation the Eastern text had primacy and authority even in the West during the early Middle Ages, so that it could hold its own against the Apostles' Creed. Even the efforts of post-Vatican II reformers in behalf of the Apostolicum have been unsuccessful. What dictated this preference over the Apostolicum, apart from ecumenical considerations, was apparently the realization that the capitally important profession of Christ's divinity in the Roman liturgy should remain well counterbalanced against the necessary new emphasis (which the sacrifice of the Mass in particular calls for) on Christ's humanity and on his human-high-priestly role.

The Credo was inserted into the Mass with the regulation that it should be recited by the whole congregation. The Eastern Churches followed this ruling, though among the Greeks it was recited by one person as representing the community. In the West, too, all joined in the recitation. As Bishop Herard of Tours puts it in his Capitula of 858 (Hardouin 5:541) the Credo, along with the Gloria, Sanctus, and Kyrie, is the responsibility of the congregation ("it is to be sung by all," *a cunctis canatur*).

The very fact that the Credo was to be said by everyone presupposed that it should be projected in a plain recitative tone, but since the people could not cope with the Latin text, their role was soon transferred to the professional singers of the *chorus clericorum* ("the clerical singing-group"). Vocal polyphony seized upon the Credo as the vehicle of some of its most sublime tours-de-force. No doubt the mysteries of our faith were glorified this way, but in the process it was overlooked or forgotten that this glorification of the mysteries was the very *raison d'être* of the whole Eucharistic Prayer of the Mass. Happily the restoration of the people's language has here also restored a sound order of things.

7. GENERAL INTERCESSIONS

Just as the Introductory Rites conclude with the priest's Prayer (Collect), so the Liturgy of the Word is brought to a close with the Prayer of the Faithful or *General Intercessions* (*oratio universalis*). Some such concluding prayer was in general use during the early days of the Church, the more so since in those times the celebration of the Eucharist did not necessarily follow the Liturgy of the Word. The close connection of these petitions with the proclamation of the Word preceding it is affirmed in the Euchologion of Serapion, who captions it as the prayer recited "on getting up from the homily." In the Roman liturgy the Solemn Petitions of Good Friday, which follow the reading of the Passion, are a precious remnant of ancient tradition and a classic of their type. But with the limitations of the ordinary Eucharistic celebration, the General Intercessions could hardly be expected to take on such grand proportions.

In the Egyptian liturgies from ancient times the General Intercessions have had three units (*hai treis*) identical in structure, each consisting of a call to prayer, invocations of the faithful, and the priest's prayer (Brightman 121f.; 160.; 223–25). In the Byzantine liturgy, too, this three-unit structure is discernible, but with this difference that the deacon's litany stands out more prominently than the priest's prayer (375–82). The primary thrust of this prayer, as may be seen in Justin's account, is always the great, general intentions: for the Church, for bishop and clergy, for peace in the world, for a good harvest, for country and for city, for the sick and the poor and the needy, for the dead, for the forgiveness of sins, for a holy death.

In the Roman Mass vestiges of the Prayer of the Faithful perdured to the waning of the patristic period. Its desuetude seems to have coincided with the introduction of the Kyrie litany, which somehow came to be looked upon as a substitute for it and was thereafter shifted to the beginning of the Mass. In the Eastern rites, in any case, the Kyrie had always been an integral part of the Prayer of the Faithful. Similarly, in several versions of the Gelasian Sacramentary we find an otherwise inexplicable concluding oration between the Collect and the "Super oblata." In the Gallican rite, on the other hand, the Prayer of the Faithful must have been so popular that even after this rite had been replaced by the Roman observance, a substantial remnant of the old heritage was preserved and new texts were also composed. In his collection of ancient canons, Regino of Prüm (d. 915) reproduced a prayer of the old type, in several parts (De Synodalibus Causis 190; PL 132:224).

In France up to the present century the *prières du prône* (prayers of the sermon), derived from an ancient tradition, usually had a fixed, two-part structure and were recited after the Gospel. As Père Gy brings out, their significance and their pastoral value have been rediscovered only in our own time.[176] Elsewhere, as in Germany, there remains only the memory that after the sermon (if it had been preached with the Mass) any prayers could be recited, either by the priest alone or by the whole congregation, and that these were usually just thrown together without any order or form. But from about 1940, under the influence of the Eastern tradition, the liturgical movement in these countries has been attempting to revive a genuine Prayer of the Faithful modeled on the ancient form.[177]

Efforts in this direction have left their mark in article 53 of the Constitution on the Sacred Liturgy. The basic outline of the

Prayer of the Faithful as indicated there has been repeated in the 1969 Ordo Missae, except that the name was changed to General Intercessions (General Instruction §§ 45–47). The Prayer of the Faithful should not merely echo the readings and the homily that have just preceded (as in fact often happened in an over-hasty development before the Council). Neither should it become an occasion for the free improvisations of the participants' reactions, as might be the temptation, say, at a Mass celebrated in a small group or in a home. Rather, it should be a prayer of petition for the Church and for the world. The Order of Mass does, however, expressly make provision for the addition of special intentions.

For the rest, one feature about the General Intercessions is that no official regulations have been laid down concerning their wording. A 1965 Vatican publication entitled "The Common Prayer or Prayer of the Faithful" (*De oratione communi seu fidelium*) which contains rules and examples was meant only as a guideline and has no binding force; the actual form is left to the imagination of local talent and to episcopal directives; only general directions are spelled out. For a basic form we have the model of the litany: invocations and some form of response alternating between leader and community. The priest should pronounce the invitatory to the intercessions and, importantly, he should, in accordance with ancient liturgical law, collect and sum it all up in his concluding prayer.

IV. OFFERTORY

With the Offertory the chief part of the Mass begins. If we consider it separately from the Canon, we do so not because it has an importance of its own. Actually, to draw a parallel with what we have already seen, the Offertory is to the Canon what the Introductory Rites are to the whole Mass. Vatican II calls this part of the Mass "the Liturgy of the Eucharist" in contradistinction to the Liturgy of the Word. As distinguished from the Mass of the Catechumens, it has also been traditionally called "the Mass of the Faithful." According to ancient Church prescription the catechumens were permitted to hear the Word of God and even participate in the Prayer of the Faithful that followed; but at the celebration of the Eucharist only the baptized were allowed to be present, since this part of the Mass came under the "discipline of the secret" (*disciplina arcani*).

From this point forward, no longer the bishop's cathedra or the priest's sedile or the lector's ambo, but rather the altar is the locus of the Eucharistic celebration. The priest now goes to the altar, and remains there for the rest of the celebration. In many of the Eastern liturgies the act of approaching the altar became more than just a change of position; it constituted a liturgical act of its own, surrounded with a cluster of prayers.[178]

1. The Offertory in the Eastern Liturgy

Particularly impressive is this ritual in the episcopal liturgy of the East Syrians (Malabars and Chaldeans). After the Liturgy of the Word, conducted at the raised platform (*bema*) in the middle of the church with the bishop presiding, the priest appointed for the purpose now leaves the bishop and goes up to the sanctuary, praying the while and halting three times en route for a deep inclination. Three times he genuflects before the altar and kisses it, first to his right, then to his left, and finally in the center (Raes 83). Likewise in the Roman Ordo (Andrieu OR 2:93), we find the rubric of saluting the altar with a kiss at this point, as at the beginning of the Mass.

The next item on the agenda is the preparation of the bread and wine, and this need not entail a formal liturgical act; Justin Martyr speaks of it as a purely practical step. It was only after the exaggerated spiritualism of the Gnostics necessitated the defense of earthly creation and its importance that we find St. Irenaeus laying emphasis on the material element of the Eucharist, in which the "firstlings of creation" are offered up. So, as we saw above, it was at this time that Tertullian and St. Cyprian published the very first reports indicating that the faithful bring gift-offerings (Part I, ch. 3).

Since the fourth century the preparation of the offerings has been clearly included in the regular course of the liturgy in all the rites, irrespective of whether the people are given a special role in it. But now since the Liturgy of the Word preceded the Eucharistic celebration, two options were possible; the offerings could be prepared either before or after the Liturgy of the Word. The Roman and the East Syrian liturgies opted for the second solution, which was originally favored elsewhere as well.

Later on, throughout the East in general, the preparation of the offerings was anticipated and joined to the opening rituals (Raes 62–75). With the eighth century the preparation of the gifts in the Byzantine liturgy evolved into an elaborate ritual, the so-called "bringing in" or *proskomide,* which is performed by the priest with the assistance of the deacon at a special table, the *prothesis* ("place of setting before"). To the accompaniment of Scriptural words and of prayers, the "Lamb" is first separated from the bread that has been set out. Wine and water are poured into the chalice. Then a large number of particles is removed from the same bread and set apart in remembrance of the saints as well as of the living and the dead. The gifts are then incensed and covered with a threefold veil (*velum*). A prayer recited by the priest concludes this first part of the oblation rite.

After the prayers concluding the Liturgy of the Word the gifts are carried to the altar in the Great Entrance. Preceded by torchbearers and thurifer, the deacon and the priest carry the host and the chalice — both covered with a veil — through the nave of the church to the sanctuary while the *Cherubicon* (the "Cherubic Hymn") is sung. The beginnings of this ritual may be recognized as early as about 390 at the time of Theodore of Mopsuestia, who saw in it a proleptic reference to Christ as he was led to be sacrificed (Mingana 222). The Expositio of the old Gallican Mass refers to a similar entrance with the sacrificial gifts at this very point of the Mass (pp. 17f. in Quasten edition).

2. THE OFFERTORY IN THE WESTERN LITURGY

a) Offertory procession

The Western liturgy, on the other hand, has never known anything but the preparation of the gifts at the beginning of the Eucharistic liturgy, and that in a simple form; anticipation of the act, as in the Dominican rite, was the exception. Even then, participation of the people was strongly emphasized: the Offertory procession of the faithful was introduced. Nor was this procession entirely unknown in the Eastern liturgies. In Byzantium on solemn occasions the Emperor brought his sacrificial gifts to the altar; and there is evidence that in Egypt up to very recent times the faithful used to bring bread and wine for the Eucharist, though it was only in the West that the practice ever developed fully. As is borne out by the Ordines Romani from the end of the seventh century, in the form the procession took in Rome, the Pope, flanked by the archdeacon and his assistants, came down toward the people and personally accepted the nobles' gifts of bread while the archdeacon took their oblation of wine.

When the Roman liturgy spread to Gallo-Frankish territory, this ritual became the Offertory procession proper. Medieval expositions of the liturgy liken it to the procession of people who paid homage to the Lord on Palm Sunday. While bread and wine were gifts brought by the faithful, other items might also be offered, especially such as were destined for use in the church — oil and candles, for instance. Finally, from the eleventh century on, all these gifts were gradually replaced by legal tender.

For several centuries the Offertory procession was a part of Sunday Mass, and as such was enjoined in various decrees during the Carolingian era. In individual country parishes in southern Germany it was still being observed in the early twentieth century. In the late Middle Ages, however, it was imposed on the faithful as a regular duty only on the four major feast days of the year; and after the Council of Trent, it no longer appears among ecclesiastical regulations. But the Offertory hymn was preserved from ancient tradition. Called the *offertorium* (or *antiphona ad offertorium*), this hymn had originally been meant as an accompaniment to the Offertory procession.

b) Evolution of the rite

Next, the priest had to place the gifts upon the altar, and this he did to the accompaniment of prayer. In the older Roman liturgy the Prayer over the Gifts ("Oratio super Oblata") was the only prayer within the confines of the Offertory rite and, like every prayer, it was recited aloud. But when, under Eastern influence, it became customary during Carolingian times to recite this prayer in a low voice on the reasoning that as a sacrificial prayer it already belonged to the sacred depths, the entire action of the Preparation of the Gifts came to include other prayers recited silently; but for a long time these were classified as wholly private.

Thus evolved the prayers the priest recited when receiving

the gifts from the deacon, a prayer for offering the bread and another for offering the wine, and other prayers for both together ("In a spirit of humility"; "Receive, O holy Trinity": *In spiritu humilitatis; Suscipe, sancta Trinitas*); also other prayers at several points for blessing the gifts of bread and wine, first separately and, again, both together. At the commingling of water and wine the popular formula from the eleventh century was found in the old Roman sacramentaries as a Christmas Collect beginning with the words, "God, you made man's nature" (*Deus, qui humanae substantiae*).

A formal gesture of offering had not always been associated with these prayers. On the evidence of Italic manuscripts, until the thirteenth century bread and wine were simply placed upon the altar (MRR 2:58 n. 86). In the Carolingian kingdom the gifts were usually incensed ritually as a conclusion to the Offertory, and this ritual was then broadened to include the solemn incensing of clergy and people with the accompaniment of special prayers. Then followed the washing of hands, which seemed the only natural thing to do after the priest had handled the thurible and in some cases even the material gifts of the faithful.

Yet this was not the original place, and still less the original meaning, of the liturgical washing of hands. There is evidence that it was performed *at the very start* of the Liturgy of the Eucharist as a symbol of the interior purity with which one wanted to enter into the sacred mystery, as is borne out in the East as early as in the fourth century in the Mystagogical Catecheses of Jerusalem (5:2). Moreover, according to the first Roman Ordo, the Pope washes his hands *before* going to the altar in order to receive the gift-offerings of the clerics (Andrieu OR 2:92f.); and it is the washing of hands at the *beginning* of the Offertory that is prescribed for bishops in the Ceremoniale Episcoporum (1.11:11) up to the present time.

The adoption of the inaudible tone for the prayers, which converted the Oratio super Oblata into a Secreta, had another effect as well; the priest had to continue praying in a low voice during the whole Canon. According to the reasoning behind this practice, the celebrant alone should enter into the holy of holies before God; but before stepping through the door of the Preface (so to speak), he should in some way take leave of the congregation and commend himself to their prayer. This was the genesis of the "Pray, brethren"

(*Orate, fratres*) which made its appearance at the end of the eighth century, more or less coinciding with first reports of the *sotto voce* recitation of the Canon. Incidentally, the "Orate, fratres" was for a long time addressed to the assisting clergy, and only in the late Middle Ages came to be addressed to the congregation: *Orate, fratres et sorores* (MRR 2:86).

3. THE NEW ORDER OF MASS

Those entrusted with the Mass reform imposed by Vatican II pondered whether the Offertory should not be restored to its original simplicity, i.e., shortened more or less to what was practically necessary, plus the Prayer over the Gifts as its conclusion. As they realized, since the essential event of the Mass must begin only now, attention should not be deflected from it by an overblown Offertory ritual; in other words, the sacrifice of the Mass as the Church's sacrifice is performed only in the Consecration and should not be eclipsed by the occurrence of an independent, autonomous sacrifice of the Church. Moreover, the consensus was that the priest should not recite long, inaudible prayers while music is being sung.

The new Order of Mass takes a middle course. The symbolism contained in the act of placing the gifts upon the altar has been clarified, not suppressed. The Offertory procession of the faithful is encouraged. Even the gesture of elevating the gifts in a movement of offering has been retained.

On the other hand, nearly all the accompanying prayers originating in the Carolingian era have been dropped, and only one short sentence accompanies the double action. The formulas that have been introduced for this purpose are from ancient times, probably the very words used at the blessing of bread and wine in a Jewish meal at the time of Christ. Ligier has reconstructed this Jewish blessing over the bread thus: *Benedictus tu Deus noster, rex universi, qui producit panem de terra* ("Blessed are you, our God, ruler of the universe, who brings forth bread from the earth"); and over the wine: . . . *rex universi creans fructum vitis* (". . . ruler of the universe, who brings forth the fruit of the vine") (Hänggi-Pahl 6–7).

In other words, the renewed Offertory formula embodies a threefold idea: the bread and wine are products of this our earth and thus symbolize our world and our life; they also signify the work of our hands and our daily labor; and they are offered here as the matter or material disguise for what they will become in the Eucharistic mystery: the bread of life, the spiritual drink. This interpretation at the same time confirms from another angle that the "offering" (*offerimus tibi*) is not intended in an absolute, self-sufficient sense.

The mingling of water, whose symbolism was underscored by St. Cyprian (as noted in Part I, ch. 3), has been saved as a venerable tradition; but of the former Christmas Collect only the essential words have been retained, i.e., that what was initiated in the Incarnation should now be fulfilled in this sacrament, and that we are to have a share in the divinity of him who became man for us. For Cyprian the action had an even broader implication, that of Christ drawing his Church unto himself.

The prayer "In a spirit of humility" (*In spiritu humilitatis*), which had always served as an emphatic summary of the process of offering and as such was recited with a deep inclination (MRR 2:51f.), has been retained unchanged for the very reason that it gives apt expression to the "invisible sacrifice" of the heart as the interior meaning of all exterior offering.

The washing of hands has likewise remained in its accustomed place. Its exclusively symbolical meaning, underlined also in the General Instruction on the Order of Mass (§ 52), is unmistakable. It makes its point to all peoples in all times; and the requirement that especially one presiding over the most sacred of actions ought to be pure has universal appeal. This mentality was so natural to the early Christians that Tertullian, in his work on prayer (De Or. 13), had to assure them that it was not necessary to wash the hands each time before they were raised to God in prayer. To a literal-minded and technically oriented generation such symbols may have become unfamiliar, but perhaps for this very reason they have not become altogether superfluous.

The "Pray, brethren" (*Orate, fratres*) has also been kept, though the original ground for its introduction, namely, the reverential silence in which the Canon was prayed, no longer applies. It has somewhat the same function as the "Let us pray" (*Oremus*) in other places in the Mass now that the "Oremus" is no longer said at the beginning of the Offertory (or, if it is said, serves solely to introduce the General Intercessions). In place of the pause meant for silent prayer after the "Oremus," we now have the prayer "May the Lord accept" (*Suscipiat*), which came into use everywhere after the eleventh century.

V. THE EUCHARISTIC PRAYER

1. HISTORICAL EVOLUTION OF THE EUCHARISTIC PRAYER

The cell from which the most important part of the Mass developed had its origin in Christ himself. It is the account of the institution of the Eucharist at the Last Supper, with the sacred words of Consecration framed in a thanksgiving prayer. Since, as we have seen, the Eucharist was being celebrated long before the accounts were preserved in the New Testament, its oldest formulation was not contingent upon the biblical versions but was at first perpetuated through liturgical usage alone. In fact, no one wording had been settled upon at the time.

a) Treatment of the Institution narrative

According to Fritz Hamm's historical findings,[179] in both the East and the West there were impressive developments that headed in the same direction though quite independently of each other. Moreover, at a very early stage the tendency was to keep the words over the bread and those over the chalice as closely parallel as possible. Thus, in both texts the great Eastern liturgies applied the one word *thanksgiving* to *eucharistesas, eulogesas, hagiasas*. Similarly, they added to the words over the bread the words proper to the chalice (as reported in Matthew 26:28): "for the forgiveness of sins." This same tendency found its way into the Roman Canon, where certain embellishing words recur in both places, as well as the identical wording of the expanded "giving thanks to you he blessed it and gave it to his disciples saying" (*tibi gratias agens benedixit deditque discipulis suis dicens*).

The second tendency with regard to the Institution account in the liturgy was to conform its wording as closely as possible to the biblical text. The Roman canon assimilated almost all the elements of the biblical account, with the notable exception of the Paul/Luke tradition of the words "to be given for you" over the bread. In

E. C. Ratcliff's *The Institution Narrative* this omission is explained by the fact that the text of the Roman Canon was based on Matthew 26:26-28.

The third tendency, betrayed in the Eastern texts as well as in the Roman Canon, is to embellish. Thus, e.g., the Lord takes bread *and* chalice "in his holy and venerable hands." Astonishingly enough, in the very midst of the words over the chalice, the words "mystery of faith" (*mysterium fidei*) were already inserted in the sacramentaries of the sixth and seventh centuries. The phrase was borrowed from 1 Timothy 3:9, where of course it occurs in quite another context, namely, that the deacons must be sincere believers in "the mystery of faith." It may have become associated with the Consecration of the chalice by reason of the fact that responsibility for the chalice was the deacon's task.

b) Setting of the narrative

Concentration of interest on the Consecration in the Middle Ages led theologians to consider the Institution narrative in isolation from its context. Yet its place is within the framework of the thanksgiving prayer already emphasized in the biblical accounts. The mandate to repeat the action was unanimously understood by the ancient Church to include the thanksgiving prayer as well. There was no rigid norm for determining the content and composition of the thanksgiving prayer. It could simply advert in passing to the primary object of thanksgiving, the mystery of Christ; but it could also develop this point in a fairly detailed exposition. It could place the act of thanksgiving in one simple phrase; or it could describe it in grandiose and solemn terms, calling upon angelic choirs to join in singing the praises of the Lord. It was in this spirit that the Sanctus was inserted in all the liturgies at a very early period, first in the East and then in the West.

In liturgies of the West Syrian and Byzantine type, the solemn language in which thanksgiving and praise are clothed, and its majestic sweep enveloping both heaven and earth, possess the whole section up to the Sanctus. The object of thanksgiving — God's gracious intervention in man's history — is unfolded only after the Sanctus, and either by detailing God's role in the Old Testament (as in the older form of the Anaphora of Basil from the fourth century, or even in the Anaphora of James), or by describing at some length the work of redemption beginning with the Incarnation (as in most later anaphoras of the West Syrian liturgy). In many cases, too, the Gallican-type liturgies followed this route, the transition being usually provided by the linking phrases in the post-Sanctus: *Vere sanctus, vere benedictus Dominus noster Jesus Christus, qui . . .* ("O our truly holy, truly blessed Lord Jesus Christ, who . . .").

The Egyptian liturgies develop the theme of thanksgiving with a short reference to the history of salvation at the very beginning of the Eucharistic Prayer, and then proceed with a grand description of the heavenly hymn of praise up to the Sanctus. But at that point they take a different path, and in the older documents an epiclesis follows. Here, too, reference is made to the hymn of the angels, not, however, to the exclamation *Holy!* but to the words: "Heaven and earth are filled with your glory." The simplest form is the one found in the sixth century papyrus of Der-Balyzeh: "Fill us also with your glory and graciously send your spirit down upon these gifts" (Hänggi-Pahl 124–26). The Anaphora of Serapion and that of Mark have the same structure, though these are wordier. In all these cases there occurs first the epiclesis and then the Institution narrative.

Basically this was the approach in the formation of the Roman Canon as well. The copulative "therefore" (*igitur*, in the prayer "Te igitur" — "We humbly pray you, therefore, holy Father . . .") serves as connection with the Sanctus and everything that precedes it. The thanksgiving prayer now continues as petition, begging God to accept and bless the gift-offerings; and in this way an epiclesis is also introduced at this point. For if we disregard the intercessions beginning here and extending to the "Hanc igitur," the "Quam oblationem" that follows is precisely what we have to identify as the consecration-epiclesis in the old Roman liturgy. Even though the person of the Holy Spirit is not mentioned here, this prayer obviously petitions God to bless these gifts, that they may become the body and blood of Christ.

The epiclesis is a legitimate element of the Eucharistic Prayer. Originally it occurred not at this point but after the Consecration, and before any reference to receiving the gifts that have now been transformed. True, even in this earlier position the Roman Canon had no Holy Spirit-epiclesis; yet there was something equivalent in the second part of the "Supplices," when we pray to God to take the sacrifice to his heavenly altar, so that those who receive from it the body and blood of Christ may "be filled with every heavenly grace and blessing." This Communion-epiclesis was then expanded in all the Eastern liturgies in such a manner that it expresses both the prayer for transubstantiation and for fruitful Communion. Its dogmatic problem has already been discussed in Part II (ch. 5).

2. ANAMNESIS AND OFFERING

In all the liturgies the anamnesis with the act of offering is more intimately related to the sacramental center of the Mass than is the epiclesis. The anamnesis proper is the first prayer after the words of the Institution narrative; or, more precisely, it is the beginning of this prayer. Since the theme of remembrance has been developed in the thanksgiving prayer and since the whole Mass constitutes an anamnesis in the broader sense, in the anamnesis proper we need only establish clearly that with our action we are fulfilling the Lord's mandate to remember him. Accordingly, only the substance of the memorial is indicated at this place, and that in very few words.

While the Roman Canon goes hardly beyond the wording of Paul (1 Cor. 11:26, the death of the Lord) or that of Hippolytus (Passion and resurrection), in the Eastern liturgies the remembrance is more richly expressed. The Egyptian liturgies use Paul's own word *Katangellete*, "Proclaim (his death)," while at the same time they encourge the people to take part by means of an acclamation.[180] This and other liturgies do not stop with the Passion, but may mention also the burial, the resurrection, the ascension, and the enthronement at the Father's right hand. The West Syrian Anaphora includes even a reference to "the glorious and fearsome second coming." If this already exceeds the scope of an actual anamnesis (= remembrance), what shall we make of a full description of the Judgment, to which a number of these anaphora extend the "remembrance"? Indeed, in the oldest of these anaphoras, that of James, the people respond with a plea for mercy at this point.

In the Gallic liturgies the anamnesis is often worded as an independent clause with a finite verb: "We recall . . . ," "We do this . . . ," "We announce . . . ," "We confess . . . ."[181] In other liturgies both East and West, it takes the participial form: "Remembering, therefore, ..." In other words, it is subordinated to the offering.

In its simplest form the "Offering" appears already in the

Eucharistic Prayer of Hippolytus: "Remembering . . . , we offer you the bread and cup" (*Memores . . . offerimus tibi panem et calicem*). A similar but more expanded expression recurs regularly at this same place in all the liturgies. In the Roman Canon it has been given very special emphasis. The gift-offerings are first described in their full value and significance, "The bread of life and the cup of eternal salvation" (*Panem sanctum vitae aeternae et calicem salutis perpetuae*); and then the act of offering is followed by a petition that God may graciously look down upon these gifts as he once did upon the sacrificial gifts of Abel, Abraham, and Melchisedech ("Supra quae"), and that he may have them carried up to his heavenly altar — a figurative way of expressing God's acceptance ("Supplices").

The unusual thing about the Roman liturgy is that the offering is expressed even before the words of Consecration, that is, not only in the Prayer over the Gifts, which has its parallel in most of the liturgies, but also in the Eucharistic Prayer itself. The first prayer after the Sanctus, i.e., the prayer serving as a transition to the epiclesis, has the sense of offering, asking God to accept and bless the gifts which are already referred to as a "holy and unblemished sacrifice" (*sancta sacrificia illibata*). That indeed is remarkable enough. The Egyptian liturgies, related to the Roman again in this respect, use similar expressions of offering in the opening section of the Eucharistic Prayer, that is, at the very beginning of the Preface.

3. Intercessions

The emphasis on the act of offering at this point during the service encouraged lingering in the same place for the great prayer of petition, the Intercessions.[182] In Egypt they are inserted into the Preface; in the Roman Canon they come after the "Te igitur."

As we have already seen, petitions for the great intentions of the Church and of humanity were embodied in the Mass as early as the second century, as borne out by Justin Martyr. And as regular and extended prayer in Justin's description, they conclude the Liturgy of the Word. Moreover, it is as a conclusion to the Liturgy of the Word that they were preserved in all the liturgies except the West Syrian and the Roman, where they disappeared at an early stage. But after the fourth century at the latest, in all the liturgies except the Gallic type, they underwent a new evolution as intercessions within the Eucharistic Prayer. The intention was to move the petitions closer into the most sacred zone of the sacrifice.

In all the East, with the exception of Egypt, this development took place after, not before, the Consecration, i.e., after the thanksgiving prayer proper was completed and the offering of the sacrificial gifts definitively expressed. As early as the Apostolic Constitutions of the fourth century, this prayer consisted of ten units, each of which opens with the formula, "We pray to you also for . . . ," or, "We offer [the sacrifice] to you also for . . . ." In the later development of the West Syrian liturgy of the Jacobites, at the beginning of each unit the deacon utters an invitation to prayer, and the priest then recites the petition.

In the Roman liturgy the Memento for the Dead was inserted at this point, first on days outside Sundays and feasts, and from the ninth century on all days. But the bulk of the intercessions followed the "Te igitur," as petition for the Church and for Church authorities [sometimes also for Christian princes, as in Austria until 1918], and as entreaty, in the first Memento, that God might remember those offering the sacrifice and those attending it.

This prayer in the Roman Canon was then extended to introduce a new element: that of establishing communion with the Church in heaven by offering to "the eternal, living, and true God" their gifts (*vota*) in communion (*communicantes*) with the glorious Mother of God [since 1962: and with St. Joseph] and with all the saints. And here the representatives of the saints in heaven, invoked by name, add up to the sacred number, twice twelve: twelve Apostles and twelve martyrs. Farther along, a parallel sacred number of martyrs — seven men and seven women — is invoked in the "Nobis quoque" appended to the Memento for the Dead. Again at the head of the list is a great saint, John the Baptist, to whom Christ himself paid the compliment of being the greatest of those born of women.

So far the intercessions were for persons who were to be commended in prayer. But then in the Roman Canon there emerged a new formula, the "Hanc igitur," with which special intentions could be mentioned. Originally used only in votive Masses, it was really a skeleton formula, and it was up to the priest to supply the intention for which he wished to pray or to offer the Mass. Since the time of Pope St. Gregory the Great, however, it has been a fixed text forming a regular and permanent part of the Canon. Except on special occasions, only the broadest intentions were now to be mentioned in it: peace in the world and our final acceptance among the elect.

Thus from the "Te igitur" onward, the Eucharistic Prayer of the Roman liturgy became almost exclusively a prayer of sacrifice and of petition, and as such, in the northern European countries, it came to be increasingly cut off from the Preface. In the Roman sacramentaries, though, it was still looked upon as forming one single unit with the Preface, for in several of the oldest manuscripts the heading "The normative sacrificial action begins" (*Incipit canon actionis*) appears before the "Lift up your hearts" (*Sursum corda*). The Eucharistic Prayer begins with the Preface and thereby sets the norm (canon) according to which the sacred action is to be performed.

4. THE SILENT CANON

But then comes Isidore of Seville with his distinction of a complex of prayers that belong to the confecting of the sacrament (*conformatio sacramenti*), that is, to the Consecration, and may be identified with the section beginning with "Te igitur." The notion of Canon has been narrowed down to just this section since the ninth century, when the Preface came to be looked upon as a not very important introduction to the Canon: merely a kind of foreword as in a book. No longer does it mean what it once had meant in Rome: the whole Eucharistic Prayer that had to be solemnly pronounced before the people and before God (*fari*— to speak, and *prae*— before, in the spatial sense). The Canon had become the holy of holies that only the priest could enter.

It was but one small step from this concept of *alone* to its practical application in the symbolic silence and stillness observed during the Canon. This practice was not new to either the Gallican or the Eastern liturgy.[183] The Canon was now prayed in a low voice, and became inaccessible to the people. The understanding of the Eucharistic Prayer in its ancient, original sense was now almost beyond the reach of even the clergy.

To a certain extent this was offset by compensating elements that crept in after the twelfth century. The elevation of the Host at the words "he took bread" (*acceptit panem*) — basically an oblation ritual borrowed from the Jewish meal ritual — became the elevation of the consecrated bread. The body of Christ is shown to the people for their veneration. The Consecration is ritually set off as the climax of the Mass. Bells ring, clouds of incense rise, all fall on their knees to adore the Blessed Sacrament. This prominence given to the decisive moment of the Mass and the veneration shown to the sacrament were in themselves certainly a gain. But the ascending curve of the Eucharistic action, moving upward in the grand sweep of thanksgiving and praise, was obscured. For the Eucharist is an ascent unto God; but with this extra emphasis on veneration and awe, attention was now concentrated rather on the opposite movement, on the descending curve.

5. THE LITURGICAL REFORM

a) General approach

The liturgical reform of Vatican II was no easy undertaking, especially when it came to the Canon. Not a few of the Council Fathers were actually in favor of leaving the Canon untouched. The ensuing Constitution on the Sacred Liturgy contains no explicit regulations on the matter, but only a general directive that the rites of the Eucharistic liturgy should be reformed with "due care . . . taken to preserve their substance" (§50). At the same time, however, the Council decreed that the reform should be such that the faithful not merely understand the rites and prayers (this was the wording suggested by the preparatory commission), but "through a proper appreciation of the rites and prayers" they reach out to and actively participate in the mystery thereby signified (§48).

If this requirement was to be met — and from the nature of the case there was no evading the consequences — then the Canon could not be left untouched. Whereupon already in the Second Instruction (*Instructio altera*) of May 4, 1967, the silence at the Canon was abolished, and bishops' conferences were empowered to allow the vernacular also in the Canon (AAS 59 [1967] 445, 448). But it was clear from the start that if the Canon was to help the people understand the mystery of redemption that becomes present in the Mass, a mere translation of the Roman Canon into the mother tongue would not be of much use. So the reform was faced with two alternatives: either to revise the text of the Canon itself, in which case the move would be in the direction of enriching the Preface and, above all, of shifting all intercessions to bring them together at the end of the Canon; or to introduce alongside the traditional Roman Canon other forms of the Eucharistic Prayer. Pope Paul VI decided upon the latter alternative.

Nor has the Roman Canon itself been left entirely untouched in the new Missale Romanum approved by the Pope on April 4, 1969.[184] For one thing the words "Through Christ our Lord. Amen" (*Per Christum Dominum nostrum. Amen*) concluding each individual section have now been dropped (or, in the English version, bracketed for optional use), since they had originated in the intercessions periodically inserted into the Canon, each with its own concluding formula. Then, most of the saints' names in the two parallel series have been set within brackets to indicate that they may be omitted. (Incidentally, along with Peter and Paul, the Apostle Andrew has remained outside the brackets. This retention is, in fact, a transfer from the embolism of the Lord's Prayer, where his name had evidently been included as a token of friendship toward Byzantium — MRR 2:285.) In combination with a good Preface the streamlined Roman Canon can be a very satisfactory Eucharistic Prayer, especially now that even on Sundays the Preface of the Most Holy Trinity, which had been in use since 1759, has been replaced by Prefaces that stress the paschal mystery.

b) The new Eucharistic Prayers

The three new "Canons" or Eucharistic Prayers II, III, and IV made public in 1968, have uniform wording for the formula of consecration in the Institution narrative. The Sanctus and the concluding doxology are from the Roman Canon. All three "Canons" contain elements of a Consecration-epiclesis as well as a Communion-epiclesis (since mention is made of the Holy Spirit). Again in the final section, all three contain intercessions with an invocation of the saints in heaven.

For the rest, Eucharistic Prayer II is substantially the one Hippolytus of Rome put in writing around the year 215 A.D. The striking thing about it is the simple clarity of its thanksgiving prayer as well as its extraordinary brevity, in particular the brevity of the transition from the Sanctus to the words of Institution. It is intended not for the community Mass on Sunday, but for week days and special situations in which a simplified form might be desired (Order of Mass, §322b).

Eucharistic Prayer IV was modeled on the anaphoras of the West Syrian Byzantine type. Accordingly, in contrast with the whole Roman tradition, it contains a description of salvation history not in the Preface but in the "post-Sanctus" position. The description begins with the history of the old covenant, and its language is saturated with biblical turns of phrase, thus presupposing a close familiarity with the language of Sacred Scripture. The claims of ecumenical interest were partly decisive in its composition.

Eucharistic Prayer III is the one that best displays the combination of Roman tradition on the one hand and, on the other, the rediscovered ideal of a Eucharistic Prayer. Since its text begins only after the Sanctus, it thus keeps to the traditional pattern of the Roman Canon: varying Preface and invariable Canon. Moreover, the Prefaces previously in use could be retained and their number even increased in the new Missale Romanum. A special advantage of Canon III is that its transition from the Sanctus to the Institution narrative strikes a compromise between the brevity of the second Canon and the length of the fourth, yet happily synthesizes the content of each. In the Prefaces, which come to a close with the Sanctus, the work of redemption has already been described; so then the Canon proceeds to speak of the fruit of redemption, the Church: the Church God gathers unto himself from all ages and all peoples, so that in this Church the pure sacrifice may be offered at all times as at this very moment.

After this general view of the reformed Eucharistic Prayer, we may now get down to some particulars that perhaps require explanation.

c) Preface and Sanctus

In every instance, the Preface opens with the conventional dialogue. In the Roman rite this dialogue has been preserved in its original simplicity, while in most other liturgies it has undergone a slight modification. But the dialogue itself is very old. In particular the invitation, *Let us give thanks to the Lord, our God*, evidently harks back to the usage of the first Christian community as described in Part I (ch. 1). In the Roman form, just as in several Eastern versions, the thanksgiving prayer always begins with the "It is our duty" (*Vere dignum*) and with the solemn address to God which is arranged, in modern punctuation, in three groups consisting of one word, two words, and three words: *Lord, Holy Father, almighty everlasting God*. The intercession itself is framed in the classic structure of Christian prayer, as is only proper in the case of the liturgy's chief prayer. We enter into God's presence *through Christ, our Lord*, whether Christ's mediatorship is explicitly stated at the very beginning, or whether reference to the mediation is replaced by a description of the mystery of Christ corresponding to the day's feast.

The new Missal offers a rich choice of Prefaces for feast days and liturgical seasons, for votive Masses and for special occasions, without however reverting quite to the principle of the oldest Roman sacramentary, which provided each Mass formula with its own Preface. This principle had led to abuses as early as in the Sacramentarium Leonianum, in which the Preface was sometimes nothing more than the description of the sufferings of a martyr or an exhortation to a moral life. The richness of the Prefaces should serve only to exhibit the mystery of redemption ever in a new light. The Preface was to be a "speaking before" (*praedicatio*) in a twofold sense: as praise of God and as proclamation before the community of the faithful.

After unfolding at some length, the thanksgiving prayers invariably modulate into a sentiment of adoration, a sentiment that was set off and climaxed all the more effectively when the Sanctus was added at a very early stage in the history of the Mass. The inspiration behind the Sanctus is the text of Isaias' vision (6:2-3), which was incorporated in the Synagogue worship during the second century after Christ at the latest. The Sanctus was preceded by an introduction in which choirs of angels ("all his servants"; Hänggi-Pahl 37) were called upon to join in singing the praises of the Lord.

It is not possible to ascertain now whether this Synagogue practice, which conceivably made its way into the Christian liturgy through Jewish-Christian circles, was what prompted the adoption of the triple Sanctus in the Eucharistic Prayer of the Christian communities at a very early age, perhaps even at the time of the Apostles. While several fourth-century documents bear witness to its use in all the Eastern liturgies, in the West even in the fifth century it was not known everywhere; it is missing from Hippolytus' Eucharistic Prayer and from others as well. In any event it is interesting to see how the Isaian text has been expanded into a hymn of praise in which heaven and earth take part. Eastern texts have made ample use of biblical quotations such as Daniel 7:10, Exodus 10:12, Hebrews 12:23, Apocalypse 4:6, Isaias 6:2-3, to compose a grand description of angelic choirs singing God's praise.

The Benedictus, the acclamation with which the crowds greeted Jesus on Palm Sunday (Matthew 21:9), was first assimilated into the liturgy in the West, and Caesarius of Arles (d. 542) was its first witness (in his Sermon 73:3; Morin 294). With the addition of the Benedictus, the triple Sanctus echoes the Apocalypse song of praise "to God and to the Lamb" (5:13 and elsewhere).

From the very beginning the Sanctus was looked upon as a hymn in which the people should take part, and was in fact the oldest congregational hymn of the Mass. This is why those Sanctus melodies that reflect the most ancient tradition are hardly more than a solemn recitative tone. Durandus (d. 1296) observes in his Rationale Divinorum Officiorum (4.34.10) that one of the functions of the organ is to provide accompaniment for the Sanctus and thereby heighten its grandeur.

d) Remainder of the Canon

A rather daring step that would not have been possible but for the introduction of the new Canons was the change made in both the wording of the Institution narrative (the embellishments added at the very heart of the text have now been dropped from the new Eucharistic Prayers) and the wording of the sacramental rite. The Roman Canon in particular has benefited by this openness to change. The clause "which will be given up for you," theologically so pregnant with meaning, has been added to the words over the bread. The puzzling "mystery of faith" has been deleted from the words over the chalice, and has now been made the cue for the people's memorial acclamation, which is also a welcome addition to the new Canons.

The idea of giving the people an acclamation at the very heart of the sacred action came up at a time in the course of the reform when no one yet dared even dream that the Canon could be recited in anything but a low voice and in Latin. This memorial acclamation was proposed with the intention of helping the faithful become more fully aware of the meaning of the action. There was a precedent for this in the Egyptian liturgies, in which the remembrance of the Lord was underlined by such an acclamation. As in these liturgies, so in the reformed liturgy (with the exception of the first and simplest form) the acclamation is addressed to Christ. This response of the people seemed quite appropriate, and it would not interrupt the progress of the priest's prayer since it would not be pronounced by the priest, but is rather a hymnic element affirming his prayer from outside.

The themes for the priest's prayer after the completion of the sacramental action are suggested by the very context. The prayer must bring out the meaning of the event itself: that what we are performing here is the Lord's memorial, the memorial of his redemptive sacrifice that was consummated in his Passion and resurrection. We are performing it in prayer before God and offer it to him as our sacrifice. And since we are taking part in it as those who receive, we hope and pray to be strengthened in the Holy Spirit and in love.

It is only at this point in the new Canons that the concisely worded intercessions begin to develop. In every Canon there is the prayer for the Church and for her supreme pastors, prayer also for the immediate parish community and for the dead, in which connection attention is then directed also to the saints in heaven. The intercessions are not always arranged in the same order of sequence. The prayer for the dead falls at the end in Eucharistic Prayer III, while in the other two it precedes the invocation of the saints. The new Canons contain no parallel to the "Nobis quoque" in which the celebrants pray for themselves following the Memento for the Dead in the Roman Canon, nor to the benediction at the words "all these [gifts]" (*haec omnia*), whose reference is far from clear.

All four Eucharistic Prayers come to a close with the solemn doxology that harks back to an ancient tradition, the "through him" (*per ipsum*), a text that is ritually dramatized by the elevation of the sacramental species. In an expanded form it is the ancient Christian doxology widely current throughout the Church in the third/fourth centuries: the praise of God "through Christ in the Holy Spirit," the classical formula underlying all Christian prayer. The expression "in the Holy Spirit," describing the dimensions from within which our praise rises up to God, is determined more precisely by the phrase "in the unity of the Spirit" quoted from Ephesians 4:2. In other words, it is the unity of the Church, the unity whose foundation is the Holy Spirit (see above, the concluding doxology in Hippolytus).

In this purview, the "Per ipsum," when expanded in the same sense, means that all praise and glory (*omnis honor et gloria*) are offered to God through Christ; but he is not alone now, for the community of the redeemed is united "with him and in him" in the glorification of God.[185] To this solemn doxology the congregation replies with the *Amen*, on whose value and significance a writer as early as Justin Martyr could lay such positive stress.

VI. THE COMMUNION LITURGY

Although it is at the Communion that the Eucharistic celebration reaches its consummation and fulfillment, it was relatively late that this action came to be set in a liturgical framework of its own. Neither Justin nor Hippolytus mentions a special prayer for Communion. The Eastern documents of the fourth century, however, do yield evidence of a special prayer for the priest to recite before Communion. In the Apostolic Constitutions this prayer opens with a litany by the deacon, and after Communion there follows a prayer of thanksgiving, which in Serapion even begins with "We thank you" (*eucharistoumen soi*). In the East the Lord's Prayer is mentioned among these prayers only toward the turn of the fourth century, as Chrysostom bears out in his Homily on Genesis (In Gen. Hom. 27:8; PG 53:251); and in the West, Augustine makes repeated mention of it.

1. THE LORD'S PRAYER

From the beginning the intention and the significance underlying the introduction of the Lord's Prayer might well have been the sentiment expressed by Pope St. Gregory the Great (Ep. Reg. 9:12; PL 77:956f.), viz., it is only proper to add to the "prayer of sacrifice" (*Oratio oblationis*) the prayer composed by the Lord himself. And yet the accent was on the petition for "our daily bread." This is obviously the point when the Mystagogical Catecheses of Jerusalem (5:11-18) and St. Ambrose's Commentary on the Sacrament (De Sacr. 5.4:24-26) proceed to explain the meaning of the Lord's Prayer in the Mass by interpreting "bread" in a sacramental sense. Even in spiritual writings commenting on the Lord's Prayer in itself, and independently of its use in the Mass, the petition for bread is often given a Eucharistic significance. Together with this, St. Augustine places special emphasis on the petition "Forgive us our sins." It was a custom obtaining in his community

205

of Hippo, he says in Sermon 351 (3:6), that at these words all strike their breast. That the Lord's Prayer was at any rate looked upon as a prayer of preparation is particularly clear from the fact that it was used at Communion outside Mass, as in the Mass of the Presanctified or in the various forms of Communion for the sick.[186]

In the liturgies of the East the Lord's Prayer was all but universally looked upon as a prayer of the people, and all the people prayed it together. Or sometimes, as in the Greek-Byzantine liturgy, the choir or one member of the choir might recite it as the representative of the people. In the West, on the other hand, it appeared most often, though not always, as the prayer of the priest, but even then with some form of participation of the faithful, who either said the last petition as in the old Roman liturgy, or responded with a ratifying *Amen* to each petition as in the Mozarabic liturgy.

In the Roman liturgy the Lord's Prayer has always been ushered in by a few words of introduction — for it certainly is a daring thing (*audemus*) to call God one's Father without preliminaries. In the same spirit the Syrian liturgies provide a preliminary prayer to it. Everywhere there is a sentence inserted at the end, the so-called embolism (insertion) of the Roman liturgy. In the Byzantine liturgy this consists only of a doxology, an expanded version of the doxology interpolated in the Matthew 6:10 text in several manuscripts. In other liturgies this prayer following the Lord's Prayer expatiates upon its last two petitions, but in the Roman Mass, upon only the last petition, and then in a low voice. The prayer then concludes with the doxology. Before long the silence of the Canon, begun at the Prayer of the Gifts in the Roman liturgy, enveloped the embolism as well. The interruption of this silence by the Preface and by the Lord's Prayer brought about a "threefold silence" which in the Middle Ages symbolized the three days Jesus lay in the tomb!

2. FURTHER PRE-COMMUNION RITUALS

Parallel with the Pater Noster and as a rule appended to it, further rituals soon evolved before Communion. In the East they usually began with a blessing pronounced over the people and with the proclamation, "The Holy to the holy!" (*Sancta sanctis*), which is found in several documents of the fourth century. Since it is an invitation to the people as well as a warning against unworthy reception of the Eucharist, in the Byzantine liturgy the people responded to it with the acclamation: "One alone is holy, one alone the Lord, Jesus Christ, in the glory of God the Father."

The blessing over the people found its way also into liturgies of the Gallic type. Its original purpose of serving as a preparation for Communion was soon lost sight of, however, and by the time of Caesarius of Arles — as we gather from his Sermon 73:2 — it had already become a blessing for those who did not communicate and could leave the assembly after receiving it (Morin 294). Later on, in the bishop's Mass this blessing came to be invested with great solemnity, and the Roman liturgy of the northern European countries took it up. On feast days the bishop was to give the blessing with mitre and crosier, in a variable formula of three parts, and the people replied with an *Amen*. The medieval benedictionals contain any number of formulas used for this blessing. Modeled at first on the Old Testament priestly blessing found in Numbers 6:22-26, these formulas have been studied only in recent times.[187]

Once the people's preparation was completed, the sacred Hosts were made ready for distribution, and part of this process was the breaking of the consecrated bread. The precedent of Jesus at the Last Supper probably lay behind the retention of the breaking of bread in all the liturgies. The true reason for breaking the bread was the problem of distributing the one piece of bread among a number of communicants before ready-made hosts and particles were introduced (in the tenth century in Germany). It is in this practical sense rather than in any symbolical way that we must understand the background of this fraction. Theodore of Mopsuestia in his catecheses (*c.* 390) construed the division of the bread as a symbol of the risen Lord's multilocational presence in his apparitions to various groups of disciples after the resurrection (Mingana 246).

Soon, however, as we saw in Part I (ch. 4), the symbolism of Christ's Passion and death gained the upper hand, especially in the Eastern rites. In the Byzantine liturgy "the Lamb of God is divided and dismembered" (Brightman 393). In the Roman liturgy the symbolism of the Passion took concrete shape at this point in the "Lamb of God" (*Agnus Dei*), which was from its beginning in the seventh century the hymn to accompany the breaking of the consecrated bread. In the Eastern liturgies the fraction then became the basis for other rites such as the "signing" (*consignatio*) and the "commingling" (*mixtio*), which were added to it. In the Syrian liturgy the *consignatio* developed into a complicated ritual. In the Greek liturgy of James, first one half of the host is dipped into the sacred blood and then the other half is crossed with it. After that the second half is crossed with the first, and then the two are combined to the accompaniment of several prayers (Brightman 62f.; Raes 94–103).

While in the oldest documents the commingling of the two species, during which a particle of the host is dropped into the chalice, was interpreted as the union of the two species to constitute one single whole — the body and blood of the one Christ — the Syrian documents seem to indicate that a deeper significance was attached to this action. After Christ's body and blood had been re-presented under the two separate species by the double Consecration, and his Passion and death had thereby been symbolized, the sacred gifts had to be re-presented now before Communion as the food of immortality, as the living unity of the risen Lord's body and blood.[188]

This commingling ritual, which in every case has only a symbolical meaning, has been part of the Roman Mass ever since the first Roman Ordo, in which it was placed immediately before the Communion. At this same period but slightly earlier in the Roman Mass, i.e., between the Pater Noster and the Pax Domini, another commingling took place. This ritual had its origin in the usage of the "leaven" (*fermentum*), a particle of the sacred Host sent by the Pope to the presbyters of churches in the immediate neighborhood as a token of unity. Later on, the two comminglings were combined at the latter point in the Mass.

3. Communion and Post-Communion Rites

After these preliminaries there follows the Communion, which in all the rites and according to the oldest documents was received in hierarchical order, first by the celebrant, then by the assistants, and finally by the people. In early Christian times the Communion rite must have been conducted everywhere in the manner described in the Mystagogical Catecheses of Jerusalem and represented in the well-known Codex of Rosano (*c.* 500). The faithful approach the priest and receive the sacred Host from him; to the priest's words "The body of Christ," they reply "Amen." At the time of Hippolytus the distribution was already accompanied by a similar phrase with the same meaning.[189] The communicant then consumed the sacred gift, and "with head bowed in an attitude of adoration and reverence" he went to receive the chalice, which by common custom the deacon held.

The communion of the chalice has been retained in the Eastern liturgies up to the present time (Raes 103–106), but almost everywhere now there is practically only one manner of giving it: the consecrated particle is dipped into the sacred blood and given to the communicant, sometimes with the help of a little spoon, as in the Byzantine rite. Only among the Copts, Ethiopians, and Nestorians has the practice of giving the chalice separately been kept as the normal thing, and the sacred Host placed directly in the mouth.

In all Eastern rites the Communion is followed by another hymn, and the priest says at least one other thanksgiving prayer, which the deacon prefaces with a short litany or invitation to prayer. The Byzantine liturgy, however, has retained no more than a remnant of this prayer.

4. NEW ORDER OF MASS

a) Generalities; kiss of peace

The example of the East served as a guideline for the Vatican II Instruction issued on September 26, 1964. Thus, the Lord's Prayer is now recited or sung in the mother tongue by priest and people together. While giving Communion, the priest says, *The body of Christ*, and the communicant answers *Amen*. In principle, the Council itself permitted communion of the faithful under both species (CL § 55), which was, in fact, a common practice until the thirteenth century even in the West (at least in the form of "dipping" [*intinctio*] or with the help of a straw); the practice of Communion under both species is now being observed in an ever increasing number of circumstances.

The 1969 Order of Mass has given a new shape and look to the entire Communion ritual. A feature of the Roman rite from ancient times is that the kiss of peace is given at this point, directly before Communion. In ancient Christian practice, as Tertullian notes, this kiss of peace was looked upon as the "seal" put on prayer (De Or. 18, *signaculum orationis*). Within the Mass it was given at the end of the Liturgy of the Word and to this was now added a new dimension, i.e., it was to be a token of brotherly love, in the spirit of Matthew 5:23-24, before the offering of the sacrifice.

While the other liturgies kept the kiss of peace in this position and in this spirit, Pope Innocent I in his Letter to the bishop of Gubbio (25:1) in the year 416 advocated the present location. As it is hardly possible now to revive the kiss of peace in its original form, which in ancient cultures was a spontaneous gesture of greeting even in public, attempts are being made to resurrect elements from tradition and to recharge them with new and relevant meaning.

Already at the time of Augustine (Sermon 277), the *Pax vobiscum* was said. In the American Order of Mass the phrase is rendered: "The peace of the Lord be with you always." With their response to this greeting the people affirm their desire and longing for peace. In ancient times the greeting was, at the same time, a cue and an invitation to all the faithful to exchange the kiss of peace, each with his immediate neighbor (congregations were divided into groups according to sex). In the first Ordo Romanus the prescription still prevailed: "After the Pope has given the kiss of peace, all others do the same" (*deinde ceteri per ordinem et populus*).

But already in manuscripts of the tenth century the rubric runs: "Then to the others in proper order and to the people" (*deinde ceteris per ordinem et populis*; Andrieu OR 2:98); this shows that over the years it had become customary that the kiss of peace should come from the altar and be passed on as a blessing emanating from there. After the thirteenth century the *osculatorium*, the "kissing board" or Pax-board, came into use at this ceremony (first in England): each one received the board in turn, kissed it and passed it on.

The new Order of Mass lays down no detailed directives, but merely suggests the possibility that with the words "Let us offer each other the sign of peace" (*Offerte vobis pacem*), the deacon could explicitly call upon the people to exchange the kiss of peace; it has been left to bishops' conferences to work out further details "in accord with the customs of the people" (General Instruction (§56b). This has not been officially implemented in many countries, as, for instance, the United States.

The action itself has gained in importance by the fact that the prayer for peace, "Lord Jesus Christ, you said to your apostles" (*Domine Jesu Christi qui dixisti*), which since the eleventh century had been the celebrant's private prayer to be recited quietly after the "Pax Domini," has now been placed before the peace salutation and is recited aloud. The proximity of Communion is justification enough for addressing a prayer here to Christ against the usual rule.

b) Other Communion rituals

The Agnus Dei, which follows, has now been taken out of its isolation. The connection of this invocation with the breaking of the sacred Host has been re-established, and thus its original significance has been restored (at least in instances of actual fraction) insofar as what is broken is not only the celebrant's host but also the hosts for the Communion of the faithful or concelebrants (Order of Mass §56c). The Agnus Dei is an invocation to Christ and recalls his sacrificial death, but at the same time it has something of the overtones of a hymn of victory offered to the triumphant Lamb of the Apocalypse.

The fraction is followed by the commingling of the two species, a practice taken over from the East, as we have seen. Though the symbolism of this commingling has lost much of its appeal for moderns, still it has been left untouched out of piety. The commingling is accompanied by the old formula that since the reform of 1570 had begun with "May the mingling avail us . . ." (*Haec commixtio*) as distinguished from the earlier "May the mingling take place" (*Fiat commixtio*); hence no support is given the view that not only the two species are here united, but also the very body and blood of Christ. The prayer is recited in a low voice, as is one of the two Communion prayers stemming from the Middle Ages — prayers, incidentally, that were meant as much for the faithful as for the priest. In the reformed liturgy of 1969 this is the only instance of a rather long prayer that is still recited in a low voice. It affords the people a moment's pause for recollection and silent prayer just before the reception of the sacrament.

The hierarchical order according to which the celebrant communicates first has been retained. But the *Instructio altera* of May 4, 1967, lays down the rule that priest and faithful should say the "Lord, I am not worthy" (*Domine, non sum dignus*) together, so that any suggestion of separation of the Communion of the people from that of the priest may be avoided. The priest shows the people the sacred Host with the words, "This is the Lamb of God." This happy contribution of the sixteenth century is a final invitation, and corresponds somewhat to the Eastern "Holy to the holy." To it is newly added an exclamation abridged from the Apocalypse

(19:9), "Happy are those who are called to his supper," which evokes once more the mood of the Church fulfilled in heaven.

The traditional formula assigned to the celebrant before receiving the Host, "May the body of Christ bring my soul to everlasting life" (*Corpus domini nostri Jesu Christi custodiat animam meam in vitam aeternam*), has been simplified to "bring me" (*custodiat me*), apparently as a deliberate reaction against the somewhat Platonic tendency of the Middle Ages to overaccentuate the spiritual.

The Roman Mass has always been distinguished from the other liturgies by virtue of the sober simplicity with which the celebration comes to a close after the Communion. For a long period during past centuries, the prevailing Communion-centered spirituality encouraged private thanksgiving as a compensation for the brevity of the Postcommunion ceremony. St. Alphonsus Liguori, for one, prescribed "at least a half-hour" of thanksgiving after Communion. If this seems excessive to moderns, neither should one be satisfied with the mere singing of a hymn during the distribution of Communion (albeit great freedom is now allowed in the choice of such hymns). The least that should be thought adequate is to sing "a hymn, psalm, or other song of praise," as the Order of Mass directs (§56j), or to observe instead a "sacred silence" (*sacrum silentium*).

VII. THE CONCLUDING RITE

A fully developed liturgy calls for a proper ceremony to round it off, just as it calls for an appropriate ceremony to usher it in. The congregation has to be dismissed, the people have to be taken leave of. This valedictory greeting is achieved by means of the priest's blessing, which according to a very old tradition consists of a prayer of benediction. In the Apostolic Constitutions of the fourth century the prayer is prefaced with the deacon's acclamation enjoining the people to bow their heads. This is the form in which the benediction is found in all the Eastern liturgies, and the precedent for the Prayer over the People of the Roman liturgy.

The concluding rituals of the Mass illustrate the tendency to expand and augment. Thus, the "inclination prayer" (*oratio inclinationis*) is followed by a further prayer of benediction or formula of blessing. In the Byzantine liturgy a concluding hymn, the "sending away" (*apolysis*), prolongs it still more; and after that, to the accompaniment of Psalm 33, blessed but unconsecrated bread is distributed as a substitute for the sacred Host to those who have not communicated, whence its name "substitute gift" (*antidoron*).[190] The ceremony is further lengthened by additional concluding rituals. Generally in the Eastern Churches the ablution of the objects used in the Mass comes only after all these rituals.

The various additions that terminated the Mass of the Roman liturgy until the Instruction of 1964 are still fresh in memory. After the "Placeat" ("May the homage of my service please you") preliminary to the blessing, and after the blessing itself, there were still the Last Gospel and then the prayers of Leo XIII — not to speak of other local appendages inspired by the piety or preoccupations of individual dioceses and parishes. The postconciliar reform has abolished all but the most essential elements of these concluding rituals. And their meaning has now been keynoted by the salutation, "The Lord be with you," which does not call attention to the Postcommunion as it did before the reform, but introduces this Concluding Rite as a self-contained unit.

1. The Blessing

As a rule the blessing itself is still imparted in the familiar form. Basically it is modeled on the bishop's parting "May the Lord bless us [or: you]" (*Benedicat nos [or: vos] Dominus*) conferred in answer to the plea of individual groups for blessing, as is borne out by the oldest Roman Ordines (Andrieu OR 2:108, 227). According to Roman custom, for a long time it was reserved to the bishop alone to impart the blessing in public, though in Gaul priests were permitted to bless if the bishop was present. Since about the eleventh century, however, popular pressure has led to permitting the priest to impart the blessing in the simple formula mentioned above at the end of the Mass. As this was a concession to the demands of the people, it is not surprising that in most monasteries where there was no congregation the question of imparting this blessing never arose, at least up to the late Middle Ages.

The new Order of Mass notes that on certain occasions the blessing might be given in another form, i.e., in one of the several liturgical traditions, with the formula *Benedicat vos* as the conclusion. One such form would be the Prayer over the People mentioned earlier. In the Leonine Sacramentary this prayer is incorporated in every Mass as the final formula; with the passage of time, however, it occurred less often. In the Gregorian Sacramentary it is restricted to the Lenten season, Sundays excepted, that is, to the days dedicated to the Church's public penance. Accordingly, without much change in text this prayer came to be adopted as the formula for blessing penitents. Another form was the one found among the formulas used for the pontifical blessing in the Gallican liturgy, as mentioned in the preceding chapter. On given occasions this too could be employed for the blessing imparted by the priest.

In the old Roman Mass the dismissal ceremony itself is a simple affair consisting of the unadorned announcement, "Go, it is over" (*Ite, missa est*). The Eastern formula is the less prosaic "Go in peace" (from Luke 7:50). The Roman formula just mentioned was in use also as a conclusion to secular meetings, as we may gather from the first letter of Bishop Avitus of Vienne (*c.* 518): "The signal for dismissal is given" (*missa fieri pronuntiatur*; PL 59:199). In this sense the word *missa* was used in the form of *minsa* even at the imperial court of Byzantium as a technical term for the conclusion of an audience, and hence still has its original meaning: *missio = dimissio.* Its translation into a living language naturally tends to be rather free as well as somewhat richer than the original. At any rate the plain statement, "The Mass is ended," would certainly not be a faithful translation of its spirit or meaning.

Another enduring legacy of ancient tradition is the kiss with which the priest takes leave of the altar, corresponding to the kiss with which he greeted it at the beginning. In the Mass of the West Syrian Jacobites, where this gesture has been stylized into an important ritual, the priest takes leave of the altar as of a personal being, with some endearing words of farewell. In the Roman Mass greater authenticity and weight are now conferred on this gesture by the fact that it is no longer placed before the blessing (for in this context the altar kiss was misinterpreted as a gesture of receiving the blessing before imparting it to the people), but after it, so that its valedictory character stands out unmistakably.

VIII. DEGREES OF SOLEMNITY IN THE MANNER OF CELEBRATING THE EUCHARIST

Although the structural framework of the Mass is fixed and recognizable in whatever setting its celebration takes place, still its actual presentational format may vary from time to time, and vary principally according to the manner in which the Church is present at the celebration. The basic, standard form will always remain the service for which the ecclesial community assembles on Sunday. The Constitution on the Sacred Liturgy outlines the ideal when it upholds the Eucharist celebrated by the bishop as the true image of the Church:

> The Church reveals herself most clearly when a full complement of God's holy people . . . exercise a thorough and active participation at the very altar where the bishop presides in the company of his priests and other assistants (§41).

Under present circumstances this ideal may be realized only rarely. The large congregation of an episcopal diocese is divided into parishes. The pastor presides over the Eucharist of the parish community gathered together on Sunday. Besides the Sunday Eucharist of the parish community there is the Mass celebrated on weekdays and attended by smaller, more or less random groups. Finally, there is the Mass said by the priest without a community. Here then are the basic categories: the bishop's pontifical Mass, the priest's parish Mass on Sundays and feast days, the weekday Mass, the private Mass.

In reports preserved from the early centuries the Mass was almost always presided over by the bishop, though occasionally a Mass entrusted to the priest is mentioned in passing from the time

215

of St. Ignatius of Antioch, as in his Letter to the Smyrnaeans (8:1). A highly developed form of the pontifical Mass is described in the documents of the original Roman liturgy. The first Roman Ordo tells us of the Pope's "station Mass" in which the whole city participated (Andrieu OR 2:65-108). The participation of the papal court and of a large number of clerics together with bishops of the immediate neighborhood has left its special mark upon the ritual; and it acquired other characteristics through the necessity for a special choir, the *schola cantorum*.

1. MASS OF BISHOPS AND PRIESTS

Before long in northern European countries the ritual of the first Roman Ordo was edited for the bishop's pontifical Mass, and defined in the Ordines IX, X, and VII (Andrieu 2:327-36; 349-62; 293-305). The bishop, surrounded by the clergy of the See city, presided over the celebration. At his entry he was preceded by seven acolytes and a thurifer. During the Fore-Mass he took his seat in the apse, behind the altar (*retro altare*). When he walked he was flanked by two assistants after the manner of ancient Oriental court ceremonial (*sustentatio* — the gesture of support).

In the northern European countries, as the above-mentioned Ordines gained ground during the eighth-tenth centuries, this same procedure (with the exception of the *sustentatio*) came to be applied also in the priest's Mass whenever the corresponding preconditions were fulfilled, as for example, in the daily Mass of monastic and canonical communities. It was only at the turn of the millennium that a clear distinction emerged between the bishop's pontifical Mass and the priest's high Mass. The first clear evidence of such a distinction is to be found in the liturgical descriptions of John of Avranches (d. 1079; De Off. Eccl.; PL 147:32-37). This is the origin of the solemn Mass (*missa sollemnis*).

From now on, the seven torchbearers and the seat in the apse were reserved for the bishop alone, and a priest could not claim them. The priest's assistants no longer comprised the entire number of the clergy available, but simply a deacon and a subdeacon (in certain cases after the twelfth century he might be allowed also a priest assistant). There are other minor distinctions as well, e.g., with regard to the celebrant's position at the Gloria and the Credo, or the precise moment at which he washes his hands (MRR 1:200-204).

There are no documents to inform us as to the evolution of the priest's Sunday Mass in the titular churches of Rome during the early period. Probably the conspicuous difference in ritual consisted in the absence of the choir, and the consequent omission of chanting at the Introit, Offertory, and Communion. The assistance of a deacon was, however, part of the normal course. St. Cyprian prescribed that the priests who went to prisons in order to celebrate Mass for imprisoned Christians should be accompanied by a deacon (Ep. 5:2; CSEL 3:479); and in one of his homilies, St. John Chrysostom points an accusing finger at those wealthy Christians who owned entire villages and yet did not bother to erect a church or maintain a priest and a deacon to celebrate Mass on Sundays (In Acta Ap. Hom. 18:4-5; PG 60:147-48).

While the Eastern Churches have retained to the present the practice of the deacon's assisting the priest at Mass, in the West a minor cleric took over the function of the deacon at a very early stage of liturgical development. There are, however, rare exceptions to this custom. For one, in the conventual Mass of the Carthusians even today a deacon only, and no lesser minister, assists the priest at the altar. Hence, when we speak of the "Mass with a deacon" (*missa cum diacono*), we should have the basic form of the priest's Sunday Mass in mind.

In addition to the Mass with a full ecclesial assembly, from earliest times (as noted above) Mass has also been celebrated without the complement of a congregation; examples would be Mass for a smaller circle like that of mourners in case of death, or for a family on a special occasion. Too, in Rome and elsewhere there were domestic oratories in which the Eucharist was celebrated. We shall consider this more in detail in Part IV, chapter 6. Since no special ritual was evolved for the home Mass, evidently there was to be no solemnity of any kind in such settings.

2. PRIVATE MASS

Finally, as we have seen (in Part I, ch. 5), since the early Middle Ages there has been the purely private Mass, in which the priest alone along with a server offers the sacrifice. Most frequently this is the votive Mass celebrated for someone who is not expected to participate. Nor did any special ritual develop for the private Mass, except that in the texts of the variable parts as well in the Preface the accent is on petition. In the Carolingian empire after the eighth century there were Mass texts in which the prayers (Collects, Preface, Hanc igitur) were all phrased in the singular. A typical case has the title "Mass which the priest is to sing for himself" (*Missa quam sacerdos pro se ipso debet canere*).[191] It is in this period that we hear of episcopal decrees against the *missa solitaria*, the Mass celebrated without even a server.

The reform under Pope St. Pius V, as incorporated in the Missal of 1570, distinguishes two chief forms of the Mass: the *missa conventualis* and the *missa privata*. Regulations concerning the bishop's pontifical Mass came only later, in the Caeremoniale Episcoporum of 1600. The conventual Mass presupposes collegiate and monastic churches with a large number of clerics taking part in the Divine Office sung in choir. This Mass is always celebrated as a solemn Mass with deacon and subdeacon and with chanting.

Besides this, the Pius V Missal recognizes the private Mass without chant and with only one server. The question of other participants arises only insofar as mention is made of "those standing around" (*circumstantes*) who keep kneeling throughout the Mass (except at the Gospel) and listen to the prayers the priest pronounces aloud. It is this private Mass that now comes to define the liturgical image of the Mass in general. The situation "where sometimes the priest sings the Mass without deacon and subdeacon" is looked upon as an exception (Ritus servandus 6:8). In the centuries that followed, however, this *missa cantata*, as the Mass of the individual priest with his congregation later came to be known, became in fact the most important form of the Mass.

The above categories of Masses corresponded to the conditions prevailing in the sixteenth century when every larger church could boast a college of priests to assist at a solemn Mass, and when the sacramental priesthood was believed to be rightly and duly emphasized by faithful adherence to the medieval separation of altar and people.

3. THE LITURGICAL MOVEMENT

It was a reaction to this isolation of the priest and devaluation of the people's role that the liturgical movement made rapid strides from 1909 onward, under the changed conditions of our age. A provisional solution was found in the so-called dialogue Mass (*missa dialogata*), which became popular after 1920. The faithful were instructed to join in the responses, a lector took over the readings, a leader read the priest's prayers in the language of the people while the priest read them in Latin in a low voice. After Pope Pius XII had recognized such endeavors in principle by way of his 1947 encyclical *Mediator Dei*, long before Vatican Council II was announced, the Instruction of September 3, 1958, "Sacred Music and Sacred Liturgy," issued by the Sacred Congregation of of Rites but approved "in a special way" by Pope Pius in one of his last acts on earth, gave directives in line with the above-mentioned temporary solution (see TPS 5.2 [1958-59] 230-50).

Vatican Council II then initiated the radical reconstruction of the liturgy with deliberate accent upon the Mass of the people of God. No longer does the private Mass, nor, for that matter, the high Mass, define the standard. The separation between altar and people has been removed. The only distinction allowed in the 1969 Order of Mass of the Missale Romanum is that between Mass with a Congregation and Mass without a Congregation.

Coinciding more or less with the notion of the private Mass, Mass without a Congregation has, apart from the absence of participants and the omission of singing, only one distinguishing characteristic, viz., certain words otherwise addressed to the congregation (e.g., invitation to the Penitential Rite and to the Sign of Peace, and the "Ite, Missa est") are dropped and the Mass server takes over the role of the people. As for the changeable parts of the Mass without a Congregation, a compromise solution has been hit upon; if need be, the priest himself reads the Entrance and Communion Antiphons.

The "common form" of the Mass with a Congregation (General Instruction §§78, 82–126) presupposes that the celebrating priest is flanked by a reader (lector), a cantor, and at least one minister (server). Whenever possible, a deacon may assist the priest; this provision is by the way of being a revival of the *missa cum diacono*. The reading of the Gospel and assisting with the chalice or the book are mentioned as special tasks of the deacon (§§78, 127–41). The reading of the First (and Second) Lesson(s) and assistance with the book by the side of the celebrant, once assigned to the subdeacon as his special function (§§142-52), are now performed by other ministers.

4. Concelebration

An improvement in the Vatican II liturgical reform was the revival of the concelebrated Mass. In the early Middle Ages the celebration of the Eucharist in common by all the priests present took place as a matter of course in monastic and canonical communities, as it has continued to do in the Eastern Churches. Since there was never a doubt whether in such a ceremony each individual priest exercised his priestly power, the traditional practice in which only one priest recited the Eucharistic Prayer (including the words of Consecration) was never called into question. We read of one exception to this usage, when for a time during the eighth century in Rome, on four major feasts the cardinal priests recited the whole Canon along with the Pope (Andrieu OR 2:131).

In this sense the Roman liturgy's service for Maundy Thursday, in effect until 1964, was, but for its absence of formality, a genuine continuation of the older concept of the Eucharistic celebration in common: one priest celebrated the Mass, and the other priests present received Communion. With the thirteenth century (Andrieu 2:349; 3:270f.), concelebration became the practice at the ordination Mass in the Roman liturgy, as an immediate exercise of the priestly Orders just received, as well as an expression of fellowship with the bishop. Hence, at the Ordination Mass the newly ordained priests recite with the ordaining bishop both the prayers and the words of Consecration.[192]

At Vatican II it was largely the representatives of monastic orders who pressed for a wider application of concelebration, in the hope of eradicating the situation in which every day each monk first said his private Mass and thereafter attended the conventual Mass at which no one received Communion. The larger point at issue was to substitute concelebration on still other occasions such as congresses and pilgrimages for the unnatural spectacle of large numbers of priests each saying his private Mass in a corner (of a hotel ballroom, perhaps). Apart from the stipend problem that would arise,[193] another question complicated the matter and rendered a proper evaluation of concelebration more difficult. Assuming the same level of devotion, was an individual priest's celebration with the full exercise of his priestly powers to be considered of higher value than his participation "in lay fashion" (*modo laicorum*) with Communion at a Mass celebrated by some other priest? Pius XII had repudiated the view that a Mass in which a hundred priests participate with devotion is "the same" as a hundred Masses they might celebrate individually.[194] As has been pointed out, however, this might well be true of the nature of the act that is placed a hundred times in the latter case, but it does not necessarily hold good with regard to the fruit, the spiritual value, which might in fact be the same in both cases, if one accepts the view concerning the *fructus missae* explained in Part II, ch. 7.[195]

So then, if the question is to find the best liturgical form in which several priests can celebrate the Eucharist together (a devout and worthy attitude being presupposed), silent concelebration (where one priest fulfills the sacramental requirements and the others assist as silent participants) would have to be preferred to verbal concelebration (where all perform the sacramental sign together), inasmuch as silent concelebration is a more perfect expression of the Eucharist as a sign of the Church's unity.[196]

Although in the Vatican II reform concelebration was reinstated primarily as a substitute for the accumulation of private Masses, the practice soon came to be adopted for the sake of enhancing the solemnity of a festive occasion through an enriched form of the *missa sollemnis*. The larger congregation on such occasions in the nave is looked upon as calling for a correspondingly larger representation from the clergy at the altar.

This brings us to another impressive form of solemn Eucharistic service (with or without concelebration), that is, a ceremony in which the norms of the pontifical Mass are fulfilled and moreover the faithful of the See city or even of a larger area gather around their bishop, as, for example during a pastoral visitation. This might foreshadow the revival of stational Masses, which were the custom in many See cities during the early Middle Ages, as A. Häussling relates.[197]

From another angle, and on an even broader scale, a development in the same direction has been under way for many years. International Eucharistic Congresses have been held ever since 1881, at first every year, and later on, every four years. Since 1893 (Jerusalem), they have been most often, and since 1906 (Tournai) regularly, attended by a papal representative; and at Bombay (1964) and Bogota (1968), Pope Paul himself presided. As at first these congresses had the character of a public manifestation of faith in Christ and in his presence in the Blessed Sacrament, they usually culminated in a colorful procession. But with the growing consciousness that the celebration of the Eucharist is the highest and noblest expression of the Church's life, there has grown also the conviction that the universal Church's gathering in honor of the Eucharist should find its climax in the Eucharistic celebration.

Thus did the concept of the Eucharistic Congress prove to be a magnified reproduction of the stational Mass for which the Christian people formerly gathered around the bishop's altar in Rome and other diocesan centers. This viewpoint exercised a formative influence on more recent international Eucharistic Congresses and brought about a real breakthrough at Munich in 1960.[198]

IX. ELEMENTS IN THE FORMATION OF THE EUCHARISTIC LITURGY

The various degrees of solemnity and of external form applied in the Mass correspond to the status of the ecclesial community in which the Eucharist is celebrated. The uncontested principle is that the people as well as the priest have something to do in the Mass. Thus it happens, for example, that the dialogue preceding the Eucharistic Prayer has been preserved in all the liturgies known to us. But the emphasis given to the people's role may vary.

1. PARTICIPATION OF THE PEOPLE

Sacramental participation consists in reception of the sacrament. As their counterpart to this reception, as early as in the third century the people were inspired with the idea that they should contribute the material gifts, and this was the genesis of the Offertory procession. Participation through responses to the prayers was self-explanatory. According to Eusebius' Church History (7:9), Dionysius of Alexandria (died c. 264/65) counted among the privileges of a Christian the right to hear the Eucharistic Prayer, to join in the *Amen*, to stand at the Lord's table, and to receive the sacred food.

As for participation in prayer, the people were expected to say not only the acclamations but also the responses in the psalmody recited between the readings as well as during the Prayer of the Faithful, the Sanctus, and, later on, the Agnus Dei. Though neglected for a while, this participation was re-emphasized during the Carolingian reform. As late a witness as Burkhard of Worms (d. 1025) cites it as an example of sinful negligence in the Church that people do not say the response in answer to the priest's call and do not pray.[199] Thereafter this participation declined steadily, as was practically inevitable once the curtain of the Latin language precluded intelligent participation in the responses and prayers. Right up to the twentieth century all that was demanded of the faithful was that they "hear" the Mass, that they be devoutly present at it, though, as we know, there were many who ignored the minimum and participated perfectly in spirit through the use of hand missals or other interpretive aids.

Under such conditions the question naturally came up: How much of the Mass were the people obliged to "hear"? In his Liber Officialis (3:36f.) Amalarius of Metz had already answered the question for the "unlettered masses" (*vulgus indoctum*): from the Offertory to the "Ite, Missa est" (Hanssens 2:370). As we know, however, post-Tridentine moralists included also the Fore-Mass, but not as a rule the Last Gospel. With regard to non-communicants the question had been asked and answered even earlier. In the Gallican Mass they could leave when the solemn blessing was given after the Lord's Prayer; and according to the first Roman Ordo (Andrieu OR 2:102) as well as other Roman documents, any announcements that had to be made concerning the next Masses were read out before the Communion of the faithful, so that no one would miss them.

Vatican II has once more prescribed participation in the entire Mass, insisting that the Liturgy of the Word is in its way on the same footing with the other parts of the Mass (CL §56). In any case the question has ceased to be of importance, for, now that the vernacular has been reinstated and active participation of the people enjoined, hardly anyone would dream of restricting or curtailing this participation. It may be that when the distribution of Communion takes an unusually long time, non-communicants will begin to wonder at what point they may leave without missing a "principal part."

In the ancient Church the *posture* assumed by the faithful was an expression of their participation in the priest's prayer. When they were at prayer the faithful, like the priest, remained standing, facing east, with hand upraised.[200] The kneeling position was introduced only as a preliminary to the priest's prayer, when after the "Let us pray" (*Oremus*) the phrase "Let us kneel" (*Flectamus genua*) invited the people to fall on their knees. This procedure was dropped on Sundays and during the Easter season, when the people prayed standing only, in honor of the risen Lord.

The proper posture at prayers of blessing and during the Canon of the Mass was a deep inclination. Even today the Eastern rites have inclination prayers at several points. In the West the deep bow was gradually replaced by the kneeling posture, which was referred to at the synod of Tours in 813 (can. 37; Mansi 4:89) as a natural position and a normal posture for the faithful. To sit for the readings (other than the Gospel) and the sermon was simply the most natural thing to do.

During the later Middle Ages precise rules for the change of bodily position during the various parts of the Mass gradually evolved under the head of "choir rules."[201] But these rules were so severe that they could be observed only in choirs of clerics.

2. MUSIC

The Eucharist, as celebrated in the assembly of the faithful, has a festive character by its very nature as the gathering of a community in God's name and for his praise. Now, singing and instrumental music are part of a feast. At the innermost zone of the liturgy, however, at the altar where man stands face to face with God, the intimacy and seriousness of this unmediated encounter rule out music of a lighter vein. In composition as well as in delivery the priest's prayers should hardly go beyond eloquent speech and a solemn recitative tone (albeit in the Leonine Sacramentary we do find one note to the effect that the prayers are accompanied by "the necessary recitative melodies" [cum sensibus necessariis]).[202]

This restraint need not be so strictly applied, however, in the case of the clergy and people immediately surrounding the celebrant and offering the sacrifice with him. The Sanctus, at which the very choir of angels are invited to join in singing God's praise, calls for singing. From the very beginning the hymns of the so-called Ordinary (Kyrie, Gloria, Credo, Sanctus, Agnus Dei) were "choral hymns" meant to be sung, if not by the entire congregation, at least by the choir of clergy assisting at the Mass (see MRR 1:124).

On the other hand, the hymns sung between the readings required a cantor or *psalmista*, and for him there was a special book, the *cantatorium*, often richly illuminated. He was the precentor (leader of the singing), who chanted the verses for the people to respond to. Since they were always set to simple melodies that required no musical training, these responses could be handled by the whole congregation.

Again, the case was different still with regard to the hymns of the Proper: the variable processional songs sung at the Entrance, at the Offertory, and at Communion. These are somewhat more remote from the essence of the Mass, not being autonomous elements in the structure of the whole ritual but serving rather as decorative commentary or embellishment to actions already present, songs to accompany the ongoing ritual, comparable to the choruses in classical drama. For these hymns Rome had the *schola cantorum* by at least the seventh century.

During subsequent centuries the performance of the schola grew more studied and more sophisticated. The melodies were set down in neumes and preserved in antiphonaries; and, out of this, Guido of Arezzo, around the year 1025, developed the first musical notation.

With the waning of the Middle Ages came the rise of polyphony for solemn occasions. Now beauty was discovered not only in the intoning of a succession of notes to produce melody (melismas), but also in their simultaneous coordination to produce harmony. This naturally imposed greater demands on the singers' talents and training, and qualified lay persons had to be engaged; that was the beginning of professional choirs, which handled all the sung parts from then on. Some seers, Bernard of Clairvaux among them, warned against the danger of increasing secularization inherent in this development; and in a decree issued in 1324–25 Pope John XXII condemned the exaggerated embellishment of choral melodies.[203] The Fathers of the Council of Trent approved the new church music somewhat guardedly, without going on record by way of a conciliar decree.

Pierluigi da Palestrina (d. 1594) inaugurated the great age of Renaissance polyphony, for which, besides the organ, the whole range of orchestral instruments was increasingly pressed into service. If all such means at the disposal of Renaissance music had served to adorn only an occasional feast-day Mass in the cathedral, the effects might have been well worth it. But the regrettable thing was that now this elegant musical service was attempted in city and country, Sunday after Sunday. Probably such a grand façade compensated in some measure for the personal experience of the mystery that was denied many people and for the entry into the sanctum to which they no longer had access — though, of course, for many others the mystery was experienced without any help from the vernacular or from physical participation. And who can estimate the spiritual, mystical value of the aesthetic experience of a magnificent polyphonic Mass?[204] The liturgical renewal of the twentieth century inevitably precipitated a crisis for church music. New solutions will be found only gradually, and they will vary according to culture and country.

3. The Other Arts

For the performance of the Eucharist not only words and music but also material things are required; hence the deployment of physical, spatial forms in the shaping of the liturgy. As in music, these material forms, while adding external adornment and grandeur, likewise became ever richer and richer in themselves. As early as St. Augustine's time, vessels of gold and silver were in use. The table became a stone or marble altar, and it was covered with precious linen. Then pictures and images were placed on it, and this eventually led to the construction of grand Gothic and Baroque high altars.

The priests wore unusual vestments, a stylized form of late Roman formal attire, in increasingly expensive materials. The symbolism of light and incense was incorporated at a very early stage in liturgical development, to point up the exalted nature of the ceremony under way. By the time of Constantine all the treasures of the earth, all the talent and inspiration of architects and artists, were put at the service of a basilica abuilding. Nothing was too good for God.

4. Principles for Use of Art in Liturgy

From the religious viewpoint the Eucharistic celebration in the assembled community is the greatest of all events, the high point of our earthly existence. It has the magnetic power to draw all arts unto itself, to bring them to their perfection and noblest expression during the divine service. At the same time, however, with good reason and an undertone of clear warning, Vatican II prescribed that "the rites should be distinguished by a noble simplicity" (CL §34; see also §124).

Our own age is questioning the artistic forms of expressing the holy, especially forms stemming from an ancient tradition. It is the question of the sacral versus the profane — indeed, of the most egregious desacralization.[205] Undeniably the past two thousand years have left us an overabundance of forms, many of which are no longer understood as expressions of what they were originally meant to convey, so that they obscure the holy rather than reveal it. Such forms are often taken in isolation from their original context (in which alone they have real meaning) and are attributed an independent value. People cling to them merely because they have been handed down, as though through long usage in the religious sphere they had received a special kind of consecration, had become sacralized, holy. As such they are in stark contrast to the simplicity and interiority we encounter in the writings of the New Testament.

To be sure, cultic forms and nomenclature proper to Old Testament tradition are employed in the New Testament writings, but only as symbolic figures pointing to the conditions and tasks of Christian life, not to the nature of the liturgical service of the new covenant. Something new has begun. Holiness itself, God himself, has come into this world in the person of Christ. The "You alone are holy" (*Tu solus sanctus*) refers to God. It is God's armor, too, against the deifications and the sacralizations of the ancient pagan world. For the world is indeed God's creation, but it has been given to men to dwell in and to use. In itself it has no particular claim to sacredness.

In Christ something new has entered the world, something that must leaven all creation and sanctify it. "It was his intent to sanctify the world by his most merciful coming" (*mundum volens adventu suo piissimo consecrare*), says the Roman Martyrology of the birth of Jesus in its epitome of the Christmas mystery.[206] This leaven of holiness spreads from Christ through his Church; and because it is a visible Church, its work of spreading the leaven requires visible and tangible forms. In Baptism and in the Eucharist the Church seizes upon material creation in its leavening process. The symbolism inherent in the sacraments is enhanced and explained by means of the liturgy, and this expansion simply reflects the reverence with which we receive the holy. The Church receives with veiled hands, so to say, what God grants it.

The development of the sacramental sign of such forms as help us to encounter the holy has also another function: to keep us, human beings endowed with body and senses, from failing to recognize the holy and spiritual, from missing it by overlooking or misunderstanding it. Finally, our Lord himself instituted the Eucharist within the framework of a sacral meal and within sacral forms that still belonged to the promise of the Old Testament and had to be superseded by new forms, forms in which the Church in its progress through the centuries would strive to give worthy expression to the new.

5. AUTHENTICITY AND ORDER

The concrete forms through which the liturgy seeks to fulfill its function must remain in a state of perpetual tension between *authenticity* and *order*. On the one hand, they should embody authentic expression of the spiritual and the interior. The priest, serving as the community's representative, should express what he himself feels and the community feels; or, better still, what both ought to think and feel in accordance with their divine vocation. And this, on the other hand, implies that the expression should be governed by order.

The larger the community, the greater the need for order. It is not surprising that with the rapid growth of communities in the West as well as in the East during the fourth century, the shape of the liturgies quickly crystallized, leaving little — sometimes regrettably too little — to the personal decisions and choices of the priest. During the past centuries this has been particularly true of the Roman liturgy, with its strong centralization since the admittedly necessary reform of Pius V. The collection of decrees issued by the Congregation of Rites during the first three centuries since its foundation in 1588 comprises 5,993 entries.

Vatican II has struck a middle course between rigid centralization and individual freedom. The fixed order has not been thrown overboard. The tradition of a uniform Roman liturgy has been retained. At the same time, important matters have been left to the discretion of national bishops' conferences and to individual bishops (CL §§22, 37–40, 57). Further, the new Order of Mass of 1969 leaves the option to the celebrating priest at several points, even on the question of the Eucharistic Prayer.

In certain areas (as, for example, with regard to incense, the Pax, the pause for silent prayer after Communion), the new Order of Mass (56i) suggests a ritual that may be employed "when convenient" (*opportune*). Such relaxation was the outcome not only of the principle of decentralization but also and especially of the recognition that the Church celebrating the Eucharist is not simply the universal Church as such, but in each instance a specific ecclesial community assembled in one specific place. To such a concrete community the opportunity for normal growth must be granted within, of course, the framework of unity.

Probably before long, this latitude too will crystallize into a fixed order according to the customs and practices of each individual place, not out of indifference or indolence but because even freedom of choice should be governed by objective attitudes and not be allowed to degenerate into mere whim or arbitrariness. Concrete experience will show all the more clearly that *it is but a utopian fancy to want each celebration of the Eucharistic liturgy shaped anew through the creative spontaneity of liturgical experimenters.* For what Karl Rahner has said with regard to Christian piety in general holds good with regard to the liturgy and to the Eucharistic celebration in particular: "The Christian living of tomorrow is faithful and obedient to the spirit of true Christian religion when it has a taste for that which is solidly established, practiced and has already taken shape, for that which is 'the practice' — in short, for forms of devotion which are established institutions in the Church. It will cease to be faithful and obedient in this sense if it allows itself to be swayed by undisciplined emotions." [207] The Church itself is an institution because it is visible. It needs institutions and makes use of institutions insofar as these are suitable means for revealing and fostering its inner life.

PART FOUR

The Spiritual and Pastoral
Aspects of the Mass

I. EUCHARISTIC PIETY AND CHRISTIAN LIFE

Now that we are clear on the theological "matter of the Mass" and the liturgical form it has taken, what remains to be explored is the question of its application, the question, namely, of the way the Mass affects — or should affect — the whole life of the Church and of the individual Catholic.

1. "EUCHARIST" AS CENTER OF SPIRITUALITY

That the Eucharist is the center of Catholic spirituality is a truism that has been repeated often during the past centuries; thus, e.g., Pope Pius XII in *Mediator Dei*: "The mystery of the most holy Eucharist . . . is the culmination and center, as it were, of the Christian religion" (§66). Yet the meaning conveyed in this statement is far from constant, varying as it does with the occasion provoking it.

During the Baroque age after the Council of Trent, the Eucharist was cherished as the very heart of piety, but it was the perduring sacrament reserved in the tabernacle, exposed in the monstrance for veneration, and carried in solemn procession through streets, fields, and stadiums. In biographies of pious Catholics of the Baroque age, devotion to the Blessed Sacrament is almost invariably held up as an important trait of their sanctity, a devotion that found expression chiefly in the numerous congregations and brotherhoods of perpetual adoration that flourished conspicuously during the nineteenth century.[208] Many great saints, among them Saints Paschal Baylon (d. 1592) and Peter Julian Eymard (d. 1868), to mention but two, attained perfection in the love of God by following this path of devotion.

It must be pointed out, however, that in this perspective, one whose first premise is Christ's presence in the sacred Host, only a limited portion of the rich and multidimensional panorama of

Catholic faith comes into consideration. True, it does yield all that is necessary for an intense spiritual life: God's nearness to us, God's love, the Incarnation, the heavenly banquet begun already here on earth. But certain other elements that are indispensable for a complete utilization of our faith in all its richness (as well as for the proper preaching of the Gospel) such as the Trinity, Christ's mediatorship, the Church, remain beyond the immediate horizon in this restricted perspective.

This type of Eucharistic piety therefore stands in a certain isolation; it appears as one devotion among other devotions that, if correctly analyzed, should actually complement it. This is why we notice a shift of emphasis in the spirituality of the twentieth century. It is no longer the *Person* of Jesus Christ but an *action* that is now seen as the real heart of the Eucharist.

The Eucharist is the sacrament through which the sacrifice of the Cross is re-presented in the Church; accordingly, the real, bodily presence of the crucified and risen Lord is certainly implied and asserted. But the Eucharist extends to the salvific event of the Cross. From this as from their source flow all the other mysteries of the Christian message of salvation: here God is glorified, sin and death are conquered through the redemptive suffering of the one Mediator, hearts are set afire with love, God's people are gathered together into the one Church from one end of the world to the other, and the great banquet, which must find its consummation in eternity, is announced and begun in time. It is in the Eucharist that God continually communicates himself to man, and at the same time man gives his humble and grateful answer to this self-communication of God. Christ and the Church meet each other here.[209]

Thus the Eucharist is in the fullest sense that summation (*recapitulatio*) of which St. Irenaeus speaks in his attack on "all the heresies" (Adv. Haer. 4:17f.). All humanity is summed up in Christ. All the sacrifices of the time before Christ are more than fulfilled in his sacrifice. As A. Hamman points out, in bread and wine earthly creation too is taken up into the very heart of the mystery of the world's redemption.[210]

The Vatican document "Instruction on the Worship of the Eucharistic Mystery" (*Instructio de Cultu Mysterii Eucharistici*) made public on May 25, 1967,[211] ratifies and explains this redis-covered, more complete form of Eucharistic piety. It also points out that what is of value in the older form need not and should not be discarded. The Mass is the source as well as the focus of the veneration tendered the sacrament outside the Mass, "for the sacrament is reserved primarily for this purpose, that the faithful who could not take part in the Mass may in communion be united with Christ and his sacrifice" (§3e; see §49).

The obligation to adore the Blessed Sacrament is underlined in section 3 of the same text. The custom of "visits to the Blessed Sacrament" has been clarified in: "Prayer before the Blessed Sacrament" (*oratio coram ss. sacramento*, §50). "The Eucharistic sacrifice is therefore the source and crown (*culmen*) of the Church's entire cultus and of the whole of Christian life" (§3e; see §6). Source and crown . . . not only of the Church's cultus, but of "the whole of Christian life!" This latter attribution is really of cardinal importance and hence calls for more detailed consideration.

2. Center of the Whole Christian Life

For some Catholics — only God knows their number — life and liturgy are far apart. For some others, the liturgy, or at least the more solemn ceremonies of the old-style liturgy, are an idealization of life. Perhaps a number could also be found who went to Mass in order to escape the humdrum and routine of daily life for an hour and to let themselves be transported into a purer world by the enchanting atmosphere of mysterious stillness and strange forms, or by the ineffable Gregorian chants or the rich polyphony of some great composer. Churchgoers of this stripe, far from being attracted by the new shape of the liturgy, may be repulsed instead; for now that the language of the people has been adopted, they find themselves confronted with a liturgy that is concerned not with meeting their temperamental needs but with preaching Christ and nourishing the faith, a liturgy that is demanding indeed.[212]

Perhaps too we could refer to those who look upon the Sunday Mass as nothing more than an obligation to be fulfilled. For such, going to church on Sunday is on a par with going to the office on Monday; both actions are performed routinely, with the same sense of duty; otherwise, however, the two acts have little in common, and do not interact upon each other.

The Eucharistic celebration will have realized the full significance inherent in it only when it forms one single unit with life, only when it is a distillation, a concentrated form of Christian living. The Mass is meant to be an expression of Christian life, and only to the extent to which it is the expression of Christian life is it also its "crown." Only then can it act as a new powerhouse, a new driving force, a new help and therefore the "source" of Christian living.

This might explain why in the writings of the New Testament, in the Acts and Letters of the Apostles, we find relatively little explicit reference to the Eucharist. The stress is much more on living "in Christ." Christians are exhorted, as Paul exhorted his constituents: "Your attitude must be that of Christ . . . who humbled himself, obediently accepting even death, death on a cross" (Phil. 2:5-8). With gratitude in their hearts they should sing "psalms, hymns, and inspired songs to God," and say or do nothing except in the name of the Lord Jesus, giving "thanks to God the Father through him" (Col. 3:16f.).

They must offer their bodies (and with it their whole life) "as a living sacrifice, holy and acceptable to God" (Rom. 12:1). Only exceptionally does an expression vacillate uncertainly between sacrament and life, apparently embracing both. Thus, according to 1 Peter 2:4f., the faithful should set themselves close to Jesus Christ, so that they may become "living stones, built as an edifice of spirit, into a holy priesthood, offering spiritual sacrifices, acceptable to God through Jesus Christ."

Such is the attitude with which the faithful should come to Mass. "Faith and devotion" (*fides et devotio*) is the expression used in the Roman Canon to describe this frame of mind. Faith is the self-evident root; but this root must have grown into devotion, or, in other words, it must have flowered forth into love. St. Thomas Aquinas brings this out in the Summa Theologica (3a, 79:7 ad 2) when, commenting on Augustine, he says that the holy sacrifice "produces no effect except in those who are united with Christ's Passion through faith and charity" (*per fidem et caritatem*).

That this devotion should inform the spirituality of the Christian was clear even at the time of Justin Martyr, who described in his Apologia what happens in Baptism: "We have offered ourselves to God" (61:1). Thus the whole course of Christian living that flows from Baptism is characterized as a continual self-surrender to God. This self-surrender is realized anew in a sacramental act each time we celebrate the Eucharist. It is taken up into Christ's self-surrender, which sanctifies and quickens it. Such is the very meaning of the Eucharist. As has been observed by B. Fraigneau-Julien: "The Eucharistic sacrifice has no other raison d'être but that the Church may ever become one with the sacrifice of her head." [213]

II. THE SIGN AND THE THING SIGNIFIED

The Eucharist and Christian living should form one complete whole; yet it is necessary to distinguish the one from the other. The two elements are related to each other as sign and thing signified. St. Thomas Aquinas stressed the same point: the exterior sacrifice that is offered is a sign of the interior sacrifice with which someone offers himself (ST 3a, 82:4c). Journet has this idea in mind when he distinguishes between sacrifice in the cultic order (*ligne cultuelle*) and sacrifice in the order of love (*ligne de l'amour redempteur* [*La Messe*, pp. 134–47]). Or, in simple theological terms, the Christian life orientated toward God is itself not the sacrifice that is offered; rather, Christian life is what is signified and represented through the sacrifice.

So while, as is clear from Rahner-Häussling (p. 30), the self-offering implied in Christian living "does not . . . belong to the constitutive elements of the cultic action," still, such a self-offering is "not a merely subjective trimming that would have nothing to do with the substance of the sacrifice of the Mass."

1. THE CHRISTIAN'S SELF-OFFERING SEEKS CULTIC EXPRESSION

Christian living, which is always and everywhere the service of God and a search for God along the way of life that Christ has trod before us, needs and seeks an expression in which it may be summed up time and again, in which it may become visible before God and in the assembly of the faithful. This expression it finds in the very sacrifice of the Church in which Christ's own sacrifice becomes present. That sacrifice would have little meaning if it did not have the function of a real sign; if, that is, behind this cultic sacrifice there did not lie the self-surrender of those—or at least of one of those—who offer the sacrifice. This was true even of Old Testament sacrifices, and it is precisely why the prophets came out against outward sacrifices devoid of interior significance. "What care I for the number of your sacrifices? says the Lord. I have had enough of whole-burnt rams and fat of fatlings. . . . Your hands are full of blood! Wash yourselves clean!" (Isaias 1:11, 15f.).

This is all the more true of the New Testament. Warning against a misunderstanding of the New Testament sacraments as being all-sufficient in themselves, Paul quotes as an example the lot that befell many Israelites in the desert: "By the cloud and the sea all of them were baptized into Moses. All ate the same spiritual food. All drank the same spiritual drink (they all drank from the spiritual rock . . . and the rock was Christ), yet we know that God was not pleased with most of them, for they were struck down in the desert" (1 Cor. 10:2-5). Without the interior attitude, the outward sign is worthless and in effect a lie, however holy the sign might be in itself.

The Old Testament people knew this well. They knew that exterior sacrifice without its interior motivation could not penetrate into God's presence, but that, in an emergency, interior sacrifice without the exterior could. Hence the prayer of the psalmist: "My sacrifice, O God, is a contrite spirit" (51:19). And the three young men in the fiery furnace could pray that their contrite soul, their humble spirit, their readiness to die might be acceptable to God as their sacrifice (Dan. 3:38-40). That is why their prayer ("In spiritu humilitatis . . .") was incorporated in the Ordo Missae at an early stage in liturgical history by way of concluding the preparation of the sacrificial gifts, and has also been retained in the reformed Missale Romanum of 1969. It is this spirit, above and beyond all exterior sacrifice, that ultimately matters before God.

As we have already seen in Part I, chapter 5, St. Augustine was so preoccupied by this meaning of sacrifice that when he finally came to define sacrifice he left out the sign altogether and spoke only of the thing signified. Thus, for him sacrifice was "that work by which one adheres to God in a sacred covenant" (City of God 10:6); all works of Christian love and mercy, all acts of self-conquest are sacrifice, and in this sense the Church herself as the community of men seeking God becomes for Augustine a sacrificial gift. For the Church's own self-offering its teacher and model is Christ its Head (ch. 20). Thus Augustine is squarely opposed to any notion that cultic sacrifice has an absolute value of its own.

Classic Protestantism not only ignores cultic sacrifice in the very definition but also excludes it from church service in favor of purely interior sacrifice. This is spiritualism pushed to the extreme; but it was, as we have seen (in Part I, ch. 7), a reaction against the liturgical practice of a time when belief in the objective and absolute efficacy of the cultic sacrifice had reached superstitious proportions; and the reaction persists today, even though the abuses against which it reacted no longer exist. As Peter Brunner argues, the anamnesis of Christ's sacrifice should not be mingled with the offering of our own sacrifice.[214] Interestingly enough, despite all their mistrust of man's spiritual capabilities, even Protestants cannot avoid laying stress on the self-offering of the faithful as a basic requirement of Christianity. By and large this self-offering finds no cultic expression in "low church" liturgy, but when it does, as in individual Agendas, the material gifts of the faithful are officially prescribed or recommended merely as a symbol of their self-offering.[215]

2. THE CHIEF CULTIC EXPRESSION IS THE EUCHARIST

The primary cultic expression of the self-offering implied in Christian living is the Eucharistic sacrifice itself. To express this self-offering is the very purpose for which the Eucharist has been put at our disposal. As the Church's sacrifice, the sacrifice of Christ re-presented in the Mass should be a sign of our own self-surrender.

Every sacrifice, even the Church's sacrifice in the Eucharist, is characterized by its function as a sign. Every sacrifice falls under the genus *sign* (*est in genere signi*), as the Scholastics put it. It is of the very essence of a sacrifice that sacrificing deprives oneself of something in order to present it to the Godhead as an indication of one's subjection. The notion that the offering itself could gratify or placate the Godhead was a distortion that came in only later. To anyone with an enlightened concept of the Godhead, the gift-offering itself could never amount to anything but a sign. The offering of first fruits or flowers, the incense rising from the altar, the blood that is poured out — all this could and should be only a sign, signifying that man with all his possessions belongs to God and is subject to his rule, and recognizes and accepts this relation. Malachi (1:8) compares sacrifice to the tribute a subject renders to his overlord: only a noble, flawless gift may be offered to a prince.

In the New Testament the life of Jesus was a total service and glorification of the Father, culminating and epitomized in the surrender of blood and life on the Cross. This surrender, this obedience unto death, became a towering sign of his life and work.[216] The sign and the thing signified were in this case so completely coterminous that only with difficulty may they be distinguished from each other. The Cross was henceforth to be *the* visible expression signifying that God has been duly glorified and that a new and everlasting covenant has been established in Christ.

The question may now be legitimately raised, whether the Redeemer's body and blood, which were the decisive sign of his self-surrender, may not serve also as a sign of our surrender of our own selves. In *The Lord's Supper* J.-J. von Allmen (the Protestant theologian cited earlier), while vigorously affirming the sacrificial character of the Eucharist, has brought up another interesting consideration, albeit (as he admits) not a crucial one. According to von Allmen, while Christ's sacrifice, which becomes present in the Eucharist, is first and foremost the sacrifice of reconciliation, and this is its real, primary meaning, there is actually a second reason for the Institution at the Last Supper. Jesus wished to leave his chosen ones an outstanding example. Considering our weakness, however, we can speak of this only with a certain reserve, says von Allmen; for otherwise "it would only be the example of romantic heroism easily deflated by a little reason, a little prudence, a little timidity" (p. 91).

While Jesus' self-surrender can never be approximated by our own self-surrender, it is the ideal toward which we should strive, the ideal we should daily affirm and draw courage from, even though we are still so far from him and often unfaithful. It is the challenge to a genuine Christian ethic. It is the call echoing down through the centuries: Follow me! And it is this call that has been translated into human terms in the God-Man's unique example. It is the tempting call of the eagle that spreads its wings and invites its young ones to soar into the skies on its pinions — in the lovely figure of Deuteronomy 32:11.

So then the Church's sacrifice in the Eucharist should really be the sign through which we express and renew our personal self-surrender. Hence it is not enough to say, as is sometimes said, that we should offer ourselves also in the Mass, that we should unite our sacrifice with Christ's sacrifice, as though it were a matter of two separate, independent sacrifices and not a sign *and* the thing it signifies.[217] If, following St. Augustine, we sometimes give the name of sacrifice to the thing signified alone, namely, to the toils of life borne in a Christian spirit, to good works, and to their encapsulation in prayer, then we should be aware that we do so in a metaphorical mode; it may be warranted, but theologically it is inexact.

III. VEIL OF MYSTERY OR VISIBLE PRESENTATION

If the Eucharist as the Church's sacrifice should indeed constitute the sign signifying the continual moral striving of her children, then the fundamental question arises again at this point: How best may this sign, insofar as it lies within the Church's hands to give it shape, be translated into concrete terms in order that it may fulfill its function as effectively as possible? This is the question underlying all attempts at liturgical reform or liturgical development. Should liturgy be a genuine symbol that reveals the sacred without lifting the veil of the mystery, or should it be a literal re-presentation exposing the mystery to the light of reason and expressing its meaning in prosaic terms?

If we ask what history has to tell us on the matter, we shall find that symbolic elements were not wanting in the very first stages of liturgical development. Bread and wine and the words of Institution were charged with deep meaning. For the rest, the ritual in those early years could not have been anything but simple, transparent, and intelligible. With the passage of time, however, the transparency and the rational clarity more and more gave way before the increasing incidence of suggestive symbolism, as may be clearly observed in what happened to the language used in the liturgy during the early Middle Ages.

1. VEILING THE MYSTERY FROM THE FAITHFUL

Since the time of Saints Hilary and Augustine the notion prevailed that the three languages used in the inscription on the Cross were sacred (John 19:19-20).[218] In the ninth century, at the time of Saints Cyril and Methodius, this idea came to be looked upon as a law of obligation, so that the sole language permitted in the liturgy in the West was the sacred Latin language. And so Latin came to stay for another thousand years, even though it was becoming unintelligible to an ever-increasing minority.

Not the least of the justifications for retaining Latin was the rationalization that it served to veil the mystery: the sacred should not be exposed to the scrutiny of the multitude. During the nineteenth century the great defender of the "liturgical language" was Abbot Prosper Guéranger, who in his monumental *Institutions liturgiques* of 1851 rehearsed in fine detail all the arguments of the past, thus giving them an erudite cachet.[219] According to Dom Guéranger the very reading of Holy Writ in the liturgy ought to be elevated and wrapped in mystery "like divine oracles" (*comme les oracles divins*; p. 70).

The tendency to veil the sacred from the eyes of the faithful, however, can be traced much farther back than Guéranger. According to St. Basil's book on the Holy Spirit (27:66; PG 32:189), the Apostles and the Fathers, the first to prescribe fixed rites in the Church, "safeguarded the dignity of the mysteries through secrecy and silence after the example of the Mosaic law"; hence it was not at all necessary that everyone should understand everything. As recounted in Part I, chapter 1, a powerful factor in making the mysterious felt in the very ritual was the attitude fostered by the fourth-century Greek Fathers who speak of the "terrible," "awesome" mystery encountered in the Eucharist.

The immediate practical application was to veil the mystery by pronouncing the sacred words inaudibly even in the assembly of the faithful. In his Pratum Spirituale ("Spiritual Meadow") Johannes Moschus (d. 619) tells of children who, while playing in a field, repeated the words of the anaphora they had heard in church, and were struck by lightning (ch. 196; PG 87:3081); and it is the present writer's theory that this story, finding its way into the lore of the West, became the standard argument for the idea that the words of the Canon of the Mass may be pronounced only in a low voice.[220]

During the Middle Ages the strange language and inaudible recitation employed to keep the mystery veiled were compounded with a highly developed ceremonial. This ceremonial was in part inherited from the tradition of the solemn Eucharistic ritual whose details, unintelligible by now, were allegorically interpreted; and in part it was the product of elaboration during the Middle Ages, as illustrated by the frequent repetition of the sign of the Cross, the altar kiss, bows and genuflections, raising of the eyes and extending of the hands. Other expressions of medieval piety may also be noted: the reverence revealed in the handling of the consecrated species and the sacred vessels, the very material of the vessels, the elegance of the altar with its superstructures, and finally a church architecture abounding in symbols.[221]

In every generation theologians have been willing to go quite far in defending symbolism and its mystery-concealing function; their defense is the outcome not only of an apologetic concern to justify the presence of customs in the Church, but also of genuine conviction. Outstanding among such men was the Oratorian Louis Thomassin (d. 1695), a real man of prayer, who found it quite proper that the liturgy, in its ceremonies as well as its language, should contain certain elements that cannot be reduced to neat intellectual categories, and even went so far as to defend the use of an unintelligible language in chanting and praying, provided that there is the will to pray.[222]

In our day we might think of David Jones, a Welsh poet-painter whose writings, notably *The Anathemata*, have identified him as a most articulate "symbolist" in art and liturgy; and Conrad Pepler, English Dominican spiritual writer, who does not believe it quintessential for perfect participation that every step in the progression of the Mass be verbalized, but rather that the deliberate explicitness of the new Order has diminished the spiritual quality of the liturgy.[223] Another critic, American this time, has called the new liturgy, on account of its wordiness, the last gasp of the anti-McLuhanites or linear men.

2. THE IDEAL OF RATIONAL CLARITY

Today we have become aware that veiling the mystery had been pushed too far, to the detriment of the kerygmatic aspect, i.e., the proclamation of the Good News that should not be separated from the Eucharistic celebration. A movement in the opposite direction that has gathered momentum during the twentieth century seeks to expose and explain what is hidden and mysterious in the rites. Vatican II has ratified this movement and made it a fundamental principle of liturgical reform; thus, the Constitution on the Sacred Liturgy has emphatically affirmed the right and duty the faithful have, by virtue of their "royal priesthood," to "full, conscious, and active participation in liturgical celebrations" (§14); for such participation is the "primary and indispensable source from which the faithful are to derive the true Christian spirit."

Accordingly, "both texts and rites should be drawn up so that they express more clearly the holy things which they signify. Christian people, as far as possible, should be able to understand them with ease and to take part in them fully, actively and as befits a community" (§21). Again, the rites should be characterized by a "noble simplicity." In the words of the Constitution, "they should be within the people's powers of comprehension, and normally should not require much explanation" (§34).

Such intelligent participation of the faithful is again explicitly stressed with regard to the celebration of the Eucharist. Incidentally, this *volte face* of emphasis came directly out of the discussions within the Council itself. For, while the proposals made by the Preparatory Commission had considered only such reforms as would help the faithful to understand thoroughly "the prayers and rites" of Mass, the final text of the Council document asserts that "through a proper appreciation of the prayers and rites they should participate knowingly, devoutly, and actively" (§48).

The subsequent liturgical reform has sought to realize this intention of the Council with the greatest consistency. Indeed, one begins to wonder whether the ideal of rational clarity has not already been pushed to the extreme. Happily, sacral forms that had become fossilized have been cleared away; but, apart from the new Eucharistic Prayers and the Prefaces, no new shoots are yet visible in the clearing.

3. STRIKING A BALANCE

In the final analysis, what we have in the celebration of the Eucharist is always a mystery, and all attempts to explain and clarify can at best bring us closer to the mystery. In the presence of the mystery itself there can never be anything but awe and adoration. Hippolytus of Rome, speaking of the final mystagogical initiation to be undergone by the newly baptized after their very first participation in the Eucharist, says: "This is the white stone of which John speaks [in Apocalypse 2:17], a stone with a new name written on it, known only to the man who receives it" (Botte 59).

It is also significant that the practice of the Church during the fourth and fifth centuries was to admit the newly baptized person, without any special introduction, to the very first celebration of the Eucharist following his Baptism; a mystagogical instruction followed only later. And even this instruction was given through images, metaphors, and above all through interpretation of Old Testament types rather than through conceptual explanations of liturgical and theological points, as is evident from, e.g., Cyril (John) of Jerusalem's Mystagogical Catecheses 4 and 5; Theodore of Mopsuestia's Catecheses on Baptism and Eucharist; and Ambrose's tracts on the mysteries and the sacraments (De Mysteriis and De Sacramentis).

The Eucharistic celebration should be the sign in which Christ's sacrifice and the Church's sacrifice become present before the faithful, a sign that reveals and yet at the same time reverently conceals the mystery. In his Commentary on the Mass (*De Missae Sacrificio*), Suárez speaks of the twofold meaning of sacrifice: the moral sense (*ratio moralis*) insofar as the sacrifice is a recognition of God's majesty, and the mystical sense (*ratio mystica*) insofar as it represents a mystery, e.g., in the case of the Eucharist, Christ's Passion (Disp. 73:2; Vivès ed., 24: 603-606). Evidently the concealment has to do with the mystical aspect primarily: the mystery is made present anew; it is expressed in words to the extent that words are capable of expressing it; it is signified in the separate species; it is projected in rites that are charged with reverence, veneration, and awe.

As a re-presentation of Christ's salvific work, the Eucharist is a sign and at the same time more than a sign. It is efficacious power, the source of grace; and as such it is the luminous darkness of faith. On the other hand, the sign must also show clearly that in the celebration of the Eucharist the community of the faithful wishes to offer its humble service to God. The mystery is proclaimed in the movement of a thanksgiving prayer; and it is this thanksgiving prayer, for which the people are asked to raise their hearts, that is recited aloud in the name of all. The thanksgiving itself becomes the offering, so that at each celebration the living com-

munity, assembled here and now, with the priest at the head, is
conscious of being called and gathered up in this movement.

For the inclusion of the community in this grand movement,
apart from the above-mentioned expression lying at the very heart
of the Eucharistic action, another special form of re-presentation
was sought from early times. The Offertory was introduced for this
purpose, and the faithful were asked to bring their material gift-
offerings. This, as we noted in Part III (ch. 4), was the clearest expression of the people's participation throughout the Middle Ages.
In this same sense, as we may recall from Part I (ch. 3), St. Cyprian
interpreted the commingling of water and wine. This symbolism of
the commingling became quite popular and important during subsequent centuries, especially in the early Middle Ages, when St.
Isidore of Seville and Venerable Bede laid great stress on it.[224] But
then this was pushed into the background in favor of new interpretations that came to be formulated in the words accompanying the
action.

This perspective on the Eucharistic celebration, which was
never completely lost from liturgical tradition precisely because it
pertains ultimately to the very essence of the Eucharist, has been
insisted upon by Vatican II in several places. Thus even here it has
shown itself to be a truly pastoral council. Through the Decree on
the Bishops' Pastoral Office, the Council exhorted the bishops to
"constantly exert themselves to have the faithful know and live the
paschal mystery more deeply through the Eucharist" (§15). And in
the Decree on the Ministry and Life of Priests, heavy stress was
laid upon the duty of priests to instruct the faithful "to offer to God
the Father the divine Victim in the sacrifice of the Mass, and to
join to it the offering of their own lives" (§5).

Moreover, "If the [Eucharistic] celebration is to be sincere and
thorough, it must lead to various works of charity and mutual help,
as well as to missionary activity and to different forms of Christian
witness" (§6). Quoting the words of the ordination ritual, the
decree invites priests "to imitate the realities they deal with" (§13).
This motive — the self-surrender of the faithful in the Eucharistic
sacrifice — could perhaps have been incorporated more explicitly
and more powerfully in the new Canons for the Mass. Nevertheless,
it does find expression in the third Eucharistic Prayer, as the effect
to be produced by the reception of the sacrament: "May [Christ]
make us an everlasting gift to you."

4. The One Mystery Both Veiled and Revealed

Ultimately the two ways, veil of mystery and visual representation, meet and merge: for what is veiled and at the same time exposed is the one "paschal mystery" (*mysterium paschale*), an expression we owe ultimately to Odo Casel, as Warnach has shown in his above-cited *Concilium* article (cf. "mystery", page 105 and note 96). Both ways lead to the same Christ who endures suffering and death, who even in his suffering is victorious and redeems the world. Both ways depend upon the same Christ event that simultaneously is an incomprehensible mystery of divine condescension and a palpable reality that seeks to embrace the whole of humanity and to lead it back to God.

The paschal mystery implies both divine mystery and man's sanctification. With good reason, then, has this become the key concept of Vatican II; nor it is confined to the Constitution on the Liturgy (CL §§5, 6, 61, 104), for it makes its appearance in other documents as well, among them the Pastoral Constitution on the Church in the Modern World, where we read: "Linked with the paschal mystery and patterned on the dying Christ, he [the Christian] will hasten forward to resurrection" (§22). For it is in this multi-dimensional complex of the paschal mystery that all human effort finds its meaning and fulfillment; where men, moved by the Spirit, "devote themselves to that future when humanity itself will become an offering accepted by God" (§38).

Thus it is one uniform plan composed of various ritual elements, one single, total sign, that the liturgy must articulate. For it is the faithful, it is the Church, that celebrates the paschal mystery in the Eucharistic liturgy. It is our mystery that is being celebrated. Hence the thanksgiving prayer contains not only the sacred object of our thanksgiving and our own grateful turning to God, but also the signs of reverence visible from the moment the priest approaches the altar to the moment he leaves it. The gestures of offering always signify both the mystery descending upon us and our encounter with it. This is true with regard to the arrangement of the altar, which is the Lord's table and our table at the same time, as well as with regard to the place of worship, the place of our encounter with Christ and with God.

This last idea was vividly brought out by the figure of Christ dominating the apse of ancient and medieval basilicas. The figure of the risen Lord, or the *majestas Domini* or a cross, met the eyes of those who entered the place provided for the holy assembly. And, as a corollary, the very place has always to be an eloquent testimony to the paschal mystery — with the accent on *paschal*. For what we celebrate in the Eucharist is not merely the redemptive Passion, the sacrifice of redemption as it was consummated on the Cross, but also the sacrifice of the risen and transfigured Redeemer; and the Cross already has its place in the splendor of the resurrection.

The liturgy has given expression to this paschal character at various places in the ritual itself. For several centuries, genuflecting, which then was looked upon as a gesture solely of humble petition and reflecting a penitential attitude, was omitted at Eucharistic celebrations. The *Flectamus genua* ("Let us kneel") preceding all the orations of a vigil (e.g., on the Ember Saturdays outside the Easter season) was dropped at the last Prayer belonging to the Mass proper. Even while praying, priest and people faced the East, the direction of the rising sun, an image of the risen Christ; and until our own time the church building itself was designed to face the East. Above all, it is Sunday, the day Christ rose from the dead, that remains the day on which the community is called together to celebrate the paschal mystery.

IV. FREQUENCY OF CELEBRATION

If the Mass is Christ's sacrifice, then it must also be a source of grace. But if we exaggerate this one aspect (which to some extent happened during the post-Tridentine period of spirituality), we may become satisfied with merely fulfilling the minimal conditions for receiving grace or conclude that the oftener we return to this source, the more grace we receive.

Long before Vatican Council II, the twentieth-century liturgical movement drew attention to the Church's sacrifice and to the idea that the people in the congregation as members of the Church are called to active participation in the Mass. It was not denied that the Mass is a source of grace, but the realization was awakened that it is far more consonant with the real spirit and meaning of the Eucharist to participate in the Mass actively and intelligently once a day and to renew one's self-surrender at that Mass, than to seek spiritual gain in mere repetition without the proper disposition. We cannot of course assume that the proper disposition is always lacking in actions that are frequently repeated; some people simply cannot keep away from what they love, and this fact may have motivated the recent Vatican relaxation of the rigid ruling against receiving the Eucharist more than once a day.

1. SUNDAY AND THE EUCHARIST

If the Mass is the Church's sacrifice, then a most proper occasion for its celebration is whenever the community of the Church is assembled. Now the Church assembles on Sunday, "the Lord's day," the day on which the Lord and *Kyrios* consummated his work through the victory of his resurrection. Hence, from the Church's infancy onward, Sunday has been characterized by the celebration of the Eucharist as the memorial day of redemption. Since the Church assembles for this purpose, the Eucharist becomes the sacrifice offered by Christ along with his Church. The Eucharist is the sign of the paschal mystery that unites Christ and his Church.

Now, the essential thing about a sign is that it should be understood and applied in accordance with its significance. The sign of the Eucharist as the Redeemer's sacrifice finds its most proper application if Mass is performed on the memorial day of redemption (Sunday), and in the assembly of the community. It was only after the fourth century that certain other memorial days came to be placed on a par with Sunday: Christmas and Ascension everywhere, and local feasts on memorial days of martyrs revered especially in the community.

In early Christian times this identification between Sunday and the Eucharistic celebration was so self-evident that we hear of no commandment binding everyone to attend Mass. It is simply the day of the community's plenary assembly, and everyone who could come was expected to be present and "not cause the body of Christ to be short of a member," as the Syrian Didascalia put it. The first known document imposing a law of Sunday obligation for the individual Christian is canon 21 of the Synod of Elvira, held at the beginning of the fourth century. The canon apparently threatened with temporary excommunication a person who lived in the city and did not come to church on three successive Sundays; but after studying the question J. J. Guiniven discounts this canon as evidence for the point at issue.[225] Later on, in both East and West, the canon was interpreted to several different effects.

The view must also have been current that the obligation to attend the celebration of the Eucharist concerned not simply the individual but the corporate community. For there are indications that during the fourth century, even in large cities like Milan and Carthage in the West and Alexandria in the East, there was only one Mass on Sundays; and that was celebrated by the bishop. Simply for reasons of insufficient room it must have been impossible for the entire Christian community to participate in a single service.[226] The manifestation of the congregation's unity around the Lord's table seemed more important than the participation of all the members. The same principle continued to operate in the medieval practice of the so-called parochial obligation. The Sunday Mass at the ninth hour brought together all who belonged to the parish, but evidently those who had to stay at home by reason of domestic and family duties were not obliged to be present.

That the principle of one community Mass on Sundays and feast days has perdured until the present is borne out by the fact of the pastor's duty to "apply" his Sunday Mass to his congregation. On principle, since the pastor celebrates the Eucharist on Sundays and feasts *with* his parish community, on these days he may not accept a private stipend Mass. In the purview of the practice and regulation concerning stipends, he has already received his stipend from the community as a whole; and to the community he therefore applies "the fruit" of the sacrifice. It would violate the spirit of this age-old principle either if the obligation were retained with regard to obsolete holy days, or if particular dioceses were exempted from this obligation and hence could bind priests to require a stipend not for themselves but for the needs of the diocese.[227]

Only toward the end of the Middle Ages was the obligation binding the individual to attend Sunday Mass mitigated to the extent of permitting him to choose a church outside his parish. For a long time episcopal synods resisted granting this option, as we learn from A. Franz's *Die Messe im deutschen Mittelalter* (pp. 15–17); finally in 1517, Pope Leo X decided in favor of freedom.[228]

After that it became the task of moralists and canonists to define the individual's Sunday obligation. For one thing, it is characterized as a grave obligation, and one that requires bodily presence and at least a minimum of religious disposition. Then it concerns presence and worship at the whole Mass, and that approach involves distinctions as to what are the essential and what the non-essential parts of the Mass.

2. MODERN CONDITIONS AND ADAPTATIONS

Obviously, insistence upon the obligation and upon the gravity of guilt can serve as a negative motivation force, a means that has not always proven ineffective. After all, in both Old and New Testaments God has repeatedly used the sanction of punishment. Moreover, pastoral concern will frequently be exercised to inculcate in the faithful an understanding of the real meaning of the Sunday celebration and to foster a sense of community. Furthermore, while the availability of a broad choice of Masses (at every hour of the day and in every section of a city, so that it is easy for the faithful, even for tepid Catholics, to fulfill their obligation) is ideal pastorally, certain observations are still in place.

Even though nowadays it is rarely possible to realize the objective of the single community celebration, it is good to recall what Vatican II has to say on the matter. The Council sees the ideal realized when, as we quoted earlier, "a full complement of God's holy people, united in prayer and in a common liturgical service (especially the Eucharist), exercise a thorough and active participation at the very altar where the bishop presides in the company of his priests and other assistants" (CL §41, with obvious reference to the letters of St. Ignatius of Antioch to the Magnesians, Philadelphians, and Smyrnaeans). It is in such a celebration, the Constitution insists, that "the Church reveals herself most clearly." This holds good alike for every local church, every parish, every congregation gathered around its pastor, as is clear from the Dogmatic Constitution on the Church (§26).

Nevertheless, in the existential conditions of our time, certain "ad-hoc" alternatives have become necessary. Since the entire community of a huge city parish cannot be accommodated at one single Mass, the assembly must be divided into several smaller groups, and the parish Mass repeated as many times as is necessary. Likewise, the rhythm of life in the industrial age has made it necessary to shift many public functions to the evening. Thus, since World War II the evening Mass has come into use and has restored the celebration to the actual hour of the Last Supper. Although for several centuries this practice was known only as an exception (as F. Zimmermann indicates[229]), since the Motu Proprio *Sacram Communionem* of March 19, 1957, it has been accepted as normal pastoral practice for every day of the year.

Anticipation of the Sunday Mass on Saturday evening goes even a step farther. Theologically this innovation could readily be justified on the ground that, according to the view borrowed from Judaism and continued in liturgical practice, Sunday begins on the preceding evening with First Vespers. This does not in any way change the fact that Sunday is and must remain *the* Lord's Day as it has been since Apostolic times. Apart from conditions of accommodation and distance, what was considered as further ground for anticipating the Sunday Mass to Saturday evening was the new concept of the weekend holiday that begins on Saturday, not on Sunday.

An important consideration also was the fact that for certain circles (sport groups and the like) a meaningful Sunday Eucharist could be celebrated better and with more unction on Saturday evening than at a rushed and marginal hour on Sunday. The permission, given at first only to particular dioceses (in Italy, Switzerland, Argentina), was brought to public notice by the Congregation of the Council in 1964, and, at the request of the bishops concerned, extension to other dioceses is now virtually universal. The instruction "De Cultu Mysterii Eucharistici," issued on May 25, 1967, laid down more detailed regulations for the choice of the Mass formula and for the reception of Communion on such occasions (§28).[230]

3. WEEKDAY MASSES

Besides the Mass celebrated with the "full complement" of the people, the Mass said in smaller circles even on weekdays was known from the beginning, though not regularly and not everywhere. Tertullian witnesses to it at least with regard to Mass for the dead on the anniversary (*annua die*; De Cor., ch. 3); Augustine exhorted candidates for Baptism to commit the Creed (*Symbolum*) carefully to memory, but as for the Lord's Prayer, they would in any case hear it every day at Mass (Sermon 58:10-12). Elsewhere the witnesses are not so clear.[231] As for the votive Mass, we have seen in Part I (ch. 6) that its practice later on led to a questionable multiplication of Masses at times. For a long period, however, public celebration of the Mass on weekdays met with little popular enthusiasm. It has been said that the reason behind this hesitation is suggested by what St. Cyprian observed in a certain letter: the full meaning of the sacrament (*veritas sacramenti*) finds its realization only when the entire community is gathered together (*fraternitate omni praesente*; Ep. 63:16).[232]

Somewhere between a Sunday and an ordinary weekday in solemnity were the "holy" days, Wednesdays and Fridays, on which people fasted according to age-old custom. So the question arose: should not the Eucharist be celebrated on these days too? There was no consensus on this question during the first centuries. While in North Africa and Milan the Eucharist was celebrated between Sundays, in Alexandria and in Rome there was only a prayer service consisting of readings and orations.[233]

Beside these two Mass schedules there was a third observance, that of a Communion service on days of fast; this was simply a throwback to the earliest centuries when the faithful were allowed to keep the Eucharistic bread at home and receive Communion every day. In the East, during the lenten season, the celebration of the Eucharist was forbidden on all days except Saturdays and Sundays (wouldn't this imply a weekday or daily celebration?) by canon 49 of the fourth-century Synod of Laodicea (liturgical canons appear only in the fourth century, as is clear from Hefele-Leclercq 1:1021).

Then in the sixth century the practice evolved of concluding Vespers on feast days with the rite of the *proegiasmena* (i.e., the offerings consecrated beforehand), a Communion service, as is clearly borne out by the Byzantine Chronicon Paschale (PG 92:989). Syrian documents describe a rite of "the benediction of the chalice" in the same sense and on these same days; this practice may be linked to Patriarch Severus of Antioch (d. 538) in the opinion of O. Raquez,[234] though in substance it is the same as the Byzantine practice.

At an early stage in the Byzantine rite the old Communion ritual was joined to a Scripture-reading service, and the combined service developed a structure that differs from the Eucharistic celebration only in the absence of the central act of the Eucharist, namely, the anaphora. This Liturgy of the Presanctified (Brightman 345–52) is still in use today, though not on every day of Lent.[235] The Roman liturgy, following the Byzantine precedent, has had the Mass of the Presanctified (*missa praesanctificatorum*) at least for Good Friday since the eighth century. During the lenten season the complete and regular celebration of the Eucharist was introduced, at first hesitantly and only for important feasts, and then, with Pope Gregory II (d. 731), for every day of the season.

4. DAILY MASS

In the course of the early Middle Ages the custom of daily Mass came to stay. While at first it was primarily the daily conventual Mass in monasteries and collegiate churches, gradually the daily private Mass of each priest became common. In most places, however, this development was tolerated rather than encouraged, as has been noted by A. A. King.[236]

Among priests engaged in actual parish work the semipublic daily Mass, coinciding with the practice prevailing in monastic and collegiate churches, began to be a normal event even in parish churches, independently of votive Masses celebrated for individual families. From the late Middle Ages certain theologians had been advocating that each priest should say Mass every day. There is, e.g., a saying attributed to St. Bonaventure (Peltier edition, 12:281) and quoted often since the end of the fourteenth century, that the priest who does not say Mass "when he is able, deprives the Trinity of praise and glory, the angels of joy, and sinners of pardon" (*quantum in ipso est, privat Trinitatem laude et gloria, angelos laetitia, peccatores venia*). This rule, however, was not zealously heeded, even during recent centuries. As late as the 1917 Code of Canon Law, the legal, minimum requirement enjoined upon pastors was the duty to say Mass in their parish churches on Sundays and on holy days of obligation.[237]

The high value set on the private Mass corresponds to the spirit of personalism characterizing recent centuries; it corresponds also to the stress laid on the priest's consecrating power since the Council of Trent. It was the exercise of this power that became the primary expression of the priesthood. Another factor contributing substantially to the private Mass's popularity was the theological argument of the special benefit accruing from the Mass to the priest personally celebrating it. These new insights have gained such ground that moralists look upon the priest's personal devotion or a prevailing custom as sufficient reason to deviate from canon 813 forbidding the celebration of Mass without a server—if for want of a server the priest has to forego his habitual daily Mass.[238] The General Instruction of the 1969 Missale Romanum permits a Mass without server when there is "serious necessity" (§211); while Canon Law binds the priest to say Mass "several times in the year," it is up to the bishop to see that his priests offer Mass at least on all Sundays and major holydays (can. 805). The Vatican II Decree on the Ministry and Life of Priests does not abrogate existing laws, but "strongly urges" daily celebration of the Mass (§13).

5. NORM FOR FREQUENCY OF CELEBRATION AND PARTICIPATION

Church law and Church practice provide the external norm on the matter of the frequency of the Eucharistic celebration. Is it possible to arrive at another norm through theological reflection, through examination of the interior grounds?[239] As we have already seen, surrender to God's will along life's way—the way Christ has taken before us—is expected of us throughout life, and early Christians were particularly aware of this truth. It would be pointless merely to posit the sign at the moment when we are expected to *do* the thing signified, such as a work of neighborly love or the fulfillment of a duty. It would be equally pointless to place this sign when in the context of a given situation a simpler sign such as a prayer or a Scripture service should be adequate. It may well be that daily Mass has become for us the obvious thing and a matter of course because other forms of raising the heart to God have become too lifeless or rigid, or have been neglected or insufficiently developed. Rahner lays down this norm:

> Mass is to be celebrated as often as this contributes to the glory of God and the benefit of men, the other conditions . . . being of course presupposed.[240]

In other words, Mass is indicated precisely and only when and where it is the appropriate sign to express our faith and devotion or to quicken these sentiments in us. For God's glory is not increased by the mere re-presentation of the sacrifice unless it is joined to a renewed act of self-surrender on the part of those offering it. Moreover, only under this condition is it a source of grace.

It follows from the very fact that Christ instituted the Eucharist for his memorial that it must be celebrated in the Church "with a certain regularity," as Rahner points out (p. 97); for the Eucharist is now the Church's most important visible bond with her Head. The primary reason for fixing upon Sunday for the regular and periodic repetition of the Lord's memorial sacrifice was the fact that it was "the day of the Resurrection." It may well be that since each new day naturally brings with it a new beginning of our activity, the morning Mass can serve as each day's renewed overture to discover the right orientation for our lives, to enter into the mystery of Christ's self-surrender and thus establish sacramental contact with the full reality of the Christian economy of salvation.

This is one of the most positive helps toward living an intensive religious life in accordance with spiritual principles and the evangelical counsels. And this is why Canon Law specifies daily Mass as the norm for religious communities (cans. 413, 595, 1367); and of course many lay Christians are daily communicants without the urging of Canon Law.

A final consideration: the Mass service should not eliminate all other forms of devotion, whether on the personal or the community level, for then the preparation for this highest devotion would be wanting and hence the esteem for the Mass itself would suffer. In early Christian times, when daily celebration of the Eucharist was unheard of in many places, the spiritual climate was still deeply imbued with prayer that activated and sanctified not only each day but also the hours of the day; and this was not confined to monks and clerics.[241] At times, then, some other form of prayer or spiritual exercise might be substituted for Mass. This would have the advantage also of preventing daily Mass from becoming a routine exercise followed thoughtlessly and mechanically.

Daily celebration of Mass or — as the case may be — daily participation in Mass will therefore remain the norm for religious communities. It will likewise remain the norm for communities of priests. Although Vatican II made allowance for possible concelebration, the option remains fully open for private Mass in which only the server participates (CL §57, 2:2), whether it is celebrated by reason of the priest's personal devotion or for the intention of one who has given a stipend and cannot be present in person.

V. THE MASS IN PASTORAL WORK

If we were asked what a pastor can do to give the Mass the place due it in the life of his congregation so as to produce the results expected from it as Jesus' own Institution, we should answer that, first of all, the pastor himself has to celebrate Mass properly: *properly* not only in the sense that the ritual should be validly carried out and all the prescriptions faithfully observed; nor even in the sense that he should celebrate the Eucharist with personal devotion.

That would have sufficed so long as the Latin Mass, from the point of view of ritual action and language, was the province of the priest. But now that the reform initiated by Vatican II involves the whole congregation actively in the very action, the offering of Mass as well as its ritual form has once more regained its full stature as the action of priest *and* people together; and this enlarged dimension has made the Mass a pastoral matter to an unprecedented degree. In consequence it must be treated as a pastoral factor, with considerably more pastoral care and attention than was ever before demanded of the priest.

While in the reformed liturgy there is a range of options for treatment of the different sections of the Mass, the actual choice should not be left to the casual inspiration of the moment. This holds good particularly with regard to what falls to the celebrant to improvise (General Instruction §11–12). Unlike in the preconciliar tradition, the liturgical text itself should be immediately understood by the faithful, its meaning grasped even as it is being pronounced by the priest. This implies that, apart from technical helps available today, the very manner of reading should help the people to follow easily and clearly what is being read (§18).

The corollary should be evident: adequate practice and training for the reader, as well as great concern and preparation on the part of the priest, for it may be more difficult to read a prescribed text with meaningful intonation than to deliver an original sermon. It is clear that the pastor's concern should extend also to the external and visible aspects of the liturgy, to dignity of posture and movement, to the beauty of the altar and the church. Only thus can the liturgy of the Mass fully unfold its riches of instruction, grace, and blessing.

1. Central Role of Sunday Mass

For centuries, particularly the transitional centuries from the early period to the Middle Ages — an epoch co-extensive with the rise of what we call Christian or Western culture — the parish Mass on Sundays was the principal form of pastoral activity. At one and the same time the Mass was both worship and proclamation of faith. Most of the forms of pastoral service taken for granted today were still unknown then. After Baptism there was no systematic catechesis or religious education for either grownups or children. There was no religious or spiritual literature for the people; there were no church organizations or brotherhoods. Outside the See city, even the sermon was a pretty primitive affair. For all that, however, Sunday after Sunday the Eucharist celebrated in an inspiring manner could and did make up for the absence of those adjuncts to worship.

Among Christians of the East the liturgy seems to have performed a similar function during a thousand years of oppression under Islam. Catechesis and "sacred eloquence" died out simply because there were no more Christian schools and training centers; but there was a Christian liturgy in which the people took part and through which the substance of the Christian faith was passed to at least the remnant of the faithful.

Conditions have improved in the countries of the West. We have now at our disposal many ways and means of pastoral service. But how do these relate to Sunday Mass?

In our times it has been said repeatedly and with good reason that the Mass must be placed at the very heart of pastoral work. All pastoral care must radiate from the altar as from its center and source. It is clear that the Eucharist above all is alluded to when the Constitution on the Sacred Liturgy describes the liturgy as "the summit toward which the activity of the Church is directed [and] at the same time . . . the fountain from which all her power flows" (§10). In the Dogmatic Constitution on the Church the same expression is applied explicitly to the Eucharistic sacrifice, "the fount and apex of the whole Christian life" (§11). The figure, however, must be understood aright.

Under normal conditions pastoral concern should never be limited to ensuring good liturgical performance, for not all the functions of comprehensive pastoral care of souls can be identified with or generated by the liturgy alone. Pastoral concern must also involve the people who do not appear at liturgical gatherings. The preaching of the Good News should not be confined to Mass, but should go beyond the four walls of the church to reach all men and to prepare the way for this central act of Christian worship. It was in this sense that Paul declared that he had been sent not to baptize but to preach the Good News (1 Cor. 1:17). As Kirchgässner observes, "Of itself the Eucharistic celebration is not equipped to draw those outside to the Lord's table. It requires heralds to seek men first where they are found, and to speak to them so that they grasp the meaning of the invitation." [242] Hence Kirchgässner's very pertinent distinction: liturgy must indeed be "first in intention" (*primum in intentione*); but in actual practice it may be "the last to be achieved" (*ultimum in executione*).

Accentuation of the Mass should not lead to a too narrow attitude toward the Eucharist, for the ultimate goal toward which all pastoral work is directed is not the presence of Christ's sacrifice upon the altar but the redemptive sacrifice itself as it was consummated once and as it now continues to be through all centuries *the sign of our hope and the guidepost for the proper orientation of our life.* In our preaching we should never lose sight of this fact. It is only by keeping this vision clearly before our eyes that we shall be able to place the re-presentation of Christ's Passion through the Eucharist in the right perspective and to evaluate priestly activity in all its broad dimensions. In his paper before the St. Xavier College (Chicago) Symposium in 1966, Yves Congar captured the very essence of the priesthood in his happy formulation: "We are priests to offer Mass, that is, to bring men to communicate in the sacrifice of Jesus Christ. . . . this implies consecration, but consecration encompasses men and their faith is their spiritual sacrifice." [243]

2. CATECHESIS OF THE MASS

Even though ideally the liturgical aspects of the reformed Mass should be, as the Constitution on the Sacred Liturgy puts it, "within the people's powers of comprehension," so that they "normally should not require much explanation" (§ 34), still an introduction to these forms by means of catechesis and homily is far from being a waste of time. This does not mean that each text and each rite need be explained in detail. Texts and rites should speak for themselves. Thanks to the reform, historical explanation has become almost superfluous; such an explanation would be doubly difficult and hardly fruitful in our time which has little sense of tradition.

In this matter our approach should be somewhat like that of the first centuries of Christianity. Even though the Eucharist is mentioned often in the early Christian documents, we hardly ever encounter an explanation of particular practices or expressions. Justin's explanation of the *Amen* is an exception. Theodore of Mopsuestia, toward the end of the fourth century, was the first to undertake a detailed explanation of the Christian liturgy. The other catecheses for the newly baptized, which have come down to us from Jerusalem and from Milan, consider the rites only in large sections and are limited to explaining and illustrating the principles most often with the help of figures and types taken from the Old Testament, or of appropriate psalms, 21 and 32 being favored for this purpose.[244]

In our own time, under relatively stable conditions, the proper setting for systematic explanation of the Mass will always be the catechetical instruction of the young and the imparting of Christian doctrine in general. In this, though, our approach will not be that of some older books, where the Eucharist was dealt with in three separate, mutually isolated chapters devoted respectively to the sacramental presence, Communion, and finally the Mass. Rather, we shall turn to account the insights made possible to us through our return to the sources. For what was instituted at the Last Supper was not merely the sacrament of Christ's presence but the sacrament of the presence of Christ's sacrifice, namely, the Mass. As a result of the rediscovery of this broader and more unifying vision, our presentation of what Christ has entrusted to his Church should be one single, organic synthesis, a complex but indivisible whole.

The Real Presence of Christ's body and blood under the species of bread and wine becomes then one aspect of the whole mystery. No doubt it is a crucially important aspect, but at the same time there is no need to handle it at the beginning of the treatise on the Eucharist, or to isolate it from other integral aspects, but simply to consider it along with and in the context of the whole.

So, too, Communion is not a religious exercise by itself, but is rather the sacramental participation in the sacramental sacrifice. Reconstruction of the catechesis of the Eucharist, which has now become necessary because of this change of outlook, has been the subject of recent investigations such as that of H. Fischer or of J. Rodriguez Medina.[245] Both these authors study the gradual transition effected since the beginning of the liturgical movement, insofar as this change can be traced in catechetical publications.

The catechesis of the Mass will have to devote special attention to the Offertory, not to enhance its importance, but to clarify or prevent possible misunderstandings into which its theology could lead us. For on the one hand the extreme to which Scotus and his school pushed the idea of the Church's sacrifice as a self-contained and autonomous act still finds echoes in our time; and yet some theologians go to the other extreme of overemphasizing Christ's sacrifice alone, to the neglect of the Church's part. On this point there have been heated discussions at conferences on liturgical renewal, among them the study meeting organized at Vanves in 1946 by the Centre de Pastorale Liturgique of Paris and reported by Cardinal Daniélou in *Le Messe et sa Catéchèse* (pp. 154–79; 304–11) cited in note 244.

At this meeting Abbot Bernard Capelle (d. 1961) had insisted that the Offertory should not be looked upon as "an act that is incomplete yet in practice autonomous" (*acte partial mais qui serait absolu*), but as "an act that is complete in itself yet relative to and dependent on the whole" (*acte total mais relatif*); he specified this point further by claiming that the Offertory should not be thought to symbolize the self-surrender of the faithful. This position came in for vehement attack in the ensuing debate, but the debate itself failed to resolve the problem, chiefly because of the vagueness on the point of how the Church's sacrifice is related to Christ's sacrifice.

The solution must be sought in this, that, as we have brought out in Part II (ch. 4), the symbolization of the Church's sacrifice can and does embrace broader horizons than the mere sacramental act. The re-presentation of the Church's sacrifice begins already at the Offertory. In the act of offering their gifts (and this might some-times take the form of an Offertory procession), the faithful should see the first authentic expression of the surrender of self with which they are to participate in Christ's sacrifice and in his self-surrender.

3. Importance and Function of the Homily

Religious instruction in general and instruction on the Eucharist in particular, imparted in the form of a sermon and above all in the form of a homily, must embrace and guide the whole Christian life. The homily will then communicate an insight into the Mass much less by analysis of its texts and rites than by exposition and continual deepening of fundamental concepts, e.g., God as the beginning and the end; man's duty to adore and worship him; Christ as man's way to God, as man's Mediator, who stands before the Father and yet is close to man, so that men may have access to God through him; the Church as the community of those who have seen sanctified in Baptism and who, as God's people, assemble in all parts of the world to celebrate the Eucharist; the sense of trust and gratitude toward God implied and called for in the very name of *Eucharist*; and other seminal themes.

At the present time it is all the more important to insist upon these fundamental concepts embodying the very essence of the Christian message since popular piety, inherited from earlier centuries, has in general been confined to particular and limited aspects of the mystery, to one or other "devotion" and often to peripheral and superficial points of doctrine (which of course might still lead "chosen souls" to contemplative union with God). A positive presentation of the above-mentioned basic concepts, unobscured by polemics or controversial jargon, will lead to a growing appreciation of the essential content of Christian faith and to an ever-increasing joy in active participation in the Eucharist.

If the homily is to fulfill the function assigned to it in the Mass, it must (as we have observed earlier in another connection) always have a more or less mystagogical character. Taking as its starting point one or another theme from divine revelation or Christian life or the liturgy, it should ultimately move to the Eucharist being celebrated here and now. It will again and again return to one point or another that has special significance in the Eucharistic celebration, as the occasion may suggest. Thus, St. Augustine preached on the "Sursum corda" (Lift up your hearts) on several occasions and drew attention to its deeper significance, notably in the detailed development of this point in Sermon 227 (PL 38:1100f.). An ancient heritage in the tradition of patristic homilies (as ancient as the Didache, 9:4) is the theme of the one bread made of many grains as symbolizing the unity of Christians. Incidentally, the homily does not provide the only occasion within the Mass to draw attention to such themes, as is pointed out in the Instruction *De Cultu Mysterii Eucharistici* (1967, §15), in the course of explaining a decree of the Council of Trent.

4. THE MASS IS ITS OWN BEST CATECHESIS

When all is said and done, we may best invoke the basic principle with which we began this chapter, namely, that Mass properly celebrated is itself the best catechesis. This maxim acquires very concrete and immediate relevance when we recall that in their substance the classic forms of the Eucharistic Prayer (one of which Hippolytus has preserved for us in his formulary) coincide almost perfectly with the classic forms of the Creed, such as the Apostles' Creed. The only difference is in the address: the Eucharistic Prayer is addressed to God as a grateful act of praise (*praedicatio*) or profession of faith (*confessio*); the Creed is a declaration pronounced before the community of the faithful, before the Church.

Attention has often been drawn to this interrelation, in particular — interestingly enough — by Protestant scholars such as F. Kattenbusch and R. Schneider.[246] In fact it has been shown by N. A. Dahl that in the early Church the Eucharistic Prayer was the principal form of handing on the faith. In the future, too, for the majority of God's people, whose primary point of contact with the Church is the Sunday Mass, this is going to be the most important means of keeping the substance of the faith alive in their consciousness.

At the same time it must be remembered that in the Mass more than in any other case, the goal of all preaching and catechesis can never be merely knowing and understanding nor what is called active participation (if by this term only external activity is meant). The real goal is to move the faithful to turn to God in faith, hope, and love, and in this attitude prayerfully to participate in the Eucharist, in Christ's sacrifice. This prayerful participation is the summit as well as the "school" of Christian prayer.

It is the summit, since prayer in this setting is that of the faithful gathered together, the Church's prayer, led by those who in virtue of their office are called by God to do so; indeed, it is led by Christ the High Priest himself, in whose special presence it rises up to the Father. But this prayer necessarily takes such forms as are particularly suited to all Christian prayer; and so it becomes also the school of that prayer. Hence, in the Apostolic Constitution of April 3, 1969, introducing the new Missal, Pope Paul VI aptly describes prayer in the Eucharist as prayer that rises "to our Father in heaven, through our High Priest Jesus Christ, in the Holy Spirit."

This is the primitive Church's basic formula for Christian prayer. And such prayer always embraces the whole of our life and orientates it toward God. In this manner Christian living becomes a participation in the life and attitudes of Christ, and draws ever nearer to that goal that is also the goal of all pastoral care of souls.

VI. THE CELEBRATING COMMUNITY

Catholic liturgy has evolved in the form of several rites. Not only did the West differ from the East in the manner of celebrating Mass, but in the West different forms co-existed for a long time. The reason for this variegated bloom was the undeveloped character of centralized organization and administration for the universal Church; as a result regional centers were responsible for order and discipline in each distinct territory. Consequently unintended differences emerged between the liturgies of various areas; the indigenous characteristics of each place and people found their way into the very liturgy, by way of the language of course, but also by way of the mentality and theology peculiar to a given country. Thus, the Byzantine way of prayer, which is fond of addressing "Christ our God," differs from the Roman, which keeps to the more objective form of praying "through Christ." The flowery and ornate language of Gallican liturgies differs from the clear and concise or, better, theologically precise prayer language of the more law-minded Romans, as has been pointed out by the liturgiologist Edmund Bishop.[247]

Now, it is quite fitting that the particular genius of the people offering the sacrifice of the Mass should leave its mark upon the form of the celebration. Indeed, it is not unknown in the history of the liturgy — the Roman liturgy in particular — that not only the special genius and traditions of a whole people but also the local conditions, circumstances, and attitudes of a concrete community played a part in the formation of the liturgy, at least in the choice of readings and hymns, if not in the principal prayer. The stational Masses bear witness to the consideration given to the particular churches concerned, to their patron saint (*patrocinium*), their surroundings, their history. For the stational Mass in the basilica of Saints Cosmas and Damian, a popular pilgrimage shrine, the reading from Jeremias 7:1-7 is clearly intended as a warning to the pilgrims not to place their trust blindly in any particular shrine.[248]

1. ADAPTATION AND ITS LIMITS

With the passage of time, however, this principle of indigenous liturgy was gradually forgotten. In their enthusiasm for everything Roman, the Frankish churchmen took over the Mass texts just as these were found in Rome, where of course they had been composed for use on particular days dedicated to the specific stational churches of Rome and thus included readings suited to the actual occasion and circumstances of the stational churches involved. The old question has now come up again. Individual nations and dioceses, and even local parish churches, are clamoring for permission and freedom to bring to the celebration of Mass their unique, characteristic genius, at least on certain occasions.

In response, Vatican Council II deliberately left room for the adaptation of the liturgy to the "genius and traditions" of individual peoples (CL §40). This principle of diversity and adaptation will have increasing importance for peoples — especially those in mission lands — whose culture has other than Graeco-Roman roots.

Fixed readings have now been prescribed only for Sundays, major feast days, and feasts of certain saints, and even in these categories the possibility of choice is not entirely ruled out. For the remaining days, whose number as given in the 1969 Roman calendar exceeds by far the number of days assigned to saints, there is plenty of latitude in the choice of Mass formula and, within certain limits, in that of readings. By reason of the large selection of votive Masses and of Masses for various purposes (*ad diversa*), it has now become possible to adapt the Mass formulary to special circumstances and occasions. Freedom in the choice of hymns is even greater: each national church is invited to draw upon the treasury of its own sacred hymns and to increase its repertory of original works.

Despite all these new concessions, within larger territorial units today there is a hankering on the part of smaller, more or less homogeneous groups to adapt the form of the liturgy to their own taste and temperament. At present, too, there is a growing pastoral concern for young children as well as for adolescents. To be sure, adolescents have to be made to feel from the start that the parish Mass is their Mass and they should take active part in it. Yet we admit that a special form of the Eucharist adapted to their psychology, to their particular stage of maturity and development, a form that speaks to them and relates to them, would suit them better — even though this might affect the structure of the Mass.

In a Mass for children the opening should be simpler, for example; there should be only one reading, and that one a free paraphrase that would bring the Gospel message within their field of comprehension. Pastoral-liturgy experts in several countries are working toward new forms to this effect. Suggestions have already been discussed and accepted in part by the German Bishops' Conference; in fact, a similar program was drawn years ago by a catechetical leader, K. Tilmann.[249]

Can the same principle be applied in other milieus as well? In every community, in every parish, people of different psychological, social, ethnic, and cultural backgrounds are brought together, not to mention the two sexes, so different in their psychic makeup. But obviously we must draw the line somewhere if we are to avoid complete chaos or impracticable utopianism. One American writer advocates the principle, "Let each cultural group create its own celebration."[250] But it would be disastrous to apply this literally and without qualification to the Mass.

The special characteristics of a given group's spiritual and cultural heritage need not always be expressed precisely and literally in the form of a religious service, much less in the Mass. Healthy religious life has always encouraged the development of family- and folk-customs around the liturgy, so long as they do not intrude into the inner sphere of the liturgy itself. And indeed a wealth of religious customs, differing from country to country, from place to place, has grown around the feasts of the Church calendar, as we learn from sources like F. X. Weiser's *Handbook of Christian Feasts and Customs*. These accretions and new interpolations, however, must not be allowed to intrude into the inner, eternal sphere of the liturgy itself.

2. Parish Mass and Group Masses

For Sundays and feasts, the days on which the "church" comes together, the old rule must prevail: the whole assembly, irrespective of profession, education, and social background, celebrates the Eucharist in common, either in the parish church to which they belong or in some other public or semipublic oratory or chapel, which by Canon Law (can. 1249) they have the right to choose.

In view of urban conditions this is usually going to be a gathering of parishioners who are strangers to one another, all the more so since now the people have such a wide choice of Sunday Masses. Under such situations it will only rarely be possible to realize the ideal of a "parish family." But therein lies the very strength of the Eucharist, that it can cut through all differences of age, ethnic background, and state of life, and bring friends and strangers together into one community united in worship. It is St. Paul's assertion come true: "There does not exist among you Jew or Greek, slave or freeman, male or female. All are one in Christ Jesus" (Gal. 3:28).

The Lord's common table is the school of Christian living in which we learn to look upon even an outsider and a stranger as our "neighbor." Naturally the form of the celebration, too, must reflect this spirit of unity; that is why, for example, it opens with a salutation addressed to all. Congregational singing and prayer, even the act of submitting to a definite external order, can help foster an atmosphere of unity in the assembly.

This does not rule out special Masses for smaller groups, at least on days other than Sundays and feasts. In earliest Christian times this practice was taken for granted: the faithful met in their houses for the breaking of bread, as we read in Acts 2:46; and there is evidence of the practice even after the Apostolic era (MRR 1:212-15). As was pointed out in Part I, St. Cyprian is our witness that the Eucharist was conducted in smaller circles side by side with that celebrated in the midst of the whole community.

In Rome, Bishop St. Ambrose is known to have offered the sacrifice in the house of a lady belonging to a patrician family (Paulinus, Vita Ambrosii, ch. 10; PL 14:30); and while this was a special case on the occasion of a journey, the celebration of Mass in private domestic chapels was common in Rome. Apparently the titular churches of later times started out as private domestic chapels or oratories, and, when freedom of worship was granted in the era of Constantine, evolved into basilicas. That is to say: from the beginning they were meant primarily for the whole community.[251]

At any rate, when the persecutions came to an end and the Christian population exploded during the fourth century, Church observance took a more rigoristic tack, and the Synod of Laodicea (c. 360) forbade bishops and priests to conduct the sacrifice (prosphora) in private houses (can. 58). In the territories of the Syrian Church (where persecution lasted longer), the Synod of Seleucia-Ctesiphon issued a similar prohibition in the year 410. The correlation between relief from religious persecution and this new strict discipline (as explored by A. Baumstark[252]) would indicate that the practice of celebrating Mass in private houses was simply an emergency measure. Liturgical ceremonies were looked upon as the celebration of the parish community, not that of a small, special, or otherwise elite group. And as such they had to cease when there were other possibilities under free conditions.

In the West the celebration of the Eucharist in private houses was not totally forbidden. In general, canon 9 of the Second Synod of Carthage (428) merely forbade such celebrations without prior permission from the bishop (inconsulto episcopo). Tolerated to some extent, the practice survived through the Middle Ages. Castles of the nobility usually accommodated a domestic chapel, with a chaplain of its own whenever available. It was generally permitted to celebrate Mass in the house of a sick person, until the Council of Trent (sess. 22) completely proscribed the celebration of Mass in all private houses. Current Canon Law regulation (canons 1188–96), however, permits the Eucharist to be celebrated in the semipublic chapels of institutions, since these may be looked upon as serving smaller congregations.

3. THE QUESTION OF SMALL-GROUP MASSES TODAY

Withal, the question of the group Mass and the house Mass may legitimately be raised once more now that since Vatican II the move is on in several countries toward fostering the practice. A mere appeal to the general practice of antiquity as an argument in its favor is hardly valid, since, as we have seen above, it was an emergency measure then. Equally invalid is the argument that this practice should help rehabilitate the supposed meal structure of the Eucharist, as would be inferred from our comments in Part I (ch. 2). The Eucharist-as-meal argument has been closely examined and then rejected by one liturgical scholar, even though the same author is in favor of the house Mass.[253] On the other hand we have to admit that, considering the situation in the large cities, the need for Masses conducted in smaller circles is greater today than ever before.

In every living, active congregation it is not the entire parish as a body but homogeneous groups that are conspicuously involved in parish life and activity. Naturally the people forming such a group would like to celebrate the Eucharist together; for by reason of their very homogeneity and family spirit, their Eucharist is sure to yield more intimate fellowship than is possible in a large congregation; and there is a greater chance that the liturgical forms will come alive as they usually cannot come alive in a huge, heterogeneous gathering, e.g., in a more meaningful or personal way of formulating the petitions or offering the sign of peace or giving the homily.

In the opposite corner, the inner-city situation of great cities — notably at present in America, but to a surprising degree in ethnically homogeneous areas such as Scandinavia, with its "guest" laborers from some seventeen different linguistic backgrounds, almost all of them Catholic and clamoring for liturgical attention — indicates modifications of a different sort. Whether the liturgy takes place in a "storefront" chapel or a *casa* in a public-housing highrise (as in Spanish-speaking sectors of New York), it has to involve as the minimum modification the use of the native language until such time as the minority group concerned is acculturated with the larger unit of parish, city, and adopted nation. Moreover, a special family occasion might legitimately awaken a longing to celebrate the Eucharist in the family home. It would be only natural that at such celebrations (especially if they take place outside

church or chapel) certain prescriptions of the ritual might be re-
laxed, such as those concerning the celebrant's movements, or the
format of the Liturgy of the Word, or the choice of readings.

Nevertheless, if this service is to be the Eucharist that Christ
entrusted to his Church, the Church cannot leave its liturgical
actualization to the free, spontaneous improvisation of whatever
group happens to be celebrating it at the moment. (In his survey
of the situation, B. D. Marliangeas mentions among other bizarre
examples groups who play down the priest's role in favor of the
equality of all present, and have the Eucharistic Prayer said by
all.[254]) Further, it is unrealistic to imagine that the experience
gained from such experiments, which by their very nature are confined to concrete situations, could be fruitful for Mass with a whole
congregation.

Besides, pastors will have to be on their guard that such experiments do not degenerate into snobbism or elitism or sectarian-
ism or mere trendiness; and that, as house Masses celebrated in the
homes of the well-to-do or indeed the homes of minority or foreign-
language groups, they do not *emphasize* differences, whether social,
ethnic, or cultural. On the other hand, every weekday Mass could
be made a more intimately shared experience if conducted, say, in
a weekday chapel, where the normally small number of participants
who in a big church would be widely scattered, could be induced to
form a close-knit worshiping community; or if the participants
might be persuaded to move closer to the altar of a larger church!

VII. EUCHARIST AND CHURCH UNITY

1. THE EUCHARIST, CAUSE AND EXPRESSION OF UNITY

That the Eucharist is the sacrament of unity is a conviction pervading the whole history of the Church. The one bread and the one
chalice bind the many together into a unity, into the one Christ,

so that they become one single body, *his* body. Those coming to it
are not brought together by any casual camaraderie; it is Christ
who calls the partakers and includes them in his sacrifice, in the
covenant he has established through his own blood. As the theologian Fries rightly observes: "The unity of the Church does not
grow from below; it is bestowed in Christ, in the contact with his
body and blood, set forth first for sacrifice and now for our reception." [255]

Hence it is not by chance or inadvertence that the exact
meaning of the *communion of saints* (*sanctorum*) in the Apostles'
Creed remains inconclusive, i.e., whether the phrase connotes the
community existing among the saints (*sancti*), or the community
constituted by holy things (*sancta*), which would refer above all
to the Eucharist.[256] For the *communio* with Christ's body brings
about a *communio* among those receiving it. Again, it is not by
chance that the term *corpus mysticum*, which we are so accustomed
to equating with the Church, was first used to designate the sacrament of the Eucharist.[257]

In all the liturgies, therefore, it was as a community celebration that the Mass was conceived and took shape. The bearer of
the ecclesiastical office stands at the head of the congregation. He
salutes them, invites them to prayer; he pronounces the prayers in
their name (therefore in the plural), and expects their ratifying
Amen.

From the very beginning the Church showed keen, lively interest in uniting the local community in one single Eucharistic
celebration. The principle laid down by St. Ignatius of Antioch in
writing the Philadelphians of his day, "Endeavor to celebrate one
Eucharist" (4), was not forgotten even in later times. Where this
was not possible, by reason of the size of the congregation, alternatives for observing the spirit of the maxim were sought.

One such alternative was the "leaven" (*fermentum*). In this
usage the bishop sent a particle of consecrated bread to the presbyters of titular churches. These presbyters then mingled the sacred
particle in their chalice just before Communion at their own Mass,
seeing in this symbolic action their own and their congregation's
unity with their bishop in the one sacrament.[258]

Another alternative was the "station Mass." During the early
Middle Ages in Rome and in other cities, the bishop made a practice of moving from place to place within his territory and con-
voking at each place the faithful around the altar to celebrate the

Eucharist with him. This "itinerant Mass" finds a parallel in our own time on a grand scale as the Pope assembles the faithful for the celebration of the Eucharist not only in the titular churches of Rome but in the great cities anywhere on the face of the earth — Chicago, Munich, Bombay, Bogotá. Ultimately, as the third Eucharistic Prayer formulates it, it is God himself who in this sacrament gathers from age to age a holy people to himself, "so that from east to west a perfect offering may be made to the glory of your name."

In several documents Vatican II emphasizes belief in the Eucharist as the sacrament of unity. In the Dogmatic Constitution on the Church, one reads in article 3, "In the sacrament of the Eucharistic bread, the unity of all believers who form one body in Christ is both expressed and brought about" (*repraesentatur et efficitur*; the same two verbs occur also in article 11 as well as in article 2 of the Decree on Ecumenism). In article 7 on the Church: "Truly partaking of the body of the Lord in the breaking of the Eucharistic bread, we are taken up into communion with him and with one another." And in article 26: "In any community existing around an altar . . . there is manifested a symbol of that charity and 'unity of the Mystical Body, without which there can be no salvation'" (the inner quotation being from Thomas Aquinas). It is the symbol, namely, of the mutual unity and charity of the faithful.

2. The Question of Common Worship

In the Decree on Ecumenism, Vatican II comes to grips with the painful reality that it is not yet possible to celebrate this sacrament of unity with all who bear the name of Christians. Article 8 distinguishes between common prayer (*communicatio spiritualis*), which is recommended, and common worship (*communicatio in sacris*), which may not be practiced "indiscriminately." For common worship "depends chiefly on two principles: it should signify the unity of the Church and it should provide a sharing in the means of grace. The fact that it should signify unity generally rules out common worship. Yet the gaining of a needed grace sometimes commends it." [259]

The principle that common worship with separated communities is ruled out on grounds of unity is implicit in this sacrament and corresponds to an unbroken tradition of the Church, as is clear beyond all doubt in several documents of the early Church. Common Eucharist presupposed the common faith and the common confession of this faith; indeed, as a celebration of the one community united in faith and worship, it necessarily presupposed membership in this community of the faithful. Only those who belonged to the *communio* could take part in the Eucharist, and *communio* then often meant simply the visible church gathered around its bishop. Thus one authority, L. Hertling, can assert that *"Communio* is that bond of unity which binds the faithful and, above all, the bishops together into the one Catholic Church, and which does not merely consist in a common faith or sentiment." [260]

Participation in the one Eucharist was the visible sign of belonging to the community of the Church. Receiving the Eucharist from the hands of a heretical bishop or priest was tantamount to sharing his heresy. We have numerous instances of this from the time of the Arian heresy, as Hertling adduces (8–10). In his *Dialogues* 3:31 (PL 77:292), Pope St. Gregory the Great tells of St. Hermenegild (whose feast, incidentally, was celebrated on April 13 until the 1969 calendar reform) that on the Easter vigil his father, the Arian king Leovigild, sent an Arian bishop to Hermenegild, who was in prison for his faith, so that the son might receive "Communion from a sacrilegious consecration" (*sacrilegae consecrationis communionem*). Hermenegild refused to receive Communion, since this would have meant renouncing *communio* with the Catholic Church, for which he was prepared to forego even Easter Communion.

The German Protestant scholar Werner Elert, who has made a historical study of the question, arrives at the same conclusion. As he asserts in *Eucharist and Church Fellowship in the First Four Centuries*, "The gathering for worship in the early Church was not a public but a closed assembly, while the Eucharist was reserved for the saints with the utmost strictness" (p. 76). The "formative influence" in this matter is to be sought not in the "discipline of the secret," however, "but the keeping of unholy people from what is holy in accordance with the Old Testament understanding of holiness" (p. 77). In fact the *Sancta sanctis*, surviving today in the Eastern liturgies, is an exact echo of this very notion. As Elert observes further, "The separation from false teachers which we find in the Epistles (already Rom. 16:17), in Revelation, and often urged in Ignatius applies in the first place to the divine service which includes the Eucharist" (p. 114).

On the question of common worship, Elert has this to say:

> When the laity are granted the right to receive the Sacrament in another church and the clergy to celebrate it there, we have the implementation of the *communicatio in sacris*. This takes place only in full church fellowship, of which agreement in doctrine and unity in confession are the basis and condition (pp. 164f.).

And in concluding his chapter on the community of the Lord's Supper in the ancient Church, he notes:

> By his partaking of the Sacrament in a church a Christian declares that the confession of that church is his confession. Since a man cannot at the same time hold two differing confessions, he cannot communicate in two churches of differing confessions. If anyone does this nevertheless, he denies his own confession or has none at all (p. 182).

3. PRESENT POSITION OF THE CATHOLIC CHURCH

While Orthodox Churches in general have maintained this position to this day, with Vatican II the Catholic Church has favored a milder approach. "Concern for grace" has now been accepted as the guiding principle to be applied in cases of emergency. Behind this lies the theological perception that the sacraments confer grace on those who do not put obstacles to it (*non ponentibus obicem*; Denz. 1606). A further factor was the readiness to render help wherever possible in genuine Christian charity. Thus, the "Directory on Ecumenism" released by the Secretariat for Promoting Christian Unity on May 14, 1967, for the purpose of implementing the Council's Decree in practical, specific terms, rules that vis-à-vis the separated Churches of the East, which have a valid priesthood and valid sacraments, the faithful may under certain circumstances and for a just reason (e.g., if one would otherwise have to do without sacraments or be unable to fulfill the Sunday obligation for too long a period) participate in the liturgy and receive Communion (see TPS, 12:3 [1966–67] 250–63).

Toward denominations taking their origin from the Reformation such a compromise is not possible. While common service of the Word and common prayer and singing are allowed and encouraged, participation of Catholics in the Protestant Communion service, for which the basis of a valid priesthood is wanting, is out of the question. Conversely, a baptized non-Catholic who cannot reach a minister of his confession may be given the Eucharist, if he believes in it in the Catholic sense, but only in case of danger of death or of grave emergency (§55). This more lenient position is warranted only because the members of these communities are not completely outside the Church but, as Vatican II explicitly owns, even these communities have genuine ecclesial elements and can therefore be called churches.

Yet even here the principle, while admitting of exceptions in case of emergency, remains the same: the Eucharist is the common celebration of those who already belong to the community of the Catholic Church and who therefore confess the Catholic faith complete and unabridged. Of course, once this basic condition has been fulfilled, there may be further conditions for worthy reception. Thus, for example, public sinners should be denied the Sacrament, and secret sinners who have not done penance are to stay away from It. The *Sancta sanctis* therefore obtains also in the Catholic Church of the West.

4. The Ecumenical Movement and Intercommunion

The longing to overcome the differences dividing Christendom has led to the ecumenical movement.[261] And this in turn has brought up the question whether it would not be possible to overcome the divisions at least partly simply by acting (*per viam facti*), i.e., by stepping across the boundaries of one's own confession to celebrate the Eucharist in common with members of other confessions. This is the question of intercommunion, and it was raised first within the various Protestant confessions and was one of the subjects brought up for discussion at the third "Faith and Order" meeting held in 1952 in Lund.[262] The fourth meeting in 1963 in Montreal still registered differences of opinion on the matter, one side arguing for unity in faith as a prerequisite, the other stressing that Christ calls all Christians to his table.

In further discussions the beginnings of mutual understanding are discernible in the fact that, thanks to the liturgical movement that has penetrated everywhere, the various confessions celebrate the Lord's Supper with greater zeal, though still separately from each other. The various Protestant confessions are sincerely searching for common formulas on the meaning of the Eucharist, focusing attention on the common faith in Christ and in the key doctrines of revelation; and the argument has been advanced that Baptism gives one the right to the Eucharist.

Reference is made also to the intercommunion permitted at

present to some extent by the Catholic Church with regard to Orthodox Christians, despite the absence of unity between the two Churches. But one sees also the difficulties inherent in the absence of the priestly office, the problem vis-à-vis the Protestants. The Eucharist celebrated together only factually without the theological basis of Church unity can result in nothing but a mere appearance of unity.

When these angles of the question came up for discussion at the World Council of Churches meeting in Upsala in 1969, the conferees significantly concluded that even among the Reformation Churches themselves, alongside the freer Protestant conception of the Eucharist there is a deep-rooted "Catholic" position that sees insurmountable barriers here, limits beyond which one cannot compromise. In general, all these tendencies and arguments show indeed a deep and sincere yearning for the one Eucharist.

On the Catholic side the yearning is equally profound. In the missions and in the diaspora the need for reunion is felt with redoubled urgency by reason of the coexistence of different confessions and cooperation in common undertakings. But the longing remains unrealizable as long as essential presuppositions are wanting.[263]

True, Baptism gives one the right to the Eucharist, and Christ invites us all to his table; but the Eucharistic table stands in his Church, in the Church of the Catholic faith and of the priestly power. This is why even in the Mass the Eucharist is celebrated only after the faithful have heard God's word and accepted it in faith. True, too, the Eucharist possesses a dynamic power orientated toward unity, but it is the unity of those who have already been united in faith. The Eucharist simply intensifies their love and their yearning for greater union.

Those who think they can force unity by taking matters into their own hands and conducting intercredal experiments in the Eucharist within private, elite circles, without concern for the Church's hierarchical order or essential differences of doctrine, labor under a false illusion. Far from performing a prophetic gesture, they rather cut themselves off from their own Church. On the same grounds it is also illusory to attempt to bring about unity first and foremost on the parish level. For a common celebration of the Eucharist it is not enough to find a common formula in matters of central dogmas of faith or even in the matter of belief in the Eucharist. Anyone who thinks that this should suffice implicitly affirms that the other doctrines are insignificant. Orthopraxis cannot take the place of orthodoxy.

With regard to the churches of the Reformation, when other questions of faith have been resolved, there remains the most difficult question of all, that of the priestly ministry. Is it possible to constitute the priestly ministry without Apostolic succession? Can this proviso be superseded or compensated for by a ministry "of desire and intention" (*in voto*)?

Where unity of faith and a valid priesthood are present, as in the Orthodox Churches, there remains the wound of schism; and complete intercommunion is ruled out by the very definition of schism. But the Catholic Church could permit restricted intercommunion with such Churches while continuing to register protest against their violation of the Church's hierarchical order at the upper levels of authority, just as two countries which have recalled their ambassadors might continue to maintain consular relations with each other. A similar relation would be possible with one or other separated confession or group with which negotiations for unity are in progress; for such negotiations already presuppose unity of faith.

Another development within the whole complex question of intercommunion, "restricted open communion," would authorize the Church to permit the reception of the Eucharist, under certain conditions, to individual Christians who belong to another confession but no longer believe in it and yet are unable to leave it. The decision in such cases, says the Decree on Ecumenism, is left to the "prudent decision" of the local bishop (§8: *prudenter decernat auctoritas episcopalis localis*).

VIII. CONCLUSION

It is a richly complex and variegated picture that has passed before our eyes in the course of our consideration of the Mass in the history of its dogma, the development of its liturgical form, and the chal-

lenge it holds out to pastoral commitment. We have been constantly confronted with new beginnings, new perspectives, new accents,
new questions. Such indeed is the richness of the mystery that
Christ has entrusted to his Church.

In the person of Christ, God stooped to become man. At the
end of his earthly sojourn the God-Man summed up his entire work
of reconciling heaven and earth in this simple sign and handed it
over to his Church, with the mandate to bear it through all the
ages as a perpetual pledge of his presence and as the center of
its own life. It was now up to the Church to protect this sign as
well as to develop it, to give it shape and form with reverence and
fidelity to the Lord's bequest and with love and concern for the
men who would gather together around it. In this manner the
sacred sign of the Eucharist became the center of a constellation of
tensions.[264]

There is the tension, first of all, between the inexhaustible
mystery on the one hand, and, on the other, the necessity of grasping
and explaining it in terms of human reason. Hence at one time
there is the reverential distance and awe, the sacred language, the
obscure symbols inherited from of old, the aversion to inquisitive
investigation; and at another time the search for clarity, the rejection of unintelligible forms and texts, the antipathy toward whatever
smacks of the magical.

There is the tension between interiority and open proclamation. Nothing touches man's innermost being so deeply as this
mystery; nowhere is the free and total response of his whole per-
sonality called for so intimately as here: the sense of astonishment
at God's condescension; of gratitude and love; the urge to surrender
his heart; the readiness to participate in Christ's sacrificial death.
And yet the Lord's death should be proclaimed aloud. The mystery
has been placed in the Church's hands, and it must be celebrated
in the gathering of the Church.

Within the Church itself, there is the tension between community and hierarchical authority. All are recipients of God's grace,
all guests at the Lord's one table. An age that proclaims equality for
all on the political plane finds it hardly acceptable that a person
who has not been empowered by the people should have prece-
dence. And yet Christ called unto himself the closed circle of the
Twelve, to whom alone he gave the mandate.

Again, there is the tension between poverty and richness. On
the one hand, not only the poverty of plain and primitive begin-

nings, but poverty and simplicity deliberately willed and chosen, a dislike of all pomp and splendor of language and attire, distrust of what musical art and dramatic forms might have to offer. And then, on the other hand, the eagerness to press into service all the riches of the earth and all the arts at the disposal of the human spirit. As was noted above, the Eucharist seems to possess a kind of magnetic power to draw all things unto Itself.

There is, finally, the tension between the free and spontaneous flow of prayer, of inspired prophetic outburst, of freshness and creativity in shaping ritual according to the times and circumstances on the one hand, and on the other the legitimate demands of tradition, of law and order. There exists the danger of growing rigid and stiff, and the equal danger of quick and senseless change for its own sake to the point of confusion, of forms being so time-bound that they soon become stale, outworn, outdated.

The ideal form of celebrating Mass, whether in large congregations irrespective of differing interests and backgrounds, or in smaller circles grouped according to every different shade of interest and background, will never be found. A form that meets all claims can be developed neither by initiative from below nor by dictation from above. It is a task that must remain forever unfulfilled. All we can hope to achieve is the continuous compromise that adumbrates and even approximates the unattainable ideal.

And yet in the midst of all this concern to give satisfactory shape to the liturgy, of all attempts at change and adaptation, there remains that which is solid, constant, stable. For two millenniums, generation after generation, God's people have been gathering together around the sacrament of the sacrifice that Christ offered on the Cross. Through all these centuries men have found divine support in it, have drawn from it strength and courage for heroic renunciation, or for mighty deeds, or even for the quiet heroism of fulfilling their duties in the silent routine of daily life. The Mass is in fact, as Journet has it, the "power of the Cross that reaches across the generations, in order to include them existentially, with all their faith and all their love, in the drama of the Passion where their place has already been predestined" (p. 96). It is the process in which Christ draws all creation unto himself. This process will continue until his Second Coming.

NOTES

[1] In *Der Paschamahlbericht Lk 22:7-14, 15-18* (Münster 1953), p. 73.

[2] In his article "Diathéke" in Kittel 2:106-34.

[3] In his article "Compositio Libri Danielis et idea Filii Hominis," in *Verbum Domini* 37 (1959) 328.

[4] For the meaning of *polloi* = all, the totality of people, see the numerous illustrations in Jeremias, *The Eucharistic Words of Jesus*, p. 172.

[5] In *Die Eucharistie in der Zeit der griechischen Väter*, 1.1:28-33; 2.12:219.

[6] The text with an introduction by L. Ligier, "Textus liturgiae Judaeorum," appears in Hänggi-Pahl 5-10.

[7] See on this point R. J. Ledogar, *Acknowledgment: Praise-Verbs in the Early Greek Anaphora*, pp. 121-24, as against J. P. Audet, who had attempted in various publications to prove that this literary genre existed in the time of Jesus — in particular in his "Esquisse historique du genre littéraire de la bénédiction juive et de l'eucharistie chrétienne," in RBén 65 (1958) 371-99.

[8] In "Schlachten und Opfern," in ZKT 78 (1956) 205.

[9] See the present author's "Accepit panem," in ZKT 57 (1943) 162-65, or pp. 277-82 in the translation, *Pastoral Liturgy*.

[10] See Averbeck 90-115 for Goetz's and Rehbach's positions.

[11] See L. Sabourin, *Rédemption sacrificielle*.

[12] In *Das Herrenmahl*, pp. 135f.

[13] Stanislas Lyonnet, S.J., "La Nature du culte dans le Nouveau Testament," in *La Liturgie après Vatican II: Bilans, études, prospective*, ed. by J.-P. Jossua and Yves Congar (Unam Sanctam 66/2 Paris 1967), p. 367.

[14] See A. Hamman, *Vie liturgique et vie sociale* (Paris 1968) pp. 161f.

[15] In "Die Gestalt der urchristlichen Eucharistiefeier," in MTZ 6 (1955) 125.

[16] See H. de Riedmatten, "La Didaché: Solution du problème ou étape décisive?" in *Angelicum* 36 (1959) 410-29; A. Hamman, *La Prière* 2 (Tournai 1963) 28f.; M. Decroos, "De eucharistische liturgie van Didaché 9 en 10," in BTFT 28 (1967) 376-98.

[17] Arguments for the Eucharistic implication are summed up in Betz, *Die Eucharistie* 2.1; 144-66; those against, in F. Schröger's article "Der Gottesdienst der Hebräerbriefgemeinde," in MTZ 19 (1968) 169-81.

[18] From Strack-Billerbeck 4:211-20.

[19] From Strack-Billerbeck 4:613f. See also 4:61f. and 72.

[20] See Harnack's *Brot und Wasser*, TU 7.2 (Leipzig 1891), 115-44, and Scheiwiler's *Die Elemente der Eucharistie in den ersten drei Jahrhunderten* (Mainz 1903), pp. 138-75.

[21] See Betz, *Die Eucharistie* 1.1:29-34; 2.12:219f.

[22] See Kilmartin's article "The Eucharistic Cup in the Primitive Liturgy," in CBQ 24 (1962) 32-43.

[23] See Averbeck 127, n. 289, on this.

[24] See C. Ruch, "La Messe d'après les Pères," in DTC 10:918-25.

[25] In his "Eucharistía und eucharistéin in ihrem Bedeutungswandel bis 200 nach Christus," in *Philologus* 69 (1910), esp. pp. 383-86.

[26] In the E. T. von Klette edition, TU 15.2 (Leipzig 1897), 98.

[27] See relevant texts in Averbeck 509f., 252, 417, 493f., 750.

[28] Consult the list in E. Dekkers, *Tertullianus en de Geschiedenis der Liturgie* (Brussels 1947), pp. 49f.

[29] See L. Ryan's article "Patristic Teaching on the Priesthood of the Faithful," in ITQ 29 (1962) 32f.

[30] See Berger's work *Die Wendung "offerre pro" in der römischen Liturgie*, LQF 41 (Munich 1965), pp. 42–60.

[31] See, e.g., P. Graff, discussed in Averbeck 353.

[32] See Odo Casel's "Die *logikè thysía* der antiken Mystik in christlichliturgischer Umdeutung," in JLW 4 (1924) 37–47.

[33] See the corresponding prayer in the Byzantine liturgy as reproduced in Brightman 341.

[34] See M. Jugie's section of the article "La Messe" in DTC, "La Messe en Orient du IVᵉ au IXᵉ siècle," 10:1317-46.

[35] See H. J. Schulz, *Die byzantinische Liturgie*, pp. 18–28.

[36] From *Acta apostolorum apocrypha*, ed. R. A. Lipsius-Bonnet, 2.1 (Leipzig 1891) 13f.

[37] See Mingana's edition of Theodore's Commentary on the Eucharist, p. 85.

[38] See O. Nussbaum's *Der Standort des Liturgen am christlichen Altar vor dem Jahre 1000* (Bonn 1965), and the present author's critique of his work, in ZKT 88 (1966) 445–50.

[39] See E. Palli-Lucchesi, "Bilderwand," in LTK² 2:467f.

[40] Published as a supplement to R. H. Connolly's *The Liturgical Homilies of Narsai* (Cambridge 1909), pp. 92–97. See further, J. Quasten's "Mysterium tremendum," in *Vom christlichen Mysterium*, eds. Anton Mayer, Quasten, and B. Neunheuser (Düsseldorf 1951), pp. 66–75, and "The Liturgical Mysticism of Theodore of Mopsuestia," in TS 15 (1954) 431–39; and G. Fittkau's *Der Begriff des Mysteriums bei Johannes Chrysostomus* (Bonn 1953), pp. 122–27.

[41] See on this the present author's work, *The Place of Christ in Liturgical Prayer*, pp. 172–238.

[42] See Brightman 318, 378; A. Raes, "De byzantijnse Vroomheid en het monophysisme," in BTFT 13 (1952) 299–305; and E. Lanne, "La Prière de la grande Entrée dans la liturgie byzantine," in *Miscellanea . . . Lercaro* 2 (Rome 1967) 303–12.

[43] Cited in Betz, *Die Eucharistie* 1.1:121-39.

[44] In the above-mentioned *The Place of Christ in Liturgical Prayer*, pp. 239–63.

[45] See M. Lepin, *L'idée du sacrifice de la Messe*, pp. 39–41, 81.

[46] *Expositio antiquae liturgiae Gallicanae Germano Pariensi ascripta*, ed. J. Quasten (Münster 1934), p. 21. See also A. van der Mensbrugghe, "Pseudo-Germanus Reconsidered," TU 80 (Berlin 1962), pp. 172–84.

[47] See K. Gamber, ed., *Codices liturgici Latini antiquiores* ² (Fribourg 1968), p. 139.

[48] In his *Kloster, Priestermönch, und Privatmesse*, pp. 70–81.

[49] See MRR 1:225f.

[50] See the present author's "Von der 'Eucharistia' zur 'Messe'," in ZKT 89 (1967), 29–40, and C. Mohrmann's "Missa," in VigChr 12 (1958) 67–92.

[51] See G. Ellard, *Master Alcuin, Liturgist* (Chicago 1956), pp. 144–73.

[52] See in this connection Part II, ch. 5, comment on Rabanus Maurus.

[53] See A. Kolping's article "Amalar von Metz und Florus von Lyon, Zeugen eines Wandels im liturgischen Mysterienverständnis," in ZKT 73 (1951) 424–64.

[54] See R. Schulte, *Die Messe als Opfer der Kirche*, pp. 159–68.

[55] On the foregoing points see J. Geiselmann, *Die Eucharistielehre der Vorscholastik*, pp. 134–41 and 221f., 218f., 349.

[56] See A. Gaudel's section of the "Mass" article in DTC 10:1009-13.

[57] See Lepin, pp. 98–112.

[58] For a survey of pertinent texts quoted during the early Middle Ages, see Lepin 37–81.

[59] See a fuller discussion of this passage in Lepin 148–53.

[60] See A. Gaudel's section of "Mass" article in DTC 10:1052-56. "Quaracchi" refers to the Franciscan research center at Quaracchi-Florence: edition of Alexander of Hales, 1924–48; of St. Bonaventure, 1882–1902. "Borgnet" refers to edition of St. Albert by Abbé Auguste Borgnet, Paris 1890–99. The translation in process of St. Thomas Aquinas, ed. T. Gilby and others (New York 1964—) has been used where texts were available; otherwise, translations are in the "English Dominican" version (2nd ed., New York 1912–36).

[61] See E. Iserloh, "Der Wert der Messe in der Diskussion der Theologen vom Mittelalter bis zum 16. Jahrhundert," in ZKT 83 (1961) 51f.

[62] See Gaudel, p. 1068f.; also R. Dameräu, *Die Abendmahlslehre des Nominalismus insbesondere die des Gabriel Biel* (Giessen 1963).

[63] There is a critical edition by H. A. Oberman and W. J. Courtenay in four volumes (Wiesbaden 1963–67).

[64] See H. B. Meyer, *Luther und die Messe*, pp. 153–55.

[65] See H. Boehmer, ed., *Analekten zur Geschichte des Franz von Assisi* (Tübingen 1930), p. 40.

[66] On Gratian and commentators in the next paragraph, see the above-cited Iserloh article, pp. 45–70.

[67] See A. Franz, *Die Messe im deutschen Mittelalter*, p. 518.

[68] See Peter Browe, *Die Verehrung der Eucharistie im Mittelalter* (Munich 1933).

[69] See T. F. Simmons, ed., *The Lay Folks Mass Book* (London 1879), pp. 131–33, 366–71, as well as Franz, pp. 36–51.

[70] See Francis Clark, *Eucharistic Sacrifice and the Reformation*, pp. 73–98, and also the Gaudel article, DTC 10:1080–84.

[71] The edition of Nicholas of Cusa is that of J. Faber (Paris 1514), republished Frankfurt 1962; cf 2:64r, and see again Franz, p. 308.

[72] Werke 6:357, 368f., All our Luther quotations are from the Weimar (German) edition, 1883—. American readers may find corresponding passages in the ongoing translation ed. Jaroslav Pelikan and others (St. Louis and Philadelphia 1957—).

[73] For detailed instances of this, see Meyer's *Luther und die Messe*.

[74] According to Iserloh, *Der Kampf um die Messe in den ersten Jahren der Auseinandersetzung mit Luther* (Münster 1952), p. 43.

[75] From Cajetan's Opuscula Omnia (Lyon 1558), p. 341. See also Iserloh's above-cited article, "Der Wert der Messe . . . ," pp. 71–76.

[76] The topic is surveyed in Averbeck 137–51.

[77] See also Meyer, pp. 161–66.

[78] In Averbeck 26f., 207, and 493. For Melanchthon's position (below), see Averbeck 34–41.

[79] See Francis Clark's work, pp. 102f., 159–68, and 380–409; Gregory Dix, *The Shape of the Liturgy*, pp. 640–69; and C. W. Dugmore, *The Mass and the English Reformers* (New York 1958), pp. 157–71.

[80] See N. M. Halmer's article "*Die Messopferspekulation von Kardinal Cajetan und Ruard Tapper*," in DTF 21 (1943) 187–212.

[81] In *The Shape of the Liturgy*, p. 626.

[82] See Lepin 297–326.

[83] In his section of the "Mass" article in DTC 10:1143–1316. A similar but more chronological sequence was devised in Lepin 335–720.

[84] Per Francis Clark, in *Eucharistic Sacrifice and the Reformation*, pp. 394–409.

[85] 21:648-79 in the Vivès edition of the *Opera* of Suárez.

[86] Appearing in *American Ecclesiastical Review* I: "The Notion of Sacrifice," 33 (July 1905) 1–14; II: "The Sacrifice of the New Law," 33 (September 1905) 258–72; and paraphrased in Lepin 619.

[87] From the 1939 original of *Meditations before Mass* (Westminster, Md., 1959), entitled *Besinnung vor der heiligen Messe*, 2 (Mainz 1939) 76; in later editions this statement was dropped.

[88] See W. L. Boelens, *Die Arnoldshainer Abendmahlsthesen* (Assen 1964), and Averbeck 381–452, esp. 436–38.

[89] See L. Bouyer's *Eucharist* (Notre Dame, Ind., 1968), pp. 396–442, on the general perspective of rediscovery of tradition among Anglo-Saxon Calvinists, in the Scottish Church, at Taizé, in the Church of South India, and in the Lutheran Liturgy of 1958 (the result of collaboration by eight groups of American Lutherans). For similar developments in the Evangelical Church of Germany, consult Averbeck 527–74.

[90] See, e.g., the compact presentation in the monograph by A. Grail and A. M. Roguet, "Eucharistie," in vol. 4 of *Initiation Théologique* (Paris 1952); in A. Piolanti, ed., *Eucaristia* (Rome-Paris 1957); or in J. Betz, "Eucharistie," in

Handbuch theologischer Grundbegriffe, ed. Heinrich Fries, 1 (Munich 1962) 336–55.

[91] In the 1964 revision, 4:16, pp. 247–528; and 3:2 in the first edition of 1941. The Scheffczyk study appears in *Pro Mundi Vita. Festschrift zum Eucharistischen Weltkongress,* ed. Theology Faculty of Ludwig-Maximilian University, Munich (Munich 1960), pp. 203–22.

[92] For examples of such argument, see Averbeck 789f.

[93] See Averbeck 776–805; K. Rahner, "Current Problems in Christology," in *Theological Investigations* 1 (Baltimore 1961), pp. 154–56; the article on this council by P. T. Camelot and its bibliography, NCE 3:423–26.

[94] See among others, Peter Brunner, "Zur Lehre vom Gottesdienst der im Namen Jesu versammelten Gemeinde," in *Leiturgia* 1 (1954) 210–12, 229–32.

[95] In his "Der Gedächtnischarakter des alt- und neutestamentlichen Pascha," as quoted in B. Neunheuser (ed.), *Opfer Christi und Opfer der Kirche,* p. 83. The second quotation appears on p. 87.

[96] For the theological state of this question, consult the conferences "De praesentia Domini in communitate cultus" by B. Neunheuser ("Evolutio historica et difficultas specifica") and by K. Rahner ("Synthesis theologica") at the Theological Congress in Rome 1966, in *Acta Congressus internationalis de theologia Concilii Vaticani II* (Vatican 1968), pp. 316–38. See also V. Warnach, "Symbol and Reality in the Eucharist," in *The Breaking of Bread, Concilium* 40, Pierre Benoit and others, eds., December, 1969. For a general survey of the subject, the following may be useful: T. Filthaut, *Die Kontroverse über die Mysterienlehre* (Warendorf 1947); J. Betz, *Die Eucharistie* 1.1:197–201; 242–59; V. Warnach, "Mysterientheologie," in LTK² 7:724–27.

[97] See Betz's *Die Eucharistie* 1.1:242–51; similarly Michael Schmaus in his *Katholische Dogmatik* 4.16:397f. Schmaus, however, lays special stress on the dramatic representation contained in the ritual.

[98] See Gottlieb Söhngen, " 'Tut das zu meinem Gedächtnis': Wesen und Form der Eucharistiefeier als Stiftung Jesu," in Karl Rudolf (ed.), *Pascha Domini:*

Fragen zur Liturgie und Seelsorge (Vienna 1959), pp. 64–90.

[99] See also Y. Brilioth, *Eucharistic Faith and Practice* (New York 1961) pp. 63f.

[100] In *Die Eucharistie* 1.1:140-342, and LTK² 3:1154f.

[101] See K. O'Shea, who in his "Sacramental Realism," ITQ 30 (1960) 129–42, explains Thomas Aquinas' lines from ST 3a, 77:5 ad 2 thus: "The Eucharist is the perfect sacrament of our Lord's passion, because it contains Christ Himself who endured it."

[102] See L. Monden, *Het Misoffer als Mysterie* (Roermond 1948), pp. 114–18; C. Baumgartner, "Bulletin d'histoire et de théologie sacramentaires," in RSR 44 (1956) 295–97; R. Lachenschmid, "Heilswerk Christi und Liturgie," TP 41 (1966) 211–27.

[103] See A. Cody, *Heavenly Sanctuary and Liturgy in the Epistle to the Hebrews* (St. Meinrad, Ind., 1960), pp. 199–202, and the Schildenberger article cited in note 95, pp. 89–94.

[104] See Averbeck 672–85, 736–38, and its Index entries.

[105] Among others the following Protestant writings are relevant on this issue: Brilioth's *Eucharistic Faith and Practice,* p. 283; Thurian's *The Eucharistic Memorial*; A. M. Allchin's "The Eucharistic Offering," in StLit 1 (1962) 101–14; Von Allmen's *The Lord's Supper,* ch. 4: "Living Bread and Sacrifice," pp. 75–100. Among those of the opposition, see O. Kock, *Gegenwart oder Vergegenwärtigung Christi im Abendmahl* (Munich 1965), and texts in Averbeck 676–85.

[106] For expressions of this position see Averbeck 219–21; K. Plachte, *Das Sakrament des Altars* (Berlin 1955), pp. 404–408.

[107] Thus, e.g., the comment in P. Brunner's article "Zur Lehre vom Gottesdienst," in *Leiturgia* 1 (1954) 358. See also M. Seemann, *Heilsgeschehen und Gottesdienst. Die Lehre Peter Brunners in katholischer Sicht* (Paderborn 1966) pp. xiv–xv.

[108] See H. B. Meyer's *Luther und die Messe,* pp. 256–59.

[109] See Averbeck, 540–42, 545f., 552–54, 558–62. For the "offering" see esp. pp. 553 and 561f.

[110] See *The Eucharistic Liturgy of Taizé,* tr. by John Arnold (London 1962), p. 48.

[111] See R. Schulte, *Die Messe als Opfer der Kirche,* p. 81 for Bishop Braulio; p. 36 for Isidore of Seville.

[112] From *The Church Teaches: Documents of the Church in English Translation,* tr. by John F. Clarkson, S.J., et al. (St. Louis 1955), p. 292, no. 740.

[113] See Pope Pius XII's address *Magnificate Dominum* of Nov. 2, 1954, in TPS 1:4 (1954) 375; also K. Rahner, "Die vielen Messen als die vielen Opfer Christi," ZKT 77 (1955) 94–101, and corresponding pages in its English expansion, *The Celebration of the Eucharist* (designated as "Rahner-Häussling"). More on this work in Part IV, note 239.

[114] For discussion of this question, see J. A. de Aldama, "De sacramento unitatis christianae seu ss. Eucharistia," in *Sacrae Theologiae Summa* 4³ (Madrid 1956) 329–31.

[115] In his *Katholische Dogmatik* 4.1:412-17.

[116] In his chapter, "Die Prosphora in der patristischen Theologie," in the Neunheuser volume, *Opfer Christi und Opfer der Kirche,* pp. 114f.

[117] In "Neue Beiträge zur Epiklesenfrage," JLW 4 (1924) 169–78.

[118] See Rahner-Häussling 29–31; and C. Baumgartner's above-cited article in RSR 44 (1956) 282: "L'expression cultuelle constitutive du don que l'Eglise doit faire du Christ, d'elle-même et du monde à Dieu."

[119] See in this connection our comment on Peter Lombard in Part I, ch. 6.

[120] Appearing in *Worship* 45:1 (1971) 13–21.

[121] In his section of the "Mass" monograph in DTC 10:1284-86.

[122] See Yves Congar, "L'Ecclesia, ou Communauté chrétienne sujet intégral de l'action liturgique," in *La Liturgie après Vatican II,* pp. 241–82.

[123] Isidore is cited in Schulte's *Die Messe als Opfer der Kirche,* pp. 36 and 40; Walafrid Strabo, on p. 144; Florus of Lyon, p. 162.

[124] For other examples see MRR 1.196, n. 7.

[125] See C. McGarry, "The Eucharistic Celebration as the True Manifestation of the Church," ITQ 32 (1965) 325–37.

[126] See B. Schultze, "Eucharistie und Kirche in der russischen Theologie der Gegenwart," ZKT 77 (1955) 257–300.

[127] See C. Baumgartner's survey, "Bulletin d'histoire et de théologie sacramentaires," RSR 50 (1962) 275f., in which he comments critically on the above-cited Schulte work.

[128] See G. C. Mitchell, "Theologians and the Offerer of the Mass," ITQ 25 (1958) 13, in which he quotes approvingly the present author's argument in MRR 1:190.

[129] Cited in Schulte, *Die Messe . . . ,* pp. 167 and 57.

[130] See B. D. Marliangeas' paper, " 'In persona Christi' — 'in persona Ecclesiae,' " in *La Liturgie après Vatican II,* pp. 283–88.

[131] As we read in J. Lécuyer's *Le Sacrifice de la Nouvelle Alliance* (Le Puy-Lyon 1962), pp. 223f. Peter Lombard is cited on p. 224.

[132] See also F. Holböck, *Der eucharistische und der mystische Leib Christi* (Rome 1941), p. 236.

[133] See consideration of Plachte's *Das Sakrament des Altars* (1955) in Averbeck 221.

[134] See also Rupert Berger, *Die Wendung "offerre pro" in der römischen Liturgie,* p. 244.

[135] See J. Geiselmann, *Die Abendmahlslehre an der Wende der christlichen Spätantike . . . ,* p. 47.

[136] See O. Perler, "Logos und Eucharistie nach Justinus I Apol. c. 66," in DTF 18 (1940) 296–304.

[137] In "Le récit de l'Institution eucharistique dans l'anaphore chaldéenne et malabare des Apôtres," OrChrPer 10 (1944) 216026.

[138] *The Church Teaches,* p. 279, no. 717.

[139] The Heiming transcript appears in "Palimpsestbruchstücke der Syrischen Version der Jakobusanaphora aus dem 8. Jahrhundert in der Handschrift add 14615 des British Museum," in OrChrPer 16 (1950) 195f.; that of Rücker, in LQF 4 (1923) 14.

[140] In his article "Epiclèse" in DTC 5:194-300, esp. pp. 248–61. For the pres-

ent Orthodox position, see C. Kern's "En marge de l'Epiclèse," in *Irénikon* 24 (1951) 166–94.

[141] The findings of various studies in this field have been summed up in J. P. de Jong's article "Epiklèse," in LTK 3²:935-37.

[142] See on this Rahner-Häussling 18–21.

[143] In his paper, "Revelation in Word and Deed," in *The Word; Readings in Theology* (New York 1964), pp. 267f.

[144] In his article "Christ's Action in the Mass," TS 27 (1966) 89.

[145] See ST 2a2ae, 70–86, and also G. L. Bauer, "Das Heilige Messopfer im Lichte der Grundsätze des heiligen Thomas," in DTF 28 (1950) 11.

[146] See Lutheran Church, Book of Concord, *Die Bekenntnisschriften der evangelisch-lutherischen Kirche* (Göttingen 1959), p. 801, and also p. 1010.

[147] See summary of his "Wie verhalten sich die Begriffe . . ." (1950), in Averbeck 493.

[148] See his foreword to the German edition of Max Thurian's famous work *Eucharistie*, p. xxxvii.

[149] For further samples of such criticism see Averbeck 141, 493, 519, 782.

[150] See Warnach's "Das Messopfer als ökumenisches Anliegen," in *Die Kirche und der heutige Mensch* (Maria Laach 1955), p. 88.

[151] As reproduced in Kleinheyer's *Die Priesterweihe im römischen Ritus* (Trier 1962), p. 160.

[152] From Book II: *The Sacrifice of the Church*, p. 227.

[153] Michel's comment appears in the "Mass" article ("La Messe") in DTC 10:1301; McCormack's article was published in *Worship* 37 (1963) 30–39.

[154] K. Rahner, "Thesen über das Gebet 'im Namen der Kirche,'" in ZKT 83 (1961) 321–24; trans. as "Some Theses on Prayer 'In the Name of the Church'" in *Theological Investigations* 5 (Baltimore 1966) 419–38.

[155] On the origin of the Mass stipend from the Offertory procession, see MRR 2:23-26. On the *offerens* see De la Taille, *The Mystery of Faith and Human Opinion* . . . , (London 1930), pp. 81–196; K. Mörsdorf, "Messstipendium," in LTK² 6:354f.

[156] For discussion of this decree see Rahner-Häussling 55f., n. 27.

[157] The Schmaus work is *Katholische Dogmatik* 4; the Von Allmen, *The Lord's Supper*, p. 100.

[158] In the collection *The Unfinished Reformation*, ed. Hans Asmussen and others (Notre Dame, Ind., 1961), pp. 113–47: "Catholic Truth in the New Testament. I. The Life of the Church." Trans. by R. J. Olsen from *Katholische Reformation* (Stuttgart 1968). See also Averbeck 763.

[159] For relevant material see Averbeck 787–805.

[160] In his "Oblatio Ecclesiae. Bemerkunger zu den neuen eucharistischen Hochgebeten der römischen Liturgie," in TLZ 94 (1969) 241–52. The quotation is from p. 251.

[161] In his "Die Eucharistie in der Didache," ALW 11 (1969) 10–39.

[162] See "The Original Form of the Anaphora of Addai and Mari," in JTS, 30 (1928–29) 23–32. For studies on this subject see Hänggi-Pahl 375–80, and also L. Bouyer, *Eucharist*, pp. 146–58.

[163] See also Clement of Rome, Letter to the Corinthians 20, and Odo Casel, *Das Gedächtnis des Herrn in der altchristlichen Liturgie* (Freiburg 1920), pp. 21–26.

[164] Quoted from his article "Revelation: Word and Deed," in the collection *The Word; Readings in Theology*, pp. 265 and 268.

[165] Quoted in A. Riedel, ed., *Die Kirchenrechtsquellen des Patriarchats Alexandrien* (Leipzig 1900), p. 273.

[166] See A. Raes' article "Un Rite pénitentiel avant la communion dans les liturgies syriennes," *L'Orient-Syrien* 10 (1965) 107–22.

[167] In "De actu poenitentiali infra Missam inserto conspectus historicus," EL 80 (1966) 257–64.

[168] See B. Capelle, "Le Kyrie de la Messe et le pape Gélase," in RBén 46 (1934) 126–44; and MRR 1:336f.

[169] See the article "Trope" by E. Leahy in NCE 14:315-18.

[170] G. G. Willis, in his *Further Essays in Early Roman Liturgy* (London 1968), pp. 108–12, doubts that the oration at the end of the Introit was originally in-

tended to be a concluding prayer, but the arguments he adduces are not convincing.

[171] This point is considered by C. Vogel in *Introduction aux sources de l'histoire du culte chrétien au Moyen Âge* (Spoleto 1966), pp. 252f.

[172] In *Nichtevangelische syrische Perikopenordnungen*, LQF3 (Münster 1921), pp. 173f.

[173] For the tradition of the West, see Stephan Beissel's *Entstehung der Perikopen des römischen Messbuchs* (Freiburg 1907), and T. Klauser's *Das römische Capitulare evangeliorum*, LQF 28 (Münster 1935). On the Epistles, see C. Godu's article "Épître," in DACL 5:245–344, and W. H. Frere's *Studies in Early Roman Liturgy, 3: The Roman Epistles-Lectionary* (Oxford 1935).

[174] See Hanssens 3:186-91; A. G. Martimort, "Origine et signification de l'Alléluia de la Messe romaine," in *Kyriakon; Festschrift Johannes Quasten*, ed. P. Granfield and J. A. Jungmann (Münster 1970), pp. 811–34; R. G. Weakland, article "Alleluia," in NCE 1:321-23.

[175] See B. Capelle, "L'introduction du symbole à la Messe," in *Mélanges J. de Ghellinck* 2 (Gembloux 1951) 1003–27; and G. Ellard, *Master Alcuin, Liturgist*, pp. 174–88.

[176] In his article "Signification pastorale des prières du prône," MD 30 (1952) 125–36.

[177] See E. Lengeling, "Fürbitten," in LTK² 4:461f.

[178] See Hanssens 3:308-317, and also the survey in Raes, Introductio 84f.

[179] *Die liturgischen Einsetzungsberichte im Sinne vergleichender Liturgieforschung untersucht*, LQF 23 (Münster 1928).

[180] For the oldest form of the acclamation in Greek, see Brightman 177.

[181] For a survey of the formulas, see Lietzmann 60–68.

[182] See J. Grisbrooke, "Intercession at the Eucharist," in SL 5 (1966) 20–44.

[183] See the present author's chapter, "Heiliges Wort. Die rituelle Behandlung der Konsekrationsworte in den Liturgien," in *Miscellanea . . . Lercaro* 1: 307–19.

[184] AAS 59 (1967) 445, 448; TPS,

"New Changes in the Liturgy," 12.3 (1966–67) 244–49.

[185] See MRR 2:265f. For the author's position in the controversy with B. Botte, see the 5th (1962) German edition of that work, 2:580f.

[186] See the author's article "Das 'Pater Noster' im Kommunionritus," in ZKT 58 (1934) 552–71.

[187] See N. M. Denis-Boulet's article in A. G. Martimort, ed., *L'Eglise en prière* (Paris 1961), pp. 422–24. The English translation of this work, *The Church at Prayer — Introduction to the Liturgy* (New York 1968), does not contain this article.

[188] See J. P. de Jong in several studies of the subject: ALW 3:1 (1953) 78–98; 4 (1956) 245–78; 5 (1957) 33–79; TU 64 (1957) 29–34.

[189] See Botte 56, *Panis coelestis in Christo Jesu* ("This is the bread of heaven in Christ Jesus!"). Since the end of the fourth century several documents show only the simple phrase "The body of Christ"; see MRR 2:388.

[190] See the P. Joannou and W. Dürig article on "Eulogie," LTK² 3:1180-81.

[191] See K. Mohlberg, ed., *Das fränkische Sacramentarium Gelasianum* (Münster 1939), pp. 249–52. On the *missa solitaria* see MRR 1:225f.

[192] Historical background may be found in A. Cornides, "Concelebration" and its bibliography, in NCE 4:103-105; J. de Puniet, "Concélébration liturgique," in DACL 3:2470-88; and A. A. King, *Concelebration in the Christian Church*.

[193] For an interpretation of this decree see Rahner-Häussling 106–111.

[194] Address of November 2, 1954, in AAS 46 (1954) 668f.; that of September 22, 1956, trans. in TPS 3.3 (1956–57) 273.

[195] See K. Rahner, "Die vielen Messen als die vielen Opfer Christi," ZKT 77 (1955) 94–101.

[196] See Rahner-Häussling 105–11, with n. 23. For a convenient summary see the discussion of this work by E. J. Kilmartin in TS 28 (1967) 851f., and 25 (1964) 660–63 (review of J. C. McGowan's work *Concelebration*).

[197] In his article "Stationsgottesdienst," LTK² 9:1021f.

[198] For accounts of the Munich Congress, see *Statio Orbis. Eucharistischer Weltkongress in München 1960*; O. Nigsch, "Statio Orbis in München 1960 und Bombay 1964," LJ 15 (1965) 167–73; and any number of solid reports in English-language journals.

[199] In his Poenitentiale, § 145. See T. H. Schmitz, *Die Bussbücher und das kanonische Bussverfahren* (Düsseldorf 1898), p. 441.

[200] See F. J. Dölger, *Sol salutis. Gebet und Gesang im christlichen Alterum* (Münster 1925), and MRR 1:239f.

[201] Rubricae generales § 17 in the Pius V Missal. An earlier example is the Liber Ordinarius of Liège composed *c.* 1285 (ed. Volk, pp. 102–109).

[202] See K. Mohlberg, ed., *Sacramentarium Veronense* (Rome 1956), p. 77; also the present author's article, "Der Begriff sensus in frühmittelalterlichen Rubriken," EL 45 (1931) 124–27.

[203] In CorIC, Extravagantes . . . Communes 3.1 (ed. Friedberg 2:1256).

[204] On the spiritual importance of art in the liturgy see T. Culley's chapter, "Two Identities in Harmony," in *Hyphenated Priests*, ed. W. H. Cleary (Washington 1969). On the evolution of liturgical music see K. G. Fellerer, *The History of Catholic Church Music* (Baltimore 1961); O. Ursprung, *Die Katholische Kirchenmusik* (Potsdam 1932); Sacred Music articles in NCE, and their bibliographies.

[205] For corroboration see, e.g., E. J. Lengeling's survey, with its rich bibliography, "Sakral-Profan. Bericht über die gegenwärtige Diskussion," LJ 18 (1968) 164–88.

[206] *The Roman Martyrology*, ed. by J. B. O'Connell; trans. from 4th ed (1956) (Westminster, Md. 1962), p. 279.

[207] Karl Rahner, "Christian Living Formerly and Today," in *Theological Investigations* 7 (New York 1971) 9.

[208] For a summary view see the article by H. Vorgrimler and K. Hofmann, "Ewige Anbetung" in LTK² 3:1263-66; "Perpetual Adoration" and related articles on Eucharistic worship in NCE; and *The Eucharist Today*, ed. R. A. Tartre (New York 1967).

[209] On this read T. D. Stanks, "The Eucharist: Christ's Self-Communication in a Revelatory Event," TS 28 (1967) 27–50.

[210] In his article "Eucharistie," DSAM 4:1569f.

[211] AAS 59 (1967) 538–73; TPS, "Worship of the Eucharistic Mystery," 12.3 (1967) 211–36.

[212] This is not to deny that the aesthetic aspect is a very important stimulus to authentic participation. On this point generally, cf. T. Culley, *art. cit,* note 204, above.

[213] In "Eléments de la structure fondamentale de l'Eucharistie," RevSR 37 (1963) 344.

[214] In his article "Zur Lehre vom Gottesdienst," in *Leiturgia* 1 (1954) 358.

[215] See Averbeck 245 and 707 for fuller discussion.

[216] O'Shea sets forth a similar theory in "Sacramental Realism," ITQ 30 (1963) 133f.

[217] This is the defect in, for example, the otherwise excellent work of Nicholas Gihr (d. 1924), *The Holy Sacrifice of the Mass*, which has had 19 reprintings in the original German (see § 49.1), 23 in English (St. Louis 1955).

[218] R. E. McNally discusses this in "The 'tres linguae sacrae' in Early Irish Bible Exegesis," TS 19 (1958) 395–403.

[219] See 3:52-222, and for a brief recapitulation, pp. 76 and 166.

[220] Cf. JAJ article cited earlier, "Heiliges Wort . . . ," in *Miscellanea . . . Lercaro* 1:307-19.

[221] See J. Sauer, *Symbolik des Kirchengebäudes* (2nd ed., Freiburg 1924), and the present author in collaboration with E. Sauser, *Symbolik der Katholischen Kirche* (Stuttgart 1960). On the consequences of abandoning what he calls a "shared symbolism" see James Hitchcock's "Here Lies Community: R.I.P.," in *America* 122 (May 30, 1970) 578–81, and the reader reaction, 123 (October 17, 1970) 287ff. See also pp. 3–19 of *The Christian Vision*, ed. M. E. Evans (Westminster, Md., 1956), containing Conrad Pepler's article "The Worship of Mystery," and his later "Some Hesitations on the New Rites," *Spode House Review* 7 (1970) 73.

²²²On this read Brémond's classic *Histoire littéraire du sentiment religieux en France* 7 ('Paris 1929) 385–99.

²²³Abbot Weakland says it all in "The 'Sacred' and Liturgical Renewal," *Worship* 49 (1975) 512–529.

²²⁴As related in Schulte's *Die Messe als Opfer der Kirche*, pp. 50 and 112.

²²⁵In *The Precept of Hearing Mass* (Washington 1942). See also MRR 1:245, n.5.

²²⁶See V. Monachino, *La cura pastorale a Milano, Cartagine e Roma nel secolo IV*, pp. 54–57, 186–91; and C. S. Mosna, *Storia della Domenica dalle origini fino agli inizi del V secolo*, pp. 257f., 278f., 325–29.

²²⁷Matthäus Kaiser, "Die Applikation der Messe für das Volk nach dem geltenden Recht (II)," AKKR 130 (1961) 386f.

²²⁸In *Bullarium privilegiorum ac diplomatum Romanorum Pontificum* 3.3 (1743) 462.

²²⁹In *Die Abendmesse in Geschichte und Gegenwart*. The Motu Proprio is translated in TPS 4:1 (1957) 8f.

²³⁰Cf. Sacred Congregation of Rites, *Instruction on Putting into Effect the Constitution on the Sacred Liturgy*, TPS 10 (1964–65) 186–200; and pertinent passages in the Instruction *Worship of the Eucharistic Mystery*, TPS 12.3 (1967) 211–36.

²³¹See the Monachino work, pp. 52–54 on Milan; pp. 355f on Rome.

²³²Cited by Mosna, p. 127 of his *Storia della Domenica* . . . .

²³³See L. Eisenhofer, *Handbuch der katholischen Liturgik* (Freiburg 1932), 2:481.

²³⁴In his "Liturgia praesanctificatorum," *Liturgisch Woordenboek* 2:1565–73.

²³⁵On this point see L. Corciani, "Osservazioni su 'La Messe' di Adriano Fortescue," EL 58 (1944) 186f.

²³⁶In *Liturgies of the Religious Orders* (London 1955), pp. 20–22, 199f., 297, 347; see also MRR 1:225.

²³⁷See Canons 339, 466.

²³⁸See, e.g., J. J. Reed, "The Mass Server and Canon 29," TS 21 (1960) 256–70.

²³⁹See ZKT 71 (1949), and subsequently as a book (Herder 1951). A second, revised edition by Angelus Häussling in 1966 is known in English translation by W. J. O'Hara as *The Celebration of the Eucharist* (references in our text are to this translation). Objections based on post-Tridentine theology to Rahner's arguments have been answered by H. McCormack in the paper "Eucharistic Problems," *Worship* 39 (1965) 35–45; in particular Colman O'Neill, in *New Approaches to the Eucharist* (New York 1967), challenges Rahner's position; see R. Ledogar, "The Question of Daily Mass," *Worship* 43 (1969) 271–77.

²⁴⁰Cf. *The Celebration of the Eucharist*, p. 91.

²⁴¹See the present author's *The Early Liturgy* (Notre Dame, Ind., 1959), pp. 97–108.

²⁴²See his article "Ist die Liturgie die Mitte der Seelsorge?" in LJ 12 (1962) 88.

²⁴³From his paper "Religion Institutionalized," in *The Word in History. The St. Xavier Symposium*, p. 147.

²⁴⁴See Jean Daniélou, "La Catéchèse eucharistique chez les Pères de l'Eglise," in the CPL volume *La Messe et sa Catéchèse*, pp. 33–72; and K. Baus, "Die eucharistische Glaubensverkündigung der alten Kirchen in ihren Grundzügen," in F. X. Arnold, ed., *Die Messe in der Glaubensverkündigung*, pp. 55–78.

²⁴⁵See the Fischer study, *Eucharistiekatechese und liturgische Erneuerung, Rückblick und Wegweisung*, a dissertation of the University of Innsbruck (Düsseldorf 1959); and the Rodriguez Medina, *Pastoral y catequesis de la Eucaristía. Dimensiones modernas* (Salamanca 1966). See also J. Hofinger, *The Good News and Its Proclamation*. Post-Vatican II Edition of *The Art of Teaching Christian Doctrine* (Notre Dame, Ind. 1968), pp. 182–89.

²⁴⁶See Kattenbusch, *Das Apostolische Symbol* 2 (Leipzig 1900) 347–53; Schneider, "Die Tradierung der neutestamentlichen Heilswahrheiten in den Anaphoragebeten der Alten Kirche," *Una Sancta* 12 (Paris 1957) 29–36; Dahl, "Anamnesis," in ST 1 (1948) 69–95.

²⁴⁷In his *Liturgica Historica*, pp. 1–19: "The Genius of the Roman Rite."

[248] There are numerous other examples in H. Grisar's *Das Missale im Lichte römischer Stadtgeschichte* (Freiburg 1925).

[249] See Tilmann's "Kindermessfeier und liturgische Erneuerung," in *Die Messe in der Glaubensverkündigung* (2nd ed., Freiburg 1953), pp. 329–36. For an account of the German experience see F. Kolbe, "Eigene liturgische Feiern für Kinder und Jugendliche," LJ 19 (1969) 246f.

[250] R. W. Hovda, "The Underground Experiment in Liturgy," *Worship* 42 (1968) 333.

[251] See J. M. Petersen, "House-churches in Rome," VigChr 23 (1969) 264–72.

[252] In *Vom geschichtlichen Werden der Liturgie* (Freiburg 1923).

[253] J. H. Emminghaus, in his article "Hausmessen," TPQ 117 (1969) 314–26.

[254] In his "Réflexions sur les messes de petites groupes," MD 100:4 (1969) 130–38.

[255] In his *Aspects of the Church*, trans. by Thomas O'Meara, O.P. (Westminster, Md. 1965), pp. 94–95.

[256] See the present author's article, "Die Gnadenlehre im Apostolischen Glaubensbekenntnis und im Katechismus," in ZKT 50 (1926) 211–13.

[257] On this aspect see Henri de Lubac's *Corpus Mysticum: L'Eucharistie et l'Eglise au moyen-âge* (2nd ed., Paris 1949).

[258] See the author's contribution, "Fermentum," in *Colligere fragmenta. Festschrift A. Dold*, ed. Bonifatius Fischer (Beuron 1952), pp. 185–90.

[259] See the commentary on article 8 by Johannes Feiner in *Commentary on the Documents of Vatican II*, ed. by Herbert Vorgrimler, vol. 2 (New York 1968), pp. 102–8; and the rapidly expanding corpus of studies in English-language periodicals.

[260] In "Communio und Primat," in *Miscellanea historiae pontificiae* 7 (Rome 1943) 6. [This work has been translated into English: *Communion: Church and Primacy in Early Christianity*, trans. by Jared Wicks, S.J. (Chicago 1972); the translation is based, however, on a new German text, which was the result of revising the original text in the light of the Italian version; the new German text appeared in *Una Sancta* 17 (1962) and does not contain, in so many words, the sentence here quoted from the first edition.]

[261] On its history see Yves Congar, "Ökumenische Bewegung," in LTK²7: 1128-37; also other works by, or drawing on, Congar; and related references in NCE.

[262] See A. Marranzini, "L'intercommunione, problema teologico ed ecumenico," *Rassegna di Teologia* 10 (1969) 159–73, with bibliography; L. Renwart, "L'Intercommunion," NRT 92 (1970) 26–55; and the vast literature originating in English.

[263] See now the agreements on the Eucharist which have emerged from the Anglican-Roman Catholic commission: text of "Anglican/Roman Catholic Statement on the Eucharist" (Milwaukee, May 29, 1967), in *Documents on Anglican/Roman Catholic Relations* (Washington, D.C. 1972), pp. 3–4; text of "Agreed Statement on Eucharistic Doctrine" (Windsor, September 7, 1971), *ibid.*, pp. 47–50; and cf. commentary on the Windsor statement by Herbert J. Ryan, S.J., in *Documents on Anglican/Roman Catholic Relations II* (Washington, D.C. 1973), pp. 1–48 (this volume contains various other commentaries on and responses to the Agreed Statement).

[264] See Journet, *La Messe*, pp. 315–17.

BIBLIOGRAPHY

Note. Special editions of particular liturgical sources (e.g., sacramentaries, local liturgies) and studies are not listed here, as they are to be found in the manuals such as Martimort, Righetti, Eisenhofer, Jungmann, as well as cited in our Index.

Adam, Karl. *Die Eucharistielehre des heiligen Augustin.* FCLD 8.1. Paderborn 1908. Traces history from Tertullian on.

Allmen, Jean Jacques von. *The Lord's Supper,* tr. by W. F. Fleet. Richmond, Va., 1969. First published as *Essai sur le Repas du Seigneur* (Neuchâtel 1966) and written in an ecumenical spirit (author is a member of the Reformed Church).

Andrieu, M. *Les Ordines Romani du haut Moyen-Age.* 5 vols. Louvain 1931–61.

Arnold, F. X. "Vorgeschichte und Einfluss des Trienter Messopferdekretes," in F. X. Arnold and B. Fischer, eds., *Die Messe in der Glaubensverkündigung. Kerygmatische Fragen.* 2nd ed.; Freiburg 1953.

Averbeck, W. *Der Opfercharakter des Abendmahls in der neueren evangelischen Theologie.* Paderborn 1966.

Baciocchi, J. de. *L'Eucharistie.* Tournai 1964.

Barclay, W. *The Lord's Supper.* London 1967. A general survey of the history of the Eucharistic celebration from the beginning to the present, from the Anglican point of view.

Barrosse, T. "The Eucharist — Sacrifice and Meal? An Examination of the New Testament Data," YLS 6 (1965) 33–79. Minimizes sacrificial aspect.

Batiffol, P. *L'Eucharistie.* 5th ed., recast and corrected; Paris, 1913.

——————. *Leçons sur la Messe.* 7th ed.; Paris, 1920.

Baumstark, A. *Liturgie comparée. Principes et Méthodes pout l'étude historique des liturgies chrétiennes.* 3rd ed. (B. Botte); Chevetogne 1953. English translation by F. L. Cross, *Comparative Liturgy.* London 1958.

Betz, J. *Die Eucharistie in der Zeit der griechischen Väter.* 1.1 (Freiburg 1955); 2.1 (2nd ed. rev.; Freiburg 1964).

Bishop, E. *Liturgica Historica.* Oxford, 1918.

Botte, B. *La Tradition Apostolique de Saint Hippolyte. Essai de reconstitution.* LQF 39. Münster 1963.

Brightman, F. E. *Liturgies Eastern and Western. I. Eastern Liturgies.* Oxford 1896.

Brinktrine, J. *Der Messopferbegriff in den ersten zwei Jahrhunderten.* FTS 25. Freiburg 1918.

Brunner, P. "Zur Lehre vom Gottesdienst der im Namen Jesu versammelten Gemeinde," *Leiturgia. Handbuch des evangelischen Gottesdienstes* 1 (Kassel 1954) 83–364.

Casel, Odo. *Das christliche Opfermysterium,* ed. V. Warnach. Graz 1968. A collection of papers of this author (d. 1948), chiefly conferences to the Benedictine nuns of Herstelle.

——————. "Das Mysteriengedächtnis der Messliturgie im Lichte der Tradition," JLW 6 (1926) 113–204.

Clark, Francis. *Eucharistic Sacrifice and the Reformation*. Westminster, Md., 1960.

Cooke, Bernard. "Synoptic Presentation of the Eucharist as Covenant Sacrifice," TS 21 (1960) 1–44 (see esp. pp. 28f.).

De la Taille, Maurice. *The Mystery of Faith*. Book II. *The Sacrifice of the Church*. New York and London 1950. Trans. by Joseph Carroll, assisted by P. J. Dalton, of Book II of *Mysterium Fidei* (3rd ed.; Paris 1931).

Dix, Gregory. *The Shape of the Liturgy*. Westminster, England, 1945.

Duchesne, L. *Christian Worship. Its Origin and Evolution*. 5th ed. tr. by M. T. McClure; London 1927. First published as *Origines du culte chrétien*; Paris 1889, 5th ed., 1925. A classic history of the Occidental liturgies.

Ellard, Gerald. *The Mass in Transition*. Milwaukee 1956. Describes the situation immediately before Vatican Council II.

Erni, R., and others. *Das Opfer der Kirche*. Luzern 1954.

Fortescue, Adrian. *The Mass. A Study of the Roman Liturgy*. London 1912.

Fraigneau-Julien, B. "Eléments de la structure fondamentale de l'Eucharistie," RevSR 34 (1960) 35–61; 37 (1963) 321–44; 40 (1966) 27–47.

Franz, A. *Die Messe im deutschen Mittelalter*. Freiburg 1902.

Gaudel, A. "Le Sacrifice de la Messe dans l'Eglise latine du IVe siècle jusqu'à la veille de la Reforme," DTC 10:964-1085.

Geiselmann, J. R. *Die Abendmahlslehre an der Wende der christlichen Spätantike zum Frühmittelalter*. Munich 1933.

──────. *Die Eucharistielehre der Vorscholastik*. Paderborn 1926.

Gihr, Nicholas. *The Holy Sacrifice of the Mass*. Rev. tr., 33rd printing; St. Louis 1955. First published in 1877, the work combines theological, liturgical, and ascetical reflections on the Roman Mass.

Hamm, F. *Die liturgischen Einsetzungsberichte im Sinne vergleichender Liturgieforschung untersucht*. LQF 23. Münster 1928.

Hamman, A., and others. "Eucharistie," DSAM 4 (1960) 1553–1648.

Hänggi, A., and I. Pahl, eds. *Prex eucharistica. Textus e variis liturgiis antiquioribus selecti*. Spicilegium Friburgense 12. Fribourg, Switzerland, 1968.

Hanssens, J. M. *Institutiones liturgicae de ritibus orientalibus*. Vols. 2 and 3. Rome 1930–32.

Higgin, A. J. B. *The Lord's Supper in the New Testament*. 2nd ed.; London 1954. A solid exposition of the historical data. Author's interpretation is summed up: "The real presence was therefore not found in the Eucharistic elements, whose role rather was to recall the sacrificial death of Christ as event."

Hoffmann, A. "De Sacrificio Missae iuxta s. Thomam," Angelicum 15 (1938) 262–85.

Iserloh, Erwin. "Der Wert der Messe in der Diskussion der Theologen vom Mittelalter bis zum 16. Jahrhundert," ZKT 83 (1961) 44–79.

Jeremias, J. *The Eucharistic Words of Jesus*. Tr. by N. Perrin from 3rd German ed. New York, 1965.

Journet, Charles. *La Messe présence du sacrifice de la Croix*. Tournai 1957.

Jugie, Martin. "La Messe en Orient du IVe au IXe siècle," DTC 10:1317–46.

Jungmann, J. A. *The Mass of the Roman Rite. Its Origins and Development*. Tr. by F. A. Brunner from 2nd German ed. (1949) of *Missarum Sollemnia* (Vienna, 1948; 5th ed. rev., 1962). 2 vols. New York 1951–55.

──────. *Pastoral Liturgy*. Trans. of *Liturgisches Erbe und pastorale Gegen-*

wart (Innsbruck 1960). New York 1962. A collection of papers on questions concerning liturgy and kerygma, historical and contemporary.

—————. *The Place of Christ in Liturgical Prayer.* Rev. ed., tr. by A. Peeler from *Die Stellung Christi im liturgischen Gebet* (Münster 1925). New York 1965.

King, Archdale A. *Concelebration in the Christian Church.* London 1966.

Lepin, Maurice. *L'Idée du Sacrifice de la Messe d'après les théologiens depuis l'origine jusqu'à nos jours.* Paris 1926.

Lietzmann, H. *Messe und Herrenmahl.* Bonn 1926. A comparative view of the principal components of the Mass (e.g., anamnesis, epiclesis) to the end of uncovering its original form. His theory positing an original Eucharist without chalice has been rejected by even most Protestant scholars.

McGowan, J. C. *Concelebration, Sign of the Unity of the Church.* New York 1964. Concise historical survey, with thorough theological discussion.

McNaspy, C. J. *Our Changing Liturgy.* New York 1966.

Maertens, T., ed. *Liturgie et Communautés humaines.* Vivante Liturgie 84. Paris 1969.

Martène, E. *De antiquis Ecclesiae ritibus.* Vol. 1. 2nd ed.; Antwerp 1736. Chapters 3 and 4 contain very rich information on the Mass and liturgy of the late Middle Ages.

Martimort, A. G., ed. *L'Eglise en Prière. Introduction à la Liturgie.* Tournai 1961. English edition is by Austin Flannery and Vincent Ryan: *The Church at Prayer. An Introduction to the Liturgy,* with the collaboration of Bernard Botte, I. H. Dalmais, and others (New York 1968).

Maskell, W. *The Ancient Liturgy of the Church of England.* 3rd ed.; Oxford 1882.

Meyer, H. B. *Luther und die Messe.* Paderborn 1965.

Michel, A. "La Messe chez les théologiens postérieurs au Concile de Trente," DTC 10:1143–1316.

Mingana, A., ed. *Commentary of Theodore of Mopsuestia on the Lord's Prayer and on the Sacraments of Baptism and the Eucharist.* Woodbrooke Studies 6. Cambridge, England, 1933. Syriac and English translation (Eucharist: pp. 70–123).

Mitchell, G. D. "Theologians and the Offerer of the Mass," ITQ 25 (1958) 1–13.

Monachino, V. *La Cura pastorale a Milano, Cartagine e Roma nel secolo IV.* Rome 1947.

Mosna, C. S. *Storia della Domenica dalle origini fino agli inizi del V secolo.* Rome 1969.

Naegle, A. *Die Eucharistielehre des heiligen Johannes Chrysostomus.* Freiburg 1900. Good information; scholastic perspective.

Neuenzeit, P. *Das Herrenmahl. Studien zur paulinischen Eucharistieauffassung.* Munich 1960.

Neunheuser, Burkhard. *Eucharistie in Mittelalter und Neuzeit.* HDG 4.4b. Freiburg 1963.

—————, ed. *Opfer Christi und Opfer der Kirche.* Düsseldorf 1960.

Nussbaum, Otto. *Kloster, Priestermönch und Privatmesse.* Bonn 1961.

O'Connor, E. D. " 'Mysterium fidei' and the Celebration of Mass in Private," YLS 7 (1966) 17–71.

O'Shea, K. "Sacramental Realism. Some Thoughts on the Sacrifice of the Mass," ITQ 30 (1963) 99–145.

Piolanti, A., ed. *Eucaristia. Il mistero dell'altare nel pensiero e nella vita della Chiesa.* Rome 1957. Papers (56) covering history, theology, spirituality, and some pastoral questions.

Powers, J. *Eucharistic Theology.* New York 1967. Succinct review of the discussions of recent decades, concerning chiefly the Real Presence.

Quasten, Johannes, ed. *Expositio antiquae liturgiae Gallicanae Germano Parisiensi ascripta.* Münster 1934.

————, ed. *Monumenta eucharistica et liturgica vetustissima.* Florilegium Patristicum 7. Bonn 1935.

Raes, A. *Introductio in liturgiam orientalem.* Rome 1947.

Rahner, Karl, and A. Häussling. *The Celebration of the Eucharist.* New York 1968. Trans. by W. J. O'Hara from rev. ed. (1966) by A. Häussling of *Die vielen Messen und das eine Opfer,* by Karl Rahner (1949).

Renaudot, E. *Liturgiarum orientalium collectio.* 2 vols. Frankfurt 1847. Originally published Paris 1716. Still useful as a collection, although superseded in certain texts by recent editions.

Renz, F. S. *Die Geschichte des Messopfer-Begriffs.* 2 vols. Freising 1901–1902.

Righetti, M. *Manuale di storia liturgica.* Vol. 3: *L'Eucaristia.* Milan 1949 (3rd ed. 1966).

Rivière, J. "La Messe durant la période de la Reforme et du Concile de Trente," DTC 10:1085–1142.

Ruch, C. "La Messe d'après les Pères jusqu'à Saint Cyprien," DTC 40:864-964.

Rupprecht, P. "Una eademque hostia. Das Verhaltnis von Kreuz-und Messopfer nach dem Tridentinum," TQS 120 (1939) 1–36.

Sabourin, L. *Rédemption sacrificielle. Une enquête exégétique.* Tournai 1961.

Schmaus, M. *Katholische Dogmatik* 4.1: *Die Lehre von den Sakramenten.* 6th ed. rev.; Munich 1964.

Schulte, R. *Die Messe als Opfer der Kirche. Die Lehre frühmittelalterlicher Autoren.* LQF 35 Münster 1959.

Schulz, H. J. *Die byzantinische Liturgie. Vom Werden ihrer Symbolgestalt.* Freiburg 1964.

Schürmann, H. "Abendmahl," LTK² 1 (1957) 26–31.

————. "Die Gestalt der urchristlichen Eucharistiefeier," MTZ 6 (1955) 107–31.

Simmons, T. F., ed. *The Lay Folks Mass Book.* EETS 71. London 1879.

Solano, J., ed. *Textos eucaristicos primitivos.* 2 vols. Madrid 1952–54.

Srawley, J. H. *The Early History of the Liturgy.* Cambridge Handbooks of Liturgical Study. 2nd ed. rev.; Cambridge 1949.

Stephenson, A. A. "Two Views of the Mass: Medieval Linguistic Ambiguities," TS 22 (1961) 588–609. Holds that the Mass was taken both as *repraesentatio immolationis (in cruce peractae)* and as *immolatio* itself — the second being interpreted sometimes, esp. by the reformers, as a new slaying of Christ.

Strack, H. L., and P. Billerbeck. *Kommentar zum Neuen Testament aus Talmud und Midrasch.* 4 vols. Munich 1922–56.

Thurian, Max. *The Eucharistic Memorial.* 2 vols. Richmond, Va., 1961. Trans. by J. G. Davis of *L'Eucharistie: Mémorial du Seigneur, Sacrifice d'action de grâce et d'intercession* (Neuchâtel 1959). Author is a founding member of the Community of Taizé.

Tihon, P. "Eucharistic Concelebration," YLS 6 (1965) 1–32.

Vonier, Anselm. *A Key to the Doctrine of the Eucharist.* Westminster, Md., 1965. First published London 1925.

Wieland, F. *Der vorirenäische Opferbegriff.* Munich 1909.

Wisløff, C. *Abendmahl und Messe. Die Kritik Luthers am Messopfer.* Berlin 1969. First published Norway 1957.

Zimmermann, J. F. *Die Abendmesse in Geschichte und Gegenwart.* Vienna 1914.

ABBREVIATIONS

AH	Analecta Hymnica. Ed. G. Dreves and C. Blume. Leipzig 1886–1922
AKKR	Archiv für katholisches Kirchenrecht. Mainz 1857—
ALW	Archiv für Liturgiewissenschaft. Regensburg 1950—
ANDRIEU	Michel Andrieu, Les Ordines Romani du haut moyen-âge
AVERBECK	W. Averbeck, Der Opfercharakter des Abendmahls in der neueren evangelischen Theologie
BOTTE	La Tradition apostolique de Saint Hippolyte
BTFT	Bijdragen Tijdschrift voor filosofie en theologie. Nijmegen 1938—
CBQ	Catholic Biblical Quarterly. Washington 1939—
CorIC	Corpus Iuris Canonici
CIC	Codex Iuris Canonici, 1918
CL	Vatican Council II, Constitution on the Sacred Liturgy
CPL	Centre de Pastoral Liturgique, Neuilly-sur-Seine, Paris
CSEL	Corpus Scriptorum Ecclesiasticorum Latinorum. Vienna 1866—
DACL	Dictionnaire d'Archéologie Chrétienne et de Liturgie. Paris 1907–53
DSAM	Dictionnaire de Spiritualité Ascétique et Mystique. Paris 1932—
DTC	Dictionnaire de Théologie Catholique. Ed. A. Vacant and others. Paris 1903–50
DENZ	H. Denzinger, Enchiridion Symbolorum. 32nd ed. by A. Schönmetzer. Fribourg 1963.
DTF	Divus Thomas (Fribourg 1914–54). Superseded by Freiburger Zeitschrift für Philosophie und Theologie, 1954—
EETS	Early English Text Society. London 1864—
EL	Ephemerides Liturgicae. Rome 1887—
FCLD	Forschungen zur christlichen Literatur- und Dogmengeschichte
FTS	Freiburger Theologische Studien
HÄNGGI-PAHL	A. Hänggi and I. Pahl, eds., Prex Eucharistica
HANSSENS	J. M. Hanssens, Institutiones liturgicae de ritibus orientalibus
HARDOUIN	J. Hardouin, Acta conciliorum et epistolae decretales ac constitutiones summorum pontificum
HDG	Handbuch der Dogmengeschichte
HEFELE-LECLERCQ	C. J. von Hefele, Histoire des conciles . . . trans. by H. Leclercq
HTG	Handbuch theologischer Grundbegriffe
ITQ	Irish Theological Quarterly. Dublin 1864—
JLW	Jahrbuch für Liturgiewissenshcaft. Münster 1921–41

JTS	Journal of Theological Studies. London 1900–05; Oxford 1906—
KITTEL	G. Kittel, ed., Theological Dictionary of the New Testament
LEPIN	L'Idee du Sacrifice de la Messe
LIETZMANN	Mess und Herrenmahl
LJ	Liturgisches Jahrbuch. Münster 1951—
LQF	Liturgiegeschichtliche Quellen und Forschungen. Münster 1909–40; 1957—
LTK²	Lexikon für Theologie und Kirche. Ed. J. Höfer and Karl Rahner. 2nd (new) ed.; Freiburg 1957–65
MANSI	G. D. Mansi, ed., Sacrorum Conciliorum nova et amplissima collectio
MD	La Maison-Dieu. Paris 1945—
MGH	Monumenta Germaniae Historica
MINGANA	A. Mingana, ed., Commentary of Theodore of Mopsuestia on the Lord's Prayer
MRR	J. A. Jungmann, The Mass of the Roman Rite
MTZ	Münchener Theologische Zeitschrift. Munich 1950—
NCE	New Catholic Encyclopedia. Washington 1966
NRT	Nouvelle Revue Théologique. Tournai-Louvain-Paris 1879—
OCP	Orientalia Christiana Periodica. Rome 1935—
PG	Patrologia Graeca, ed. J. P. Migne. Paris 1857–66
PL	Patrologia Latina, ed. J. P. Migne. Paris 1844–64
QLP	Questions Liturgiques et Paroissiales. Louvain 1921—
RAHNER-HÄUSSLING	Karl Rahner and A. Häussling, The Celebration of the Eucharist
RBén	Revue Bénédictine. Maredsous 1884—
RSR	Recherches de Science Religieuse. Paris 1910—
RevSR	Revue des Sciences Religieuses. Strasbourg 1926—
SCHOL	Scholastik. Valkenburg 1926–41; Frankfurt 1949–65. Superseded by Theologie und Philosophie, 1966—
SL	Studia Liturgica. Rotterdam 1962—
ST	Studia Theologica. Lund 1947—
STRACK-BILLERBECK	H. L. Strack and P. Billerbeck, Kommentar zum Neuen Testament aus Talmud und Midrasch
TLZ	Theologische Literaturzeitung. Leipzig 1876—
TPQ	Theologisch-praktische Quartalschrift. Linz 1848—
TPS	The Pope Speaks. Washington 1954—
TQ	Theologische Quartalschrift. Tübingen 1819—; Stuttgart 1946—
TS	Theological Studies. Baltimore-New York 1940—
TU	Texte und Untersuchungen zur Geschichte der altchristlichen Literatur. Leipzig-Berlin 1882—
VC	Vigiliae Christianae. Amsterdam 1947—
YLS	Yearbook of Liturgical Studies. Ed., J. H. Miller and others. Collegeville 1960—
ZKT	Zeitschrift für katholische Theologie. Innsbruck 1877–1940; Vienna 1947—

INDEX

A listing of the principal theologians, texts, textual editors, liturgies, "schools," and· heresies mentioned by the author, whether introduced in the text or in the Notes. Works which do not appear in the Bibliography and those which are not cited fully in the Notes are listed in the Index.

TOPICAL INDEX

Uniformity and freedom, 157–158
Unleavened bread, 68, 131–132

Washing of hands, 189, 191
Water with wine, 27, 41, 191
Wine needed at Mass, 30, 40

INDEX OF LATIN WORDS

accipiam, 13
antiphonale, 66
arcanum, 51

cantatorium, 176, 225
capitulare evangeliorum, 66
chorus clericorum, 183
collecta, 161, 171
communicatio in sacris, 272, 274
communicatio spiritualis, 272
communio, 271, 273
confessio, 263
confiteor, 164, 167–168
conformatio sacramenti, 59, 68, 198
consignatio, 207–208
contestatio, 60
corpus mysticum, 271

dominicum, 41, 42

eucharistia, 12, 21, and *passim*

fermentum, 132, 238, 271

illatio, 60, 61
immolatio, 60, 61, 71
intinctio, 209

lectio continua, 175
lectionare, 66

mactatio, 71

missa, 64–65, 214
missa praesanctificatorum, 254
missa solitaria, 64
mixtio, 208
mysterium fidei, 193

oblatio, 37–39, 71, 73–75
offertorium, 188
oratio sexta, 59, 60
Ordines Romani, 66 and *passim*
osculatorium, 210

passio, 60
patrocinium, 265
praedicatio, 202, 263
praefari, 198
prex mystica, 59
psalmista, 225

recapitulatio, 234
repraesentatio, 76

sacrificium, 37–39 and *passim*
schola cantorum, 63, 165, 216, 225
secretarium, 165
statio, 63
supplicatio, 60
sustentatio, 216

velum, 187
vota, 65

INDEX OF GREEK AND HEBREW WORDS

agape, 20
alleluia, 23, 159
alla agoreuein, 69
amen, 23, 25, 27, 130, 159, 206, 207,
    222, 271
amnas, 50
anamnesis, 16
anaphora, 47
antidoron, 213
apolusis, 213

barak, 12

bema, 186
berakah, 13
birkatha-mazon, 12

cherubicon, 187
deipnon, 21
diatheke, 9
didomenon, 10

eikon, 104
ektene, 51, 52
enarxis, 162